BASIC DIGITAL MARKETING

The 5 Step Solution to Attract More Customers and Boost Sales by Promoting Your Business Online

DARRELL C. BOYCE

Results Matter
PUBLISHING

Published by Results Matter Publishing, Plainfield New Jersey
www.ResultsMatterPublishing.com

Paperback: 978-1-7341876-0-1
Ebook: 978-1-7341876-1-8

Library of Congress Number: 2022904062

First printing edition 2022.
Edited by Josh Raab
Proofread by Johanna Petronella Leigh
Cover art by Aesthetica Society (www.AestheticaSociety.ro)
Layout by Luisa Torres -Luisaferd

Printed in the United States of America

Contents at a Glance

Dedication

To my mom, Gloria.

Whenever I talk about you, I always say that you were the greatest mother in the world. Even though we did not have much financially, I always seemed to have what I needed and at times a little extra. I know you are the reason I was a good student in school. I remember all the books you got for me to read and the times you helped me with my homework.

I know you were disappointed when I went down the wrong path in high school, but I am thankful you were there when I found my way back and made the Dean's List in college. None of that would have been possible without your love and support.

I would not be the person I am today without your influence. Your personality and demeanor were an example how a good person should act and treat others. I learned from you that if you are not laughing, you are not living.

I write this book in your honor and know you would be very proud and happy that I achieved this. I love you and will always appreciate you.

Acknowledgements

To my Book Production Team:
Josh Raab, my editor. You knew exactly what this book needed from the start and helped me to bring it to life. I can't thank you enough. Johanna Leigh, my proofreader. Thank you for the love and attention you gave to this book and making my thoughts and ideas easier for readers to understand. Sebby at Aesthetica Society, thanks for designing such an amazing cover. Luisa Torres -Luisaferd, thank you for your hard work laying out this book. Your dedication to this project is deeply appreciated.

To my Virtual Book Coaches:
Steve Manning, Dr.Jeffery Lant, John Eggen, Stephen Pressfield, Dan Poynter, Jean Marie Stine, Roger C. Parker, Mitch Axelrod, and Elsom Eldridge Jr. This book would not have been written without your teachings and guidance. You provided encouragement throughout this process and always reminded me why it was important that I share my knowledge with the world in a way that only I could.

To my Mentors:
Ramon Williamson for showing me how to live my best life and teaching me that my mess was my message. Stephanie Frank for giving me assurance and validation at a time I needed it most. Michael Grant for teaching me that it doesn't matter what people think about you, it only matters what you think of yourself. Those words impacted the life of an impressionable 12-year-old. You were a great teacher and role model.

To my Virtual Mentors:
Earl Nightingale, Rich Schefren, Frank Kern, Tony Robbins, Robert Kiyosaki, Eben Pagan, Michael Fortin, Mary Bowling, Dan Kennedy, Robert G. Allen, and Michael E. Gerber. I have read your books and listened to your information products countless times. They gave me the knowledge and confidence to pursue my entrepreneurial dreams and start my own business.

To my Career Supporters:
Irene Abraham for helping me get a job with the phone company. It was a great job and opportunity that allowed me to live a very comfortable life. Jay Schwartz for hiring me when I needed to re-enter the workforce and giving me a huge advance when I needed it most. Darren Pagan for believing in me by putting me in position where I could display my talents and achieve success. Mike Henn and Benjamin Luberto for their mentoring and guidance.

To my Friends:
Ronald Abraham, Louis A. Brown III, Reggie Felder, Ronald G. Henry, Ricardo Garcia Hernandez, Diane Paralini, Richard Thompson, and Gia Trumpler. At different times in my life, you each had an important role in making school, work, or life so much easier to deal with. The most important thing you did was make me laugh so hard I cried. For that I owe you my deepest gratitude.

And Special Thanks:
Frank Sousa for investing in an enterprise I was involved in without hesitation. Alejandra Guarneros for pointing out my procrastination when I was close to finishing this book. I really needed that.

Introduction

Maybe you already started promoting your business online and are dissatisfied with the results. Maybe you are just starting your business and want to know how to become successful quickly. You've probably seen businesses that are leveraging the internet to get more customers and make more sales, and it would be unusual if you didn't want the same for your business.

The purpose of this book is to explain digital marketing in an easy to follow way, so you understand how to attract, engage, and convert customers online. Digital marketing is a broad term used to describe the use of the internet, mobile devices, display advertising, and other digital technologies for promotional purposes. This book will primarily focus on the use of the internet and mobile devices to build and promote your business. You should consider this book a starting point rather than an intensive how-to book. At the end, you'll understand what digital marketing is all about, the various strategies you can choose from, how they each work, how to use them, what pitfalls to avoid, and why investing in hiring a digital marketing specialist is a smart move.

Who Is This Book For?

Small-to-medium-sized business (SMB) owners and entrepreneurs that want to know:

- How they can use the internet to promote their products, services, and themselves.

- How the top digital marketing strategies can benefit their business.

- How to find and hire a digital marketing expert that can help create and reach online marketing goals.

If you have tried digital marketing in the past and had little to no success, or you're not sure exactly what you're looking for but know you need to market online to stay competitive, this book is for you. Individuals who are considering starting and e-commerce store or want to work at a digital marketing agency will also find this book helpful.

Why Is This Book Important to You?

As the owner of a business, or someone who has been put into a position to help grow one, you are responsible for making it successful. That means you must have the right information and take the right actions to reach whatever sales and online marketing goals you are trying to achieve.

By reading this book, you will receive the required knowledge to build a strong foundation online for your business. If necessary, you will also learn how to rebuild an existing foundation in case you got off to a bad start or made some mistakes with online marketing previously. In either situation, this book will set you up to reach any business growth goals using online marketing.

When it comes to digital marketing, you won't have to worry anymore about not knowing what exactly needs to be done, why it's important, and what your priorities are. You will be exposed to new ideas that capture your interest and understand what is possible for the growth of your business.

What is perhaps most significant is that you'll gain the ability to communicate effectively to others what digital marketing tasks you need to be done so they can work on them while you spend your time building your business.

Conventions Used in This Book

Here is a list of common phrases used throughout the book that are interchanged with other phrases or abbreviations:

Digital Marketing:	Internet Marketing, Online Marketing, Web Marketing
Small to Medium-Sized Business(es):	SMB, SMBs
Business Owner(s)	BO, BOs
Consultant	Specialist, expert, professional, strategist, DMC (digital marketing consultant)

How This Book Is Organized?

This book is divided into 5 sections and organized based on the **BASIC** signature process that I created. The acronym **BASIC** used in the title of the book stands for **Begin** to **Acquire Strategies** to **Implement** with a **Consultant.**

The process organizes the steps you must take in order to succeed with digital marketing. I'd like to briefly introduce each step to you.

- **Step 1: Begin – Understand Why You Need to Have the Right Mindset Before You Use Digital Marketing**
  We will explore the mindset you need to have before you get started with digital marketing. You'll learn about the mistakes that most business owners can make that keep them from succeeding and how the BASIC signature process will keep you from making those mistakes.

- **Step 2: Acquire – Get The Tools You Need to Succeed Online**
  We will lay out all of the different components you need to promote and sell online. Topics covered include choosing a domain name, selecting a host for your website, building a website, and getting started with e-commerce.

- **Step 3: Strategies – Use The Most Effective Digital Marketing Channels**
  We will survey various digital marketing strategies that are available to you. Step 3 takes up the largest portion of the book and you'll learn what each strategy offers and how it could benefit your business.

- **Step 4: Implement – Carry Out Your Digital Marketing Strategy**
  We will clarify what actions you should take after you have achieved a digital marketing mindset, acquired the necessary components for marketing online, and selected the strategy you want to follow. This step is about doing things that will substantially increase your results.

- **Step 5: Consultant – Get Help with Your Digital Marketing**
  We will discuss why you should strongly consider hiring an expert to help you with your digital marketing. You will find out about all of the advantages and how to go about finding a skilled professional to help you grow and promote your business.

How to Use This Book

This is a reference book, and as such, every business will not use all the concepts in this book, however, earlier chapters will set the stage for later chapters. To get the most from this book follow these recommendations:

1. Read through Chapter 1 to Chapter 4. This is where fundamental information is covered. Even if you have an established business you may have overlooked some things when you initially got started. If your intention is to not just promote but also to sell online, read Chapter 5.

2. Read Chapter 6—on content marketing—because that information is essential to almost all of the other strategies.

3. Select one of the strategies found in Chapter 7 to Chapter 14 that you are most interested in learning about and want to try implementing in your business.

4. Read Chapters 15 and 16 to learn what business concepts you need to know so whatever strategy you use has the best opportunity to work and separate you from your competition.

5. Read Chapters 17 and 18 so you know what to look for when hiring a digital marketing expert and find out some of the things they may need from you.

After reading the recommended chapters follow the advice in them. Make decisions. Take action. Measure results. Hire someone to help you. Learn about another strategy to complement one that is working or replace one that is not. If you want a complete overview about digital marketing, read the entire book.

A Few Words about Who I Am

I am a Digital Marketing Consultant and what fires me up is helping SMBs and entrepreneurs reach their business goals. I especially like helping with the parts of online marketing that can be confusing, intimidating, overwhelming, and time-consuming. My training and passion for online and offline marketing make me a perfect match for clients that need help in these areas. My mission is to help you fully realize the potential of your business by using digital marketing strategies to attract more customers.

What sets me apart and makes me different from the thousands of other web designers, internet marketing consultants or SEO specialists? You have the answer right in front of you—my **BASIC** signature process that I have developed to make digital marketing so much easier to understand. I want you to be savvy when discussing the online marketing goals of your business. This methodology makes it easy for me or any other expert you may work with to introduce ideas and explain them.

I also have the ability to take your unique knowledge, skills, and experiences, and turn them into valuable information products that you can:

- Make more money
- Demonstrate your expertise in an organized way
- Gain even more credibility among your peers and clients.

When delivered to the right person at the right time this information is going to be life-changing. If this book was meant for you, there will be something in it that will cause you to take action and attain the results that will make a difference in your business and your life.

I'm Here if You Need Me

I love teaching and talking with people all around the world. I invite you to stay in touch with me. If you got a copy of this book from another source and not directly from me, you are probably not on my mailing list. You can subscribe by visiting BasicDigitalMarketing.com/subscribe

or creating and marketing your info products let me know by visiting YourWebSolutions.info and scheduling a free strategy session. However, if you contact me with questions that can be found in the book or any of my other resources, I'll tell you to find it there first, and buy if necessary.

If you just want to let me know what you think about the book, send appreciation, make a suggestion, or point out any typos, send an email to feedback@basicdigitalmarketing.com

If you want to see what I am up to or look at some of my other resources, visit DarrellBoyce.com

Step 1: Begin

Understand Why You Need to Have the Right Mindset Before You Use Digital Marketing

In the first part of the book, we will examine 25 reasons why business owners are not successful when they try to use online marketing. You'll learn about these mistakes and ways to avoid them.

Chapter 2 gives you a clear and easy to follow process for getting started with digital marketing. You also learn how SMART goals give you clarity and your business a sense of direction.

"Mistakes are costly and somebody must pay. The time to correct a mistake is before it is made. The causes of mistakes are, first, I didn't know; second, I didn't think; third, I didn't care."

–Henry Buckley, politician

1. Avoid Making Digital Marketing Mistakes

1.1 25 Reasons Why Most Small Business Owners Fail at Digital Marketing, and Why You'll Fail Too If You Don't Use This Book

Hundreds of thousands of small business owners in the United States and around the world are missing out on getting more leads, earning additional revenue, and the opportunity to grow their businesses. Some of the reasons this is happening are:

- Most business owners are simply unaware of what is possible
- Many choose to ignore the huge impact digital marketing can have on their business
- Some are aware and try, but never get the results they expect.

My goal is to not let you be any of these business owners. I want you and your business to be known, liked, and trusted by new prospects and existing customers.

This chapter discusses the most common and self-defeating mistakes nearly all small business owners make when attempting to market online.

Your business will not reach its full potential if it can't be found online or has a very weak presence on the web. With all of the complicated, exaggerated, and conflicting information available from the various marketing gurus, it's easy to become confused and develop a lot of misconceptions about online marketing. These misconceptions cause irrational objections to form in the minds of business owners.

When you finish this chapter, you will have a better understanding of what mistakes to avoid and what you need to be thinking about before you even start any digital marketing campaigns.

The 25 reasons that follow are divided into five related but distinct mistakes. These five types of mistakes are:

- Objections
- Planning
- Limiting Beliefs
- Being Behind the Times
- Lack of Knowledge

You must not only become aware of these oversights, but you must solve them and not allow them to keep you from the success you are striving for.

1.2 Objections

Avoidable Mistake #1: You think digital marketing is ineffective.

Many people have an extremely negative view of digital marketing. They might perceive that it is simply a 'waste of time,' or they might think that it provides ineffective results when compared to more traditional marketing methods. In reality, this couldn't be further from the truth, and it is a viewpoint that usually comes from a lack of understanding of the digital marketing arena.

When implemented in the correct manner, digital marketing provides a very effective way of reaching both new and existing customers. Through having a strong online presence and implementing carefully planned digital marketing campaigns, it is possible to generate many more leads than traditional outbound marketing—but also at a much lower cost.

In addition, digital marketing affords you the opportunity to accurately reach very specific demographics. As an example, you could set up a social media campaign to specifically target 21–25-year-olds who live in New York and who also have an interest in skiing.

Digital marketing can do so much for your business. It is an effective way to reach new customers and better engage existing ones, while also allowing you to achieve faster and better results than ever before possible in history.

Whatever you do, don't ignore digital marketing.

Avoidable Mistake #2: You do not want to change the way you run your business because you are afraid you'll lose something.

Some business owners are just scared of change. They see the facts presented to them about how marketing online can change their business for the better, but they would rather maintain the status quo. Their motto is "if it ain't broke don't fix it." If you are afraid that an online marketing strategy might not work, or you're not going to get a return on your investment, it's because you don't have a plan that gives you confidence.

You don't know what to expect so you expect the worst. This is not a good way to run your business. This type of thinking is extremely limiting and actually reveals that you are not really committed to exposing your product or services to all of the people that could benefit from them. If you are afraid that you will get more business than you can handle, then the decision if you should market online is not the main challenge you need to address.

Avoidable Mistake #3: You don't understand the internet.

This is a cop-out. Do not believe for a second that the internet is too difficult for you to grasp. You don't need to learn how to do everything. In fact, I recommend not trying to learn how to do everything. Once you start getting deeper into this book and realizing that you need online marketing to propel your business forward, you'll be ready for Chapters 17 and 18 which cover how to find a digital marketing professional to help with your goals.

Avoidable Mistake #4: You think it costs too much to market online.

It is a common misconception that digital marketing is expensive and unaffordable to the majority of businesses. When times get tough for a business, the marketing budget is often the first to be tightened. But while it is certainly true that some of the initial costs of digital marketing can be a little steep, the reality is that the results generated by your online presence and digital campaigns will most likely pay for themselves and then some. That, after all, is the point.

It is certainly a mistake to view digital marketing as an upfront cost. Rather, it should be treated as a long-term investment, whereby you are willing to put money into it to gain results in the long run. In addition, it is worth mentioning that it is much better to put smaller amounts of money into a well-planned digital campaign than it is to put massive sums of money into something poorly planned and executed.

In most cases, the best approach is to put in a minimal amount of money to 'test the water,' then increase the budget once it has been proven to provide a positive return on investment. You should try to resist the temptation to throw in loads of money and simply hope that this will be enough to succeed.

Avoidable Mistake #5: You don't think you have the time for marketing online.

You're probably right. Being a business owner involves a lot of responsibilities that can occupy your time far more than you anticipated. You may not even realize you are doing the work of 10 people until some aspect suffers. Since we cannot buy more time, we need to hire help.

One of your first hires should be a digital marketing consultant. They can analyze your business and online marketing needs and provide you with strategies and systems to meet your business growth goals.

It may seem cheaper to do it yourself, but time is money and it definitely won't be faster because you still need to spend the time to learn what to do on top of actually executing. So, it can be a while before you see results. I suggest that you spend your time on what you are good at and hire someone who is good at marketing online so you can get the fastest and best results possible.

Avoidable Mistake #6: You believe online marketing is just a fad so you don't even want to bother getting started.

Wrong. The internet has been going strong since the early 1990s. It is only getting more robust and innovative daily. Potential customers and your competition know that the internet is here to stay, and your competition is taking full advantage of that all the way to the bank. It is time for you to see the potential as well.

Thousands, maybe millions of people in your own city are browsing the internet daily. Consumers have more choices than ever these days and they have to be reminded constantly that your business exists. The best way to reach them is where they spend most of their time . . . which is on the internet.

Avoidable Mistake #7: You believe that your target audience isn't online.

Sometimes business owners are reluctant to embrace digital marketing because they perceive that their target audience doesn't really use the internet. In truth, the reality of the modern world is that pretty much everyone is online, including both young and old people alike. But while it's true that a huge and diverse proportion of the population uses the internet, it is a common mistake to think that everyone uses it in exactly the same way.

The key to success with digital marketing is figuring out which methods are best to attract and engage with your particular target audience. Let's take social media marketing as an example. Many businesses assume that it is necessary to be active on all the main social media platforms, but what if your target market doesn't really use all of them? Is there any point in spending time and effort on Pinterest marketing if a large proportion of your target audience rarely uses Pinterest?

The key is to do your research and find out how your audience uses the internet so that you can target them most effectively.

Avoidable Mistake #8: You think that your competition isn't using digital marketing, so you don't need to be either.

If you think you don't need to bother much with digital marketing because your competition doesn't, you're missing out on a big opportunity. The truth is that your competition could start at any time, so why not get in before them and gain a competitive advantage?

Digital marketing is playing an ever-increasingly important role in the long-term success of businesses, so if you're not currently taking advantage of the opportunities it provides you with, the time to start is now.

1.3 Planning Mistakes

Avoidable Mistake #9: You did not take the time to set goals.

Business owners should create goals that are measurable so that they can track their progress. Great goal setting is the key to success in online marketing and in life. To accomplish those goals, you'll want to create smaller objectives that will lead to the accomplishment of the big goals. When you reach your initial goals, set new ones so your business can continue to improve. A proven process for creating goals is covered in Chapter 2.5.

Avoidable Mistake #10: You procrastinate because you don't have a plan.

If you decide to market online with poor upfront planning or no plan at or, you will be faced with a failed project. Planning gives you a roadmap to success. Through this process, you can evaluate the business environment within your niche. You'll be able to spot any problems that may come up when implementing your online marketing strategies. When following your plan, you'll know if you're on pace to reach your goal or if you need to make changes to avoid wasting additional time and resources.

Avoidable Mistake #11: You don't analyze the data from your website to measure progress and make improvements.

Your website should be equipped to capture traffic data generated from the visitors that come to/visit your site. The metrics you can look at include but are not limited to the following: number of visitors to the website, where they are located, how much time they spend on the site, and what the most popular page on your website is. All of this data and more help you determine what changes are needed for the success of your website. Learn about what metrics to track and how to do it in Chapter 15.5.

Avoidable Mistake #12: You copy what your competition is doing without doing any research.

When you want to be noticed in a competitive market, don't blindly copy your competitors' strategies. Without research, it is difficult to determine if their techniques are even effective. Do not look for them to announce what is working for them. What is working for them may not even be something that fits your style. Do your own thing based on what you have researched and the advice you receive from your digital marketing consultant.

1.4 Limiting Beliefs

Avoidable Mistake #13: You are afraid to appear as a slimy salesperson.

Just because you are selling your services doesn't mean you have to do it in a slimy way. Your customers can tell if you are trying to manipulate them. Instead, just focus on providing value to your customers rather than forcing them to say yes to your product or services.

Avoidable Mistake #14: You think you must do everything yourself.

There is no way you can do everything at the same time. Activities like accounting, marketing, customer service, ordering supplies and more can be full-time jobs on their own. While you should be considering online marketing, your focus needs to be on finding someone to do the work for you (this applies to other areas of your business as well).

A dentist, lawyer, or accountant probably don't know how to build a website. So, should they spend several days trying to learn a new tool so they can build a website? Probably not and neither should you. When you're trying to grow a business, there is a temptation to try to do everything you possibly can to save some money. Resist this temptation and start becoming more strategic.

I suggest you read a book called The E-Myth Revisited: Why Most Small Businesses Don't Work and What to Do About It by Michael E. Gerber. The author dispels the myths surrounding starting your own business and shows how commonplace assumptions can get in the way of running a business.

1.5 Being behind the Times

Avoidable Mistake #15: You rely solely on getting your clients by word of mouth.

It amazes me the number of businesses I come into contact with that claim to not need any more business. While word of mouth is a great marketing method, relying solely on word of mouth is basically putting your fate in the hands of your customers and associates. Relying on one marketing avenue will get you in trouble. Rather than relying on past customers to advertise for you, take control of the marketing of your business and know where your next source of revenue is coming from.

Avoidable Mistake #16: You invest more money on print ads than you do on internet marketing.

Small companies continue to throw away their advertising dollars on several avenues that have little to no impact on their client acquisition. The Yellow Pages, and other methods mentioned below, have been around for a very long time. People want to use what they know and what has proven to work for them. However, the methods that worked twenty years ago no longer have the same impact as they did back then. Here are a few of the antiquated methods of advertising and why they are so ineffective.

<u>Yellow Pages:</u> Even though the number of people using the Yellow Pages for reference has dropped considerably. Furthermore, ads in the Yellow Pages are not cheap. Nobody searches through their Yellow Pages if they even keep one in the home or business. People are using the web to find businesses and get information about them. The only upside to the Yellow Pages ad is that it is just one more place that people can find you.

<u>Print flyers:</u> Business owners are spending valuable time and resources putting flyers on vehicles and bulletin boards in towns and cities only to have them tossed in the garbage or on the ground. It takes time and money to design the flyer, print, and distribute it. All of this effort could be spent on other business strategies and instead to work on a web presence with a digital marketer.

<u>Ads in local newspapers:</u> Ads in local newspapers are expensive! And as with the other obsolete methods, the audience for newsprint is significantly down in recent years. People are getting the bulk of their news from the internet. Most of the contents of the newspapers are available online. One positive thing that comes out of a newspaper ad is, again, it is one more place to be seen by a potential customer. In addition, for most local papers, if you post an ad in the print version of the paper, they may put your ad on their website.

<u>Coupons in entertainment books or coupon mail packs:</u> There is a significantly smaller audience seeing and using these coupons compared to people looking for services on the internet.

1.6 Lack of Knowledge

Avoidable Mistake #17: You think digital marketing means instant results.

Some business owners believe that digital marketing provides instant results. They somehow think that they can launch an SEO campaign and their website will immediately appear at the top of Google search results, or that they can set up a Facebook page and instantly gain hundreds of new fans and customers. While it's definitely true that digital marketing can provide faster results than some more traditional offline marketing methods, digital marketing is in no way a 'quick fix' solution.

To truly succeed with digital marketing, you must have a well-planned and executed strategy. It takes a certain degree of knowledge, skill and experience to make digital marketing effective for your business, and it's vital to adopt a long-term approach. In addition, the length of time it takes to start seeing results will depend on many different factors such as experience, skill set, and industry—but even the most experienced professional digital marketing expert won't be able to achieve instant 'overnight' success.

While some digital strategies will help you start moving in the right direction rather quickly, most need time to be worked on. You also have to factor in the time it takes to plan and implement a campaign. Always keep in mind that everything takes time and that a 'slow and steady' approach is required in order to win the race.

Avoidable Mistake #18: You are marketing to the wrong target audience.

How do you know your target market is wrong? Simple, they either aren't interested in buying your product or service or they don't have the money. Take the time to identify your ideal customer also known as your customer avatar. If you start marketing before you have clearly identified your customer profile you will most likely be wasting your money in places that will never reach your customer.

Part of identifying your ideal customer is knowing where to find them. Put your online marketing efforts and dollars into places where they hang out. If you invest your money where your customers are going to see your content and ads, you will reap the benefits. Get as specific as you can. "Everybody," is not a good answer, nor is it realistic. If you have a young clientele, you may find them on Snapchat. If your customers are baby boomers, you could find them on Facebook.

Identify your niche. Once you find them make sure your business remains visible and you are giving them a compelling reason why they should spend their money with you. The more targeted your message is to your specific audience, the more success you will have with your online marketing.

Avoidable Mistake #19: You think you know what's best.

You may think that you have all of the answers and insist you are doing what's best, but nobody has all the answers. Any business owner who thinks they do has a false sense of security, and your competition is more than happy with your current knowledge of the market. If you're not competing, they don't have to worry about you. That's right, you don't need to know about the customers that you could have had and also the money you didn't—maybe because they could not find you online anyway.

Avoidable Mistake #20: You think your product or service speaks for itself.

Overconfidence is not only arrogant, but it will cost your business. Just having a great product or providing a good service is not enough to ignore online marketing. Your competition may offer the same product or service, but they're marketing online. Customers are going to see your competition online, visit their web pages, and buy from them instead of you. They are establishing a relationship with your potential customers that will be hard for you to break later on. So, while you may be doing well, you can be doing a whole lot better when you market online.

Avoidable Mistake #21: Whether the business is doing good or bad you don't want any help.

You may be the type of business owner who believes when business is good, you don't need any help, but business will not always be good. It is then that you will be grateful you have put digital marketing strategies in place to consistently bring in more customers. Even if business is good, why not strive to make it better? Or when business is bad you may feel that you don't want help or can't afford it. That is exactly when you need help the most. Find a way to make the time or financial investment in online marketing so you can always have a digital strategy working in your favor.

Avoidable Mistake #22: You think having a website is all that you need.

Many business owners believe that having a website is enough to make them successful online. While it is certainly important to have a well-designed website that is both informative and easy to use, that definitely doesn't mean you can just sit back and expect people to come to it: you must take a proactive approach.

A static website that hasn't been updated in years will do absolutely nothing for your business. Your site should be regularly updated with fresh, relevant content, and your website needs to be just one part of a bigger digital marketing strategy. Simply having a website is not sufficient for digital marketing on its own. You need to have a clear strategy in place to attract visitors to your website—for example, by optimizing your website for search engines (SEO) so that it appears higher up in search rankings or drawing in visitors through content marketing.

Avoidable Mistake #23: You think social media is digital marketing.
When most people think of digital marketing, they instantly think of social media. But in fact, social media is only one part of digital marketing, and it's definitely not the same thing. Social media marketing is marketing that is conducted through sites like Facebook, Twitter, Instagram, LinkedIn, and YouTube, etc. As an example, you might launch a special promotion to your Twitter followers, or you might use Facebook advertising to find new prospects.

Digital marketing incorporates many different things in addition to social media, such as:

- Search Engine Optimization (SEO)
- Local Search Marketing
- Email Marketing
- Content Marketing

Social media is certainly an effective tool that you should be taking advantage of, but it's also just one part of the puzzle and shouldn't be the only thing you concentrate on. A solid digital marketing strategy will incorporate many different elements that all work together to achieve a bigger overall result.

Avoidable Mistake #24: You are reluctant to ask questions.

You must remain aware of the inner workings of your business. Be ready to ask questions when hiring anyone to do digital marketing work for you or even in your everyday business. Ask your customers questions about what resources they use when they are looking for a business online.

Once you have started implementing some digital marketing strategies, don't be afraid to ask your customers what they think of them. Also, do a little research before your online marketing strategies are planned so you know if your hired professional is steering you in the right direction. When you are learning, you are growing.

Avoidable Mistake #25: You haven't optimized your website for mobile devices.

According to Statista.com, 60% of Google searches are done via mobile devices. Just 5 years ago, the figure was nearly half of that at 34%. If a potential customer were to find your site using their smartphone and it is not optimized for mobile-device viewing they will leave your site quickly. Websites designed for desktop computers and monitors are difficult to view on smaller screens. It is more important than ever for your website to be optimized for mobile devices. You can learn more about mobile websites and their importance when you read Chapter 10.3.

"Learning new systems and processes is not mandatory, but neither is staying in business."

–Bobby Darnell, author

2. Embracing Digital Marketing as a Solution

2.1 Why Digital Marketing?

I'm passionate about digital marketing because I see so many business owners struggling to find new customers and getting their name out there. Using my unique and straightforward approach, I am able to understand their challenges and help them navigate the world of online marketing to reach their goals.

Without the help of a consultant, digital marketing can quickly become overwhelming and time-consuming. There are so many opportunities for your business to capitalize on, but just how do you actually go about taking advantage of them and fitting them all into your schedule? Which digital marketing strategies should you be using, and how do you go about implementing them successfully? What about tracking the results of your campaigns?

If you are feeling more than a little weighed down and confused by digital marketing, you're certainly not alone. Thousands of business owners just like yourself are feeling overwhelmed and confused because they aren't achieving the results they would like from their efforts. Despite the opportunities digital marketing provides to businesses, many choose not to use it at all, and those who have tried it felt that their efforts were ineffective.

The strategies and technologies used for digital marketing are evolving faster than businesses can keep up with. This immediately puts many of them at a disadvantage because they now have to try and understand what has changed in order for their current online marketing campaigns to remain effective. In this chapter, I'll outline my brand of digital marketing and how it can help you understand the landscape and reach your business goals.

2.2 How I Got Started with Digital Marketing

I started out designing websites for people. Over time I realized that my clients needed more than just a website, so I began to offer them additional web marketing services. There were two types of prospects that I usually found myself talking to the most:

1. Business owners that wanted a website and believed that was all they needed.

2. Business owners that already had a website but were not interested in investing any additional money into online marketing.

The challenge that I faced with almost all of my clients was that they knew nothing about online marketing, and I found myself constantly explaining all of the various and important aspects of a digital marketing strategy. At the time, I had trouble explaining it in a way they would easily understand. There were many things I was eager to discuss with them, such as:

- What they needed before their website could be built
- What elements their website needed
- What they needed if they wanted to sell online
- Different ways to get more traffic to their website
- How to attract and convert more leads
- Why they needed to track their online marketing
- Why doing any of this was a worthy investment.

Having to repeatedly explain what was needed and what was possible became tedious and I obviously didn't do a good job at it because most of my prospects still believed they didn't need what I was offering.

Maybe I gave them too much information and they became overwhelmed, or maybe the details were too technical. Whatever the reason, there were definitely a lot of opportunities I missed to further help people marketing their business online. For those that did show some interest in online marketing, they decided to do it by trial and error rather than pay a skilled professional such as myself to do it for them.

I realized I had to do something different to get the attention of my prospects and show them why they needed to use digital marketing. I had to do something that would make talking about digital marketing easier for me, and easier for my prospects and clients to understand. I needed a way to point out the possibilities and benefits of digital marketing, along with showing that ignoring it is just a bad business decision. This knowledge was too important for any business owner to overlook.

So, I took a break from digital marketing and decided to focus on figuring out what I felt every SMB and entrepreneur needed to know about online marketing. After several years of planning, researching, and writing I created a process that would inform and convince my prospects, and anyone else that wanted to understand and talk about digital marketing.

2.2.1 What Are Six Questions That Led to My Big Breakthrough?

When it comes to digital marketing, there are usually six universal questions prospects would usually ask:

1. I need a website, what do I need to get started?
2. I want to do (.i.e., social media), where do I begin?
3. What do I need to start selling online?
4. Who's responsible for performing these activities?
5. How long will it take to do all of this?
6. How much is this going to cost?

These questions and were consistently being asked, so I wrote them down along with the corresponding answers that I saved on my computer. Over time I added more questions and answers including many that prospects did not ask me about but should have. The document I created helped me deliver the answers in a way that was clear, quick, and concise. This made it easier for anyone I talked to about digital marketing understand various concepts and learn along the way. After outlining all the information that I had researched and documented, I realized there was a sequence of activities that, when followed, would make digital marketing easy to understand, feel less overwhelming, and more likely to get the results business owners were seeking. And at that moment the **BASIC** process was created.

2.3 What Is the BASIC Process and How Does It Solve Digital Marketing Challenges?

With the intention of changing the association of the word 'overwhelm' with digital marketing, I decided to use a word to describe my process that was encouraging and made online marketing less intimidating.

BASIC stands for Begin to Acquire Strategies to Implement with a Consultant. While there were plenty of words to choose from, the word BASIC encapsulates the process perfectly in a comprehensive and unique way.

My process has five steps:

- **Step 1: Begin – Understand Why You Need to Have the Right Mindset Before You Use Digital Marketing**
You need to Begin on the right foot. We've already dug into this a bit by discussing avoidable marketing mistakes, explaining what digital marketing is, its benefits, and its challenges.

You have to know what digital marketing involves so you can decide if and how you are going to be committed to it. You should not commit to something you don't understand but far too many people do just that. You need to begin on the right foot by establishing a strong foundation of understanding about online marketing and your own goals.

- **Step 2: Acquire – Get The Tools You Need to Succeed Online**
This is where you establish your online business presence. This is also the time where you will be making some of your most important decisions and making your initial financial investments. In order to promote your business online you need to Acquire things like:

  - A domain name, web hosting, and Google account (Chapter 3)
  - Building your website (Chapter 4), and
  - Setting up e-commerce capabilities if you plan to sell online (Chapter 5)

None of the other steps of the process are effective if you do not have these components.

- **Step 3: Strategies – Use The Most Effective Digital Marketing Channels**
The information that is the most essential to digital marketing is the strategies. This is where you learn about the different methods available that are used to increase sales, get you more exposure, get more leads, attract web traffic, and much more.

The Strategies that I talk about are the most popular ones businesses are using, such as:

  - Content Marketing (Chapter 6)
  - Search Engine Optimization (SEO) (Chapter 7)

- Local Search Marketing (Chapter 8)
- Reputation Management (Chapter 9)
- Mobile Marketing (Chapter 10)
- Email Marketing (Chapter 11)
- Social Media Marketing (Chapter 12)
- Video Marketing (Chapter 13)
- Paid Online Advertising (Chapter 14)

These are the methods that bring customers back to what you Acquired in Step 2.

In this book, each strategy is discussed in its own chapter giving you a chance to select the one you are most interested in and taking time to find out more about it. The information provided will enable you to communicate these strategies to other people on your team with confidence.

- **Step 4: Implement – Carry Out Your Digital Marketing Strategy**

This step is about taking action. After understanding and preparing using Steps 1–3, now it's time to make some moves. This section covers the following:

- The importance of market research and how to do it
- How to analyze your business operation to identify a digital marketing goal you want to set
- How to make a digital marketing budget
- Why it is important to measure a web marketing campaign and how to do it.
- How to choose a digital marketing strategy to achieve your goals

In the process of Implementing, you'll want to make sure that you are distinguishing yourself from your competitors, especially if you're in a crowded market. We cover this in Chapter 16, discussing the following:

- Branding and how to build a brand people will know, like, and trust
- Six ways to become an authority in your industry
- How to use storytelling to grow your business

Regardless of the strategy you choose to move forward with, these topics are relevant for amplifying the effects of your digital marketing.

- **Step 5: Consultant – Get Help with Your Digital Marketing**

By hiring a consultant, you solve the biggest challenge of digital marketing: the need for help with an overwhelming number of things that need to be done.

When I first started writing this book, I was focused on my prospects and the most important things I wanted them to know about digital marketing. But it also made sense for me to talk about why they needed help implementing their digital marketing strategies. Even if they decided to work with another digital marketing professional, I wanted them to get more value from my advice and become more knowledgeable.

The last step of The BASIC process discusses how and why it's important to work with a consultant. In this case, a consultant is anyone that you would hire to provide you guidance and support with digital marketing. (i.e., web designer, consultant, SEO specialist, social media manager, etc.). They can be anyone from an individual freelancer you hire for only one job or an entire agency that will build and manage different web marketing campaigns for you. A professional digital marketer gives you access to a highly-trained and experienced specialist.

We will cover the following topics:

- Why you shouldn't do digital marketing alone
- What the benefits of hiring a consultant are
- What you should know about your business before contacting a consultant
- How do you find the right consultant for your business?
- What information do you need to have before interviewing a consultant?
- What do you look for in a consultant?
- Where do you find consultants?
- What questions do you ask consultants?
- What questions will consultants ask you?
- What determines the cost of digital marketing services?
- What should you be on the lookout for before signing a contract with a consultant?

There is often a steep learning curve to online marketing, so it's sometimes not worth a business owner's time investment when there are so many aspects of the business that need attention. This is why hiring and working with a consultant to handle the nitty-gritty must be considered.

2.4 Six Ways to Establish Realistic Digital Marketing Expectations

Following the BASIC process for digital marketing will do a tremendous amount of good for your business, however, you need to understand it is not a magic solution. Many business owners have unrealistic expectations in terms of what can be accomplished using digital marketing. For example, they assume results will come quickly even if they put in very little or no effort, or that using only one strategy can solve all of the challenges that their business faces.

It can be very discouraging when expectations are not met. That is why establishing expectations that are clear and realistic make digital marketing more manageable, less stressful and more fulfilling when executed properly. Here are six ways how to set realistic expectations for your digital marketing.

1. **Think Long Term:** Digital marketing is a marathon, not a sprint. Sometimes it is possible to get quick results, but there are many factors to consider such as the online marketing strategy used, type of business, target audience, product or service offered, etc. It is not realistic to expect results overnight when you start a campaign because many action steps need to be taken over a sustained period of time regardless of what strategy is used.

2. **Expect to Spend Money:** Digital marketing requires an investment. Whether it is setting up a high converting website or launching paid online advertising campaigns—almost all web marketing strategies have a cost associated with them. Also, consider the cost of hiring an agency or freelancer to implement your strategies.

3. **Prioritize Education:** When you don't know what is required, expectations can become extremely unrealistic. Once you have synthesized the information in this book, you will be able to communicate what has to get done. Share this book or buy copies for anyone on your in-house staff that is going to be handling any of your web marketing so you can understand each other when discussing plans and action steps.

4. **Create a Schedule:** Make a list of tasks to work on daily, weekly, and monthly. Allocate time to complete the tasks by creating a schedule and try to stick to it as close as possible. By following an established timetable, you will be able to stay on track and work toward any goal you have set.

5. **Do One Thing at a Time:** Don't multitask and try to do too much at once. It is better to work on a task until it is completed rather than have to worry about multiple unfinished tasks.

6. **Recognize When Help is Needed:** Digital marketing is a complex business activity that requires specialized knowledge and skills. With that in mind, there is likely to come a time when there is a task you need to be done that can't be accomplished in-house. To get the most success from digital marketing you have to be able to recognize when you need help so you can take the steps to get it.

   Getting help may look like hiring an agency to do some work for you. Perhaps it may be hiring someone new on your staff that has the abilities that you need. At the very least it could be asking a question or getting an opinion from a forum or social media page that discusses digital marketing. Whatever the situation is, it is important to get help when you need it.

2.5 What is SMART Goal Setting

Setting goals is an important part of digital marketing. Many people like to use the SMART goal setting process because it simplifies creating plans to execute. SMART stands for **Specific**, **Measurable**, **Achievable**, **Relevant** and **Time-bound**. Here's a quick overview of each part of the process:

- **Specific** goals are much more effective than setting general goals. Focusing on just one goal at a time helps to eliminate confusion and overwhelm that tends to slow down progress. When it is time to delegate tasks, having one specific goal also helps everyone involved focused on achieving it.

- **Measurable** means having a way to track the progress of your goal. You need to know if you are advancing from where you are or what you have today to where you want to be. Choose a performance metric to make your goal measurable, keep you focused, and help you meet your deadline. See Chapter 15.5.2 for examples of performance metrics worth measuring.

- **Achievable** means setting a goal that can be reached. If your goal is too big or complicated, you won't have the motivation to go for it. Do you have the resources to attain the goal? If not, then make getting them a separate goal. Plan your goal, write it out, and break it down into smaller objectives.

As you complete each objective, you'll gain confidence and will want to continue making progress.

- **Relevant** means the goal is part of a bigger plan to benefit you and your overall business objectives. The goal must be worthwhile and not feel like a waste of time.

- **Time-bound** goals have start and end dates. If your goal does not have a time limit, there will be no urgency to work toward it. Having to complete tasks and reach milestones by certain times makes you more accountable and more likely to reach your goal.

The steps above make up the standard SMART process for goal setting. But in my own practice, I add two more steps to achieve maximum success using the SMARTER process. The E stands for evaluating your goals. When a goal is being evaluated it is being reviewed to see if the action steps being taken are working or not. During this review process if anything is found that is not working or progress is really slow, then changes can be made. The R stands for Rework, so after you evaluate you can implement a change of course to better achieve your goals.

The evaluation and rework steps don't happen just once. Diligent business owners realize that goals need to be evaluated and strategies reworked continuously.

Business goals change for different reasons such as changes in the economy and business expansion. A business that has evaluated their goals consistently will not have any problems changing or resetting their goals if necessary.

Goal setting is part of the growth of any business, so use the processes mentioned above to set goals and to ensure everyone on your team is pulling in the same direction.

Step 2: Acquire

Get The Tools You Need to Succeed Online

Just like an architect needs a drafting board and a mechanic needs a wrench, you will need to acquire the necessary tools to effectively build and market your business online. The chapters in this section discuss everything you will need to establish your online presence in order to sell your products and services on the internet.

From domain names and web hosting to websites and shopping cart software, you will find out everything you need to get your business online and ready to take orders from customers.

"Embrace what you don't know, especially in the beginning, because what you don't know can become your greatest asset. It ensures that you will absolutely be doing things different from everybody else."

– Sara Blakely, founder of SPANX

3. Building Your Online Marketing Foundation

3.1 What Are the Three Critical Success Factors for Getting Your Business Online?

A critical success factor (CSF) is a term for an element, activity, condition, or capability that is necessary for your goals to be successful. CSFs are not measurable but are things that need to be done or acquired to achieve an objective.

When establishing your business online to increase its visibility and make a strong first impression, there are at least three critical success factors you will need to keep in mind:

1. A good domain name
2. Reliable web hosting
3. A Google account

Let's take a look at each of these to learn what they are and why they are so important to your success.

3.2 What Is a Domain Name and Why Do You Need One?

A domain name is unique address that represents the location of your website. A domain is like a street address for your website. Similarly, no two companies will have the exact same web address. This is how people will know to find your website. In the past, websites used to always look like this: www.websitename.com. As the popularity of the internet has grown and we started to run out of unique domain names, you can now have numerous domain extensions instead of ".com".

For instance, your website can end in .guru, .biz, .world, .agency, .partners, .tech, and hundreds more. It's also not necessary to add the "www" anymore, so your website might look like this: websitename.technology. There is a world of opportunity to purchase and utilize a unique domain name that lets you and your business shine and be found more easily.

3.2.1 What Are Five Benefits of Having Your Own Domain Name?

Your domain name is going to be one of the ways your customers find you online. That's why, if you don't already have one, it must be one of your top priorities. There are 5 key benefits of having a domain name for your business:

1. **Simplicity:** Your domain is easier to remember than a generic, cobranded domain such as "https://sites.google.com/site/hardtoremember/" or "www.ebay.com/usr/hard_to_remember".

2. **Brand Protection:** By purchasing your domain name, you keep competitors from swooping in and purchasing it. It is also recommended to buy different variations of your website address. This keeps others from buying them simply so you cannot. Another possibility is that a company with a similar name will want to use it and therefore make it harder for your company to be found on search engines.

3. **Credibility:** Prospective customers will be more likely to buy from a business with a professional, established online presence. And a good domain name provides that. When you don't invest in distinguishing your business online from your competitors it signals that you are not serious about your business.

4. **Professional Email:** When you purchase your domain name, you can set up an email address that will have the domain name in it. If you purchase websitename.com, your email address can be info@websitename.com, or anything@websitename.com. This is much more professional than if you were to use ContactMe@hotmail.com. You add another level of credibility to your company when you use an email that includes your domain name.

5. **Promotion:** Your domain name makes it easier to promote your business. You can put it on business cards, t-shirts, coupons, videos, other websites, and so on.

3.3 How to Choose a Domain Name for Your Business

Determining your domain name is not a task that should be taken lightly. Because so many domains already exist, it can be rather challenging to find a domain name that matches your business name. In fact, if your company name is not set in stone yet and you have not purchased a domain name, research what domain name is available before you settle on a business name.

Here are some factors to consider when deciding on your domain name:

- **Research the Competition:** Look at other companies in your industry and see what domains they are using. Is their brand name part of the domain? Is the service they provide in the domain name?

- **Brand, Location, Keywords:**

  - If you sell a product, will you use the name of your product in the domain or your company name?

  - Do you only service your own city? You may want to include the city in your domain name.

  - Research what keywords people are using to find you or your competition's products or services. (See Chapter 7.4.) If you are solving a problem with your services or products, use that to help determine what your best choice would be for a domain.

- **Stick with Letters:**

To avoid any confusion when communicating your domain name avoid the following characters:

- **Numbers:** If people hear a number in your domain name, they are likely to question if you mean the actual number or the written-out number. For example: "5" or "five." If a number is in your actual business name, then register both versions of your domain name. (ex: www.5dayplan.com and fivedayplan.com) Your business name will be the main domain and the other domain will be used to redirect web traffic to the main domain.

- **Punctuation & Symbols:** Hyphens, underscores, and others will be difficult to communicate to others. People could also forget about the punctuation or symbols. (ex: www.dont-use-hyphens.com.)

- **Double Letters:** This would be when the end of the first word has the same letter as the first letter in the next word. "Suzie's Scents" is an excellent example of this. The domain would be suziesscents.com but most people trying to visit the website will forget an "s" and type suziescents.com instead. Suzie would need to decide if she should purchase both versions just in case.

- **Extension (aka TLD):** A top-level domain (TLD) is the part of the domain name that appears on the right of the dot ("."). The most common TLDs are [.com], [.net], and [.org]. Some others are [.co], [.info], and [.biz]. These common TLDs all have particular guidelines but are available for anyone to get anywhere in the world. If you decide to use one of the newer domain extensions like [.services] or [.media]—make sure it is relevant to your business and not just for fun.

- **Research:** Make sure the domain you want to use is not copyrighted or trademarked. If it is, you risk having to abandon the domain at the very least. You could even risk a lawsuit if the owner of the copyright or trademark feels that you made a lot of money by using the protected name.

- **Memorable:** Avoid a lengthy domain name or one that has words that are rarely used. You want a domain that people can easily communicate to one another; often they are communicating it from memory.

You should make a list of domain names you would like to get. List the domains in the order of your preference and put the most-wanted domains at the top of the list. The list will be a helpful guide when the time comes to getting your domain. Make sure that they meet the above criteria. When you are looking for a domain, your top choice may not be available, but you may find a slight variation of it available. For example, let's say Karen has a cupcake shop. She wants to use KarensCupcakes.com, but it is not available. She may want to try KarensCupcakeShop.com or GetKarensCupcakes.com. Do not be afraid to add alternatives to your list.

3.3.1 How Many Domain Names Do You Need?

Of course, you can operate with just one domain, but there are reasons you may want to consider getting more than one. Using the example above, Karen may decide to get KarensCupcakes.com, KarensCupcakeShop.com, and GetKarensCupcakes.com and direct them all to the same website.

- **Strategic Purpose:** KarensCupcakes.com is a great domain name, it's descriptive and easy to remember. KarensCupcakeShop.com is also good because it indicates Karen has a physical location and doesn't just sell her cupcakes wholesale. In any case, having both domains allows Karen to determine how she wants her business to be represented online.

- **Added Insurance:** Purchasing multiple domain names also ensures that competitors won't be able to get domain names that will stop traffic from coming to your website. Savvy competitors can get a domain name you have but with a different extension like .net and get it ranked high in the search engines. When a potential customer does a search on a site like Google, they will see your competitor's site unless yours is ranked higher. If not, you will lose that customer and many more. Getting your website ranked high in the search engines will be discussed in Chapter 7.

If you decide to register more than one domain, make sure you don't go overboard and get too many. The cost for getting multiple domains can add up especially if you register them all at the same time. A digital marketing consultant can help you with this decision.

3.4 What Does It Mean to Register a Domain Name?

The act of securing a domain name is called domain registration or registering a domain. There are 3 components to the registration process:

1. **Registry:** This is a database that manages the domains and the information behind those names.

2. **Registrars:** They allow you to reserve (buy) a domain with the registry.

3. **Registrant:** This is the individual (you or your business) that registers the domain.

3.4.1 When Should You Register Your Domain Name?

Once you have decided what domain you want, you need to register it immediately. With so many businesses becoming aware of the need for an online presence, don't give someone else a chance to grab a domain you want before you do. If the one you want is taken, try the next one on the list you created.

3.4.2 Where Do You Register Your Domain Name?

The registrar is the company that you purchase domains from. Prices vary but you can often get a domain name for less than $20. Compare prices and services before you purchase your domain. Here are a couple of the domain registrars:

- **GoDaddy.com:** A very popular domain registrar. Some of the features included with your domain registration from GoDaddy include:
    - Domain Forwarding which redirects visitors from your new domain name to any web page you choose.
    - A privacy option so you can assign a proxy company name to your registrant details to keep them private. This privacy hinders companies that collect your information and use it for telemarketing, email spam, and junk mail.
- **NameCheap.com:** This site provides domains at a discounted rate. They include the same features as GoDaddy in addition to free WhoIsGuard for one year that will keep your registrant details private.

3.4.3 Who Should Register Your Domain Name?

As the owner of your business, you should register your own domain name. When a consultant or agency providing any type of web services registers a domain for you in their name, they'll have ownership of the domain. For you to do anything with the domain, you must work through them. That is the type of control you do not want to hand over. Keep control of your domain so you know when any renewal fees are due. You don't want to lose access to your domain because your registration has expired.

3.4.4 How Do You Register a Domain Name?

The process of you purchasing your domain will register it. When you purchase the domain, you must provide all of your personal information and that information will be added to the registrar. In the purchase process you are entering into a contract with the registrar under the terms they set forth.

How Does the Domain Purchase Process Work?

Each registrar has their own steps to registering a domain name including upselling to other optional services, but the steps below are common amongst all registrars:

1. Visit the website of the domain registrar you want to use and enter the domain name you're interested in registering and the site will show if the domain is available for purchase.

2. If the domain is available, proceed to the checkout page and pay for the domain. If it's not available, you will see a message on the screen indicating this and you will need to select another option from your list.

3. On the checkout page—or some point before—you will be asked how long you want to register your domain name for. The amount of time you choose will have an effect on registration cost. You may also be offered bundles that have web hosting and other services. I suggest you don't buy anything extra unless you are certain of what you want or you were advised by a digital marketing consultant to do so.

4. Before you pay for your domain name, make sure it is spelled correctly, that you selected the right extension(s), and that you selected the right length of time you want to register the domain for. Once you are satisfied with your registration options, you can make your payment. Note: if you accidentally register the wrong domain name some registrars will issue a refund if you contact them immediately.

5. The last step is to point the domain to your web host. This is the process of changing the DNS—domain name server—record. The DNS record is like an online phone book. Registrars keep a directory of domain names and translate them to Internet Protocol (IP) addresses. An IP address looks like 201.17.248.166 or this e6a4:79f5:5066:8900:bd51:42ec:7cae:8f1a. While

humans recognize websites based on their domain name, computers / machines access websites based on IP addresses. When you update your DNS record, it can take up to 24 hours for your domain to point to the correct address.

3.4.5 How Long Should You Register Your Domain Name For?

When you purchase your domain, you can register the domain for between 1 and 10 years. It is recommended to invest in at least 5 years. Make sure you document when you registered your domain name. Once registered domains are usually set to auto-renew after their expiration date. Make sure that your payment details are the same and the money is available to pay for the registration. You risk losing your domain if your contact information or payment information is outdated at the time the site tries to auto-renew.

Most registrars have a grace period between 20 and 30 days after the expiration date. After that, you will need to pay a recovery fee to retrieve it past the expiration grace period. If you don't pay the fee to recover your domain name you risk losing it to another business. You may get a better ranking in search engines the longer your domain registry lasts because the search engines see your commitment to your web presence.

3.5 Should You Keep or Change a Domain Name You Already Have?

Sometimes business owners register a domain name and find out later that the name was a bad choice. A bad domain name can certainly have an effect on web traffic and sales. But, with this new information you just learned you may be wondering if you should change your domain name and start over.

You want to avoid changing your domain name if you have a high amount of traffic going to an existing website. It will take time to get that traffic back if you change your domain name.

However, if you don't get much traffic at all, you may want to change your domain.

Consider the following when deciding if it would be advantageous to register and start using a new domain name for an existing website:

- Is the existing domain name on business cards or other printed materials?

- Is there a lot of traffic/leads/sales coming to the existing site?

- Where does it rank on the search engines? Is it on the first page of Google?

- How much work has gone into creating an online presence for that domain?

- Does your existing website need an overhaul?

If your existing website needs an overhaul, I suggest getting a new domain and a new website. Start fresh!

If you don't need an overhaul to an existing website but feel the current domain name is not producing the results you expect for your business, then register a new domain name and use it for your existing website. Then redirect the old domain to the new one so you don't lose visitors that may still use the old web address.

3.6 What Is Web Hosting and Why Do You Need It?

Web hosting is the process of storing websites so that other computers and mobile devices can access the content of your website from the internet. A web host is a company that provides space on their computer servers where your website content is stored. While it is possible to set up a web server yourself and host your own website, it's not practical and not recommended. Web hosting is very affordable and can be paid for monthly or annually.

3.7 What Are the Different Types of Web Hosting?

Prior to choosing the best host for your needs, you should understand that there are different types of web hosting options. You will have to determine which option matches your needs.
Web Hosting Types

1. **Shared Hosting:** With shared hosting, you are on the same server as other websites. Each website on the server has their own directory where they store files for their website. If you have less than 30,000 visitors to your website each month, a shared host is a good way to start. This option

usually comes with technical support, security upgrades, and programs that add features to your website like a shopping cart. You can get this hosting for as little as $3 per month.

2. **Dedicated Hosting:** This type of host is for high traffic websites (more than 100,000 visitors per month), or sites that are so big that shared hosting will not meet their needs. Examples would be eBay.com or Amazon.com. The web host provides more security and better performance than a shared host. The cost for this option starts around $75 per month.

3. **Virtual Private Server (VPS) Hosting:** This option is a mixture of the shared and dedicated hosting. With VPS, you are on a shared server. The difference is that certain resources are allocated to your site and other sites cannot infringe on those resources. You may use this if you want to use a specific software that is not available with a shared hosted site. You may also need a VPS if your site's CPU or memory has exceeded the capacity for a shared host. This is often the case if you have complex programming or interactive elements on your site. The cost for VPS hosting is about $20 per month.

4. **Cloud Hosting:** Whereas traditional hosting puts your website on a server in a specific geological location, cloud hosting distributes your site to multiple servers in various locations. There are many benefits to this type of setup. For instance, the servers are load-balanced so that if another website in your same cluster is taking up most of the bandwidth, it doesn't affect your site's performance because another iteration of your site at a different location can be made active. Furthermore, natural disasters or power outages at one server farm won't mean your site goes down because another location's server can be made active. Because of this unique setup, cloud hosts often charge users on bandwidth used rather than a flat fee. One downside is that security and privacy are harder to ensure because your information is stored in multiple locations.

3.7.1 Which Operating System Should You Choose for Your Web Hosting?

Just like home computers that offer choices in operating systems like Windows and Apple's macOS, web servers offer choices in operating systems. The two major ones are Linux and Windows. The overall difference between the two servers is that they use different script and database languages. If your home computer runs on Windows that does NOT need to be taken into account when deciding on your type of web server operating system.

Below is a quick overview of both operating systems:

Linux Server:

- More affordable
- Known for being reliable, stable, faster, and efficient
- Ideal for blogs, content management, and forums
- Generally, Linux is a more secure server, but it could still be the target of malicious coders.
- If you plan on a website that uses WordPress, Drupal, or Joomla (which all use MySQL and PHP) Linux is the best server option for you.

Windows Server:

- If you want to run Windows-based applications on the site like ASP.NET and Microsoft SQL, you must use a Windows server
- Could also run WordPress, but Linux is usually the more cost-effective option.

3.7.2 What Are the Main Features to Look for with a Web Hosting Plan?

There are quite a few factors to consider when deciding on a web host.

- **Reliability and Speed:** Look for a company that guarantees at least 99.5% uptime (when the site is functional).
- **Data Transfer (Traffic/Bandwidth):** Data transfer (also known as "traffic" or "bandwidth") is the number of bytes transferred from your site to visitors when they browse your site. Each time someone accesses your website, downloads files from your server, or even uploads files, bandwidth is used. Some web hosts provide unlimited bandwidth which is a nice feature.

• **Disk Space:** This relates to how much web space your site uses. Just like the hard drive on your home computer, disk space is used by text, photos, videos, audio and all other files on your website. Like bandwidth, some web hosts offer unlimited disk space.

• **Technical Support:** Look for a web host that provides 24/7 tech support. There are enough of them out there that you should be able to expect this from your web host.

• **PHP Support:** Many new programs and scripts require PHP support. Hosting companies include it with their Linux packages.

• **SSL (Secure Sockets Layer):** This is a component that provides security to your customers. While it used to be only required for sites that accept payment information, with the increase in data breaches, browsers like Chrome often block websites without SSL, and Google may even lower your search ranking. When you see https://... in a web address, the "s" signifies that the site is secure to receive and transmit private details like customer payment information. Before you commit to your web host, find out if they let you set up a secure (SSL) connection.

• **Email Aliases, Forwarding, and Autoresponders:** Don't underestimate the value of dedicated email addresses that identify your business. The ability to create email aliases allows you to create an email address for everyone that works in your business and for whatever need you may have. For example: info@yourdomain.com, contact@yourdomain.com, YourName@yourdomain.com. Email forwarding allows you to set up an email address so all of its incoming messages get redirected to one or more different email addresses. An autoresponder allows you to set up a custom email that goes out automatically to anyone that sends a message to the email address that the autoresponder is set up for.

• **Control Panel:** This is where you manage various aspects of your web hosting features. You can manage your email setup, site backup, check web traffic, install programs, change your password and much more.

• **MySQL Databases:** Databases are needed for blogs, photo galleries, content management systems, forums, and member-based websites.

• **Subdomains:** Subdomains are extensions of your domain name that you can forward to specific web addresses or directories within your hosting account. You can put an entirely different website in a subdomain. An example of a subdomain web address would be forums.yourdomain.com, support.yourdomain.com.

• **Data Backup:** Look for a web host that offers the ability to back up your website. If your site is hacked or something happens that causes your website to stop working correctly, the web host can go back to how your website looked when it was last backed up.

• **Program and Script Auto Installer:** Some features don't come with a basic website. Hosts often let you add extras to your website. Some of those include content management programs like WordPress, image galleries, calendars, polls and surveys, advertising tools, the ability to add a shopping cart, and many others.

Take your time and look through all of the features. Due diligence now saves stress later when your site grows and needs more support. Don't assume that the most expensive host offers the best services. Factor in the above features in addition to the price.

3.8 Where Should You Host Your Website

Where you host your website can be the difference between your site running smoothly and an ongoing saga of technical troubles. There are several things to consider when deciding on a web host and hundreds of companies to choose from, so picking the right one may seem like a tough decision if you're just starting out. I'll make it easy for you by listing two very reputable companies for you to research and consider.

HostGator.com: All-Purpose Hosting

1. HostGator is a very well-known web host provider that meets the needs of both Linux and Windows customers.

2. They can scale with your business because they have a variety of packages that work well for everyone—from single blogs to large-capacity, high-traffic websites and applications.

3. HostGator provides shared hosting as well as VPS and dedicated hosting services.

Bluehost.com: Great for Beginners

- Bluehost offers a variety of hosting plans for customers that are going to use WordPress for their websites.

- If you decide after your site is up that you need specific features, Bluehost allows you to easily upgrade your hosting plan.

- Bluehost has plans that allow hosting for an unlimited amount of websites on the same account. This works nicely for business owners that want to set up numerous sites.

3.9 Is It a Good Idea to Get Your Domain Name and Web Hosting from the Same Company?

It may seem logical to get your web hosting from the same company you registered your domain name with, but let's look at the pros and cons:

Pros of Using the Same Company:

- Convenience of having a single username and password to access your two of your most important web services.

- Convenience of managing your services from one control panel.

- Technical issues and questions are handled by one company.

Cons of Using the Same Company:

- If you ever get upset or dissatisfied with your web host, it will be harder to cut ties because your domain is with them. Some hosts will make it difficult for you to transfer your domain if you want to change companies.

- If your account with the company gets compromised, you could lose access to your website and domain name.

- Some companies offer a free domain name with their web services. If you decide to stop using their services but want to keep the domain name, they will sell the domain to you at a price well above the cost of normal domain registration. Make sure to read Chapter 4.7 Free Websites Aren't Really Free, and You Don't Own Them.

Convenience and security are the underlying factors in determining whether to use the same company for your hosting and domain purchase. If you want security, separate companies for each is the way to go. If you are willing to forgo some security for convenience, you can go with one company for both services.

3.10 Why Do You Need a Google Account?

Google and its suite of free and paid apps are indispensable for modern business owners. Whether it is managing your keywords, advertising, search engine results, email, or file management, there is little reason for you to not jump on the bandwagon.

Here are 11 of the best tools Google offers:

1. **Google Ads** is an advertising service for businesses that would like to show ads in Google searches and within the Google advertising network. Google Ads enables businesses to establish an advertising budget and only get charged an advertising fee when their ads are clicked on. The delivery of the ads is based largely on keywords that people enter in search and the keywords businesses are targeting.

2. **Google Analytics** is a free service for websites that provides you with insight about visitors to your web pages. Here's some of the data you will get tracked for you:

   • **Demographics:** Age, gender, location, language, etc.

   • **Social Engagement:** You will see what social networks your visitors are coming from.

   • **Traffic Sources:** You will know which search engine or website your visitors are coming from or if they came to your site simply by entering your URL. You will also know what keywords they used to find your site.

   • **Technology Used:** What browsers or operating systems are your visitors using?

   • **Mobile or Desktop:** You will know if your visitors accessed your site from a mobile device or desktop. You will know if your leads most often come from mobile or desktop.

- **Top Content:** You'll know which parts of your site are being visited most often and that will tell you what content people enjoy reading the most.

- **Lead Conversions:** Determine how many of your visitors leave without filling out a form or contacting you in some way. From this information, you can develop goals within Analytics.

3. **Google Alerts** is a service where you can have email notifications sent whenever Google discovers new or changed information you want to track. For example, you can have an alert set up for when new information appears anywhere on the internet about your business name, product, service, website, competitor, etc. You can also set up a query for industry news in specific niches.

4. **Google My Business** was formally known as Google Places and Google+ Local. The service allows you to create a free business profile to manage how your business appears on Google Search and Google Maps. By verifying and editing the business information in your profile, you help your customers find your business and vital information about it.

5. **Google Search Console (formerly Webmaster Tools)** is another free, fantastic service offered to businesses by Google. The Google Search Console provides tools that help businesses monitor and maintain their site's presence in Google Search results. It is important to know that a business does NOT have to sign up for Search Console to have their site be included in Google's search results, but doing so can help business owners better understand how their site looks from Google's point of view. This is vital to optimizing a site's performance in search results.

6. **Google Trends** provides insight to website developers showing how popular search terms and industry trends are over time. When you do a search using a web address you can view the interest in that website over time. You can also compare traffic with other websites over time by entering multiple domains all at once and separating them with commas.

7. **Google Merchant Center** allows you to upload your product listings to be displayed in Google Shopping, Google Product Ads, and Google Commerce Search.

8. **YouTube** is a fantastic way to promote your product, view instructional videos and simply finding entertaining posts from other people.

9. **Google Keyword Planner** provides you with insight as to what traffic you can expect for specific keywords. It also provides you with similar keywords you may want to target.

10. **Google Hangouts** is a video conferencing tool that helps people from all over the world connect with people. Companies can conference with anyone else with a Google account, interview candidates, broadcast webinars, and hold group meetings.

11. **Google Docs** is a web-based software that is similar to Microsoft Office. You can share documents with other Google account holders where they can also edit the same document. There are other types of programs available that you can create spreadsheets and presentations with.

Apart from Google Ads, nearly all of these services are entirely free, which makes them very attractive if you are on a tight budget.

"A website is a window through which your business says hello to the world."
– Amit Kalantri, Author

4. Establishing Your Online Presence

4.1 Why Having a Website Matters to Your Business

According to a CNBC/SurveyMonkey Small Business Survey nearly half (45%) of all small businesses in the U.S. still don't have a website. But 92% of SMBs that have a website think they are a smart marketing tactic. So why are so many small businesses continuing to ignore this vital component?

Here are the 3 main reasons:

1. **Cost:** If a business is having a hard time paying their basic bills, they don't think they can afford a website.

2. **Complexity:** If business owners want to build their website on their own, they are going to be spending hours and hours trying to learn the process of building the site, maintaining it, and then promoting it.

3. **Choices (Alternatives):** The business may prefer to take advantage of free solutions like social media. They can also put their items for sale on sites like Amazon, eBay and they feel like this is "good enough."

While these may seem like legitimate reasons, I believe they are really just excuses to justify the avoidable mistakes that were covered in Chapter 1. Many new and established business owners don't realize that a website is the cornerstone for building a web presence that will make it easier for them to promote their products and services online. Without it, these business owners are leaving money on the table by not making it easier for customers to find them. One survey found 83% of small business owners with a website feel a competitive advantage to those without one.

A website gives you the opportunity to get in front of your potential customers in ways that are not possible with other marketing methods. People are not flipping through the Yellow Pages anymore to find businesses; they are using the internet. When consumers cannot find a website for you, they are going to find your competition's website.

If you still don't have a website, you need to know why you must have one you own and control.

4.2 Why Your Business Must Have a Website You Own and Control

While there are many ways for your business to be found online without a website, those other ways limit how your information is presented and, in some cases, how much information you can share. Having your own website means you have complete control of the type and quantity of content you make available, and how it looks. This is important because if you have a lot of information about your products and services, you don't want any limitations on what you can show. You also want your website to have its own look and feel that matches your brand.

4.3 What Are the Two Main Purposes of Your Website?

There are a lot of functionalities that websites can perform these days. With your own website, you can take advantage of any of these functionalities, but to get the most out of your site you need to ensure that it fulfills these 2 primary purposes. First, it needs to make it easier for your business to make money, and secondly, it needs to capture leads for follow-up communications.

How does your website make you money?

- **Direct Sales:** If your business offers products for sale, you'll rely more on pictures of products, descriptions, a way to process sales smoothly, and keep track of transactions. You may get some inquiries or sales by phone or fax, but seriously consider the ability to process orders immediately through your website. Customers enjoy the convenience of being able to order directly online.

If you're selling more than just a few different items, plan on investing in "shopping cart" software. This allows your customer to put items in a virtual "shopping cart" and see the sales totals, tax, and shipping cost when they're ready to "check out." This additional feature will certainly increase the cost of your website development, but do brick and mortar store owners expect to run their business without counters, carts, and cash registers? Of course not. Neither can you. Selling products online means your website needs to be set up properly. See Chapter 5 to learn more about selling online.

How does your website generate leads?

- **Providing Business Details:** If you have a small business that offers local services, you probably won't be using your website to sell products. You will instead be providing information about your business and services to generate leads and quotes for interested customers. The leads can come from a phone call or a web form (aka opt-in form) on your site.

- **Providing Education:** For certain companies, providing free information can be a fantastic way to make their website useful as a sales tool without being too pushy. Providing articles and resources relevant to your industry—that your customers would find useful—is a good way of showing you're passionate about what you do and interested in providing assistance without any obligations. The key to making this useful is to promise even more information in the form of emails and then having visitors fill in the opt-in form to receive your emails. Somewhere down the line, you can convert these leads into sales. Because almost every website has an email opt-in form now, it's important you come up with enticing and original ways to inspire visitors to sign up.

Once you have your prospects' email addresses, you now have a direct communication channel to keep them informed about your business. You can send them emails with free, valuable information related to your industry as well as occasional promotional offers. Learn more about how to talk to prospects using email in Chapter 11.7 How to Write Subject Lines That Get People to Open Your Emails.

4.4 Should You Build Your Own Website or Hire a Professional?

The main reason most business owners want to build their own websites is to save money. For some businesses, the cost for a professionally designed website can range from hundreds to thousands of dollars and more depending on what their specific needs are. If you have the skills and time to build your own website, then it's worth considering. If it's going to save you money and doesn't take away time you could be spending on your business, then cutting this cost is not a bad thing.

Even if you have the time and ability to create your own website, you will still need additional time and skills to drive traffic to it in order to make money or capture leads. This is the part far too many business owners forget about. While building your own website can save you money, it doesn't mean there won't be any cost.

The 5 factors that you will want to think about when deciding whether or not to build your own website are:

1. **Cost:** How much will be saved by doing it yourself? How much will it cost to have someone else do it?

2. **Difficulty:** How hard is it to build an effective website for your business?

3. **Time:** How long will it take you to build a website? Do you have the time?

4. **Customization:** Will you be able to create a unique site that reflects your business?

5. **Maintenance:** Will you be able to maintain the site and make regular updates?

4.4.1 The Pros and Cons of Building Your Own Website

Building your own website may seem like a good idea or appear to be the only option for some business owners. Here's what needs to be considered when making this decision.

Pros of Building Your Own Website:

- **Saves Money:** You save on the initial cost of building it and long term by being able to update it.

- **Learn a New Skill:** Knowing how to build and manage a website is a useful skill for a variety of projects and businesses.

Cons of Building Your Own Website:

- **Lost Time:** Developing your own website is extremely time-consuming. You will need to learn the ins and outs of creating a website if you want to do it correctly. This is basically like training for a new career.

- **Wasted Time:** You had a grand vision and the best of intentions, but your website does not look or work the way you thought it would.

- **No Marketing Skills:** Your next task will be learning how to promote the site you just built. You don't have the same experience a professional web marketer has under their belt.

- **Your Bottom Line:** This will suffer if you are trying to build a website on your own. You are spending time developing your website while your new customer acquisition is suffering.

4.4.2 The Pros and Cons of Hiring a Professional to Build your Website

Hiring someone to build your website has its own advantages and disadvantages. Here are a few examples.

Pros of Hiring a Web Designer:

- **Saves You Time:** When you hire a professional, someone else will be responsible for building the website that you need. Instead of your having to do it, you can now spend that time working on other aspects of your business.

- **Knowledge of Search Engine Optimization:** Knowing how to get web pages ranked in search engines such as Google is an important skill. A professional designer will know how to build your site so that it is search engine-friendly.

- **Presentation:** Your site will look more professional and have design elements and functionality you probably wouldn't have thought of.

- **Expands Your Web Presence:** A professional knows how to make you look like an expert in your industry. They will suggest web marketing strategies and resources that get customers to your website.

Cons of Hiring a Web Designer:

- **Cost:** Hiring a web designer can be a big investment. Prices can range from $40 to $200 per hour for quality work, and you get what you pay for.

• **Dependency:** When you hire someone to do the job for you then you may need to keep hiring them when you need something done.

• **Qualifications:** It can be hard to determine the qualifications of a person you're looking to hire to build your site. Read Chapters 17 and 18 to learn how to select professionals to work with you.

If you don't know how to build a website, don't have the time or desire to do it yourself, then hire someone who knows what needs to be done.

4.5 Should You Refresh or Redesign Your Current Website?

If you have an existing website, you might be wondering if you should revamp it or create a new website from the ground up. Here are some factors to help you determine your best option.

What is the difference between a refresh and redesign?

With a website refresh:

- Changes can be done on specific areas of your website
- There is no downtime when the changes are made
- There will be no effect on the website's functionality
- It's easier and cheaper to implement than a redesign
- It doesn't take a lot of time.

You can think of a refresh as repainting your house. The outside looks different but the inside still is the same.

With a website redesign:

- It is more comprehensive than a website refresh
- It is more than just a visual upgrade
- Content may need to be rearranged or reentered
- If done right, the website will become more functional, get more features, and be easier to update
- It takes more time and is usually more expensive to implement than a refresh.

When redesigning a website from the ground up you are starting from scratch, but depending on the issues you're trying to address, it may be easier to build it from the bottom up than pick through to find the existing problems to correct.

4.5.1 How to Know If You Should Redesign Your Website

If you have a website and it's not performing the way you expected, then maybe it is time for a change. Here are some signs to look out for to see if redesigning your existing website is necessary:

- **Website is not mobile-friendly:** The number one reason that a website redesign may be in order is if it is not a mobile-friendly website. If your website cannot be easily viewed on a mobile device like a smartphone or tablet, it's going to have an impact on your results in the search engines.

- **Website speed or performance is poor:** If your web pages take too long to load your search ranking will suffer, and visitors will leave your site quickly. Research shows people wait 2–4 seconds for a web page to load before they give up and continue their search on another website. Some of the things that could impact the speed of your website are designs that use a lot of inefficient HTML code, JavaScript, ads, a slow web server, too many images on the page, and many more.

- **Navigation is confusing:** How easily can visitors navigate throughout the website? If navigation is difficult and complicated, you may want to consider a complete rebuild of the website.

- **It's difficult to update:** If you cannot change certain elements of the website without tinkering with the HTML, PHP, ASP, or CSS files then it is definitely time for a redesign. Modern websites are built using content management systems (CMS) that make updating a website like working with a simple word processing program.

- **You are embarrassed by your website:** Is your website old and outdated? Are you afraid of what your prospects might think of it? You have a legitimate reason to feel that way. About 75% of consumers admit to making judgments on the credibility of a business based on the design of their website. A bad website can be far more damaging to your business than not having one at all. First impressions are important, and a poorly designed website gives a bad one.

4.6 Pros and Cons of Leasing a Website

Leasing a website vs. buying is a little-known option for businesses wanting to have a website. Leasing is an alternative for business owners that are on a shoestring budget. There are companies that lease websites to business owners allowing them to make monthly payments to have access to a predesigned website. Leased websites can be beneficial because you are able to use a more dynamic website in the beginning. A website with the same dynamic functionality on a pay-upfront-website might be expensive. Leasing may be more reasonable.

Pros of Leasing a Website:

- Lower upfront costs and the monthly payments are affordable.

- Great way to test out the waters if you need a website in a short amount of time.

- The owner of the website is the one responsible for any technical problems that the website may encounter, and they are also responsible for any upgrades for the website.

- There are also tax benefits to leasing a website. While with the purchasing of a website you save on taxes within the purchase year—when leasing a website you are getting tax benefits for the length of the lease, which most likely lasts a few years.

Cons of Leasing a Website:

- Over a period of time, you will end up paying more for a leased site than you would for purchasing the site outright.

- When you stop leasing the website, you lose the internet presence associated with that website and possibly the domain name. If a leaser decides to increase the price at lease renewal time, and you do not want to pay that increase, then you will lose the website and basically have to start from the ground up with a new website—unless the company wants to sell the website to you. And by that time the website may be much more valuable than it would have been when you first started leasing a few years back.

4.7 Free Websites Aren't Really Free, and You Don't Own Them

Have you seen the commercials on TV with companies offering free DIY websites? The offer may seem like the perfect solution especially if there is a free trial, but there are a number of reasons why you should hold off using a free website. Not all free website services are the same, but here are some of the issues they commonly present:

1. **Unprofessional web address:** Website addresses like www.freewebsite.com/mybizname or www.mybizname.freewebsite.com are not professional and won't make a great first impression on customers. You will definitely need to register your own, unique domain name if you plan to go forward with getting a free website.

2. **They may use your content:** Make sure you check the fine print before you upload your content to a free website. You may be agreeing to give up your ownership rights or waiving any claims that you may have against the service provider if they use your name, content, or website in their marketing or promotional material.

3. **Forced to advertise:** Many of these companies provide free websites in exchange for advertising their own company. Somewhere on your website will be a mandatory logo with a link leading back to the host. This is free advertising for them to get more customers, but it also lets people know that you are using a free website. This can impact how you are perceived by prospects and search engines that you want to be indexed in. Your credibility may be questioned. These ads can often be removed when you agree to pay for premium service.

4. **Limits on disk space, bandwidth, or file size:** Web hosting cost money so most companies offering a free website will have one or more of the following limits:

   - How much content you can upload (disk space)
   - The amount of data transferred to user's web browsers (bandwidth)
   - The size of the files you upload (images, videos, etc.).

5. **Website load times are slow:** You can expect your website to lag because you're sharing resources with so many other free websites.

6. **Hidden cost for extras:** The ability to do things like sell online, track website user data, and add contact forms are considered premium features. You will need to pay more for these and any additional features if you want to have them.

7. **Not easy to move website:** You will not be able to transfer your entire website in the event you want to. You'll need to export the data and use it to rebuild a new site on another platform. You won't be able to take the template you got from them.

8. **Limitations:** You won't be able to truly customize your website as you will be limited to whatever the website-building software offers or supports.

9. **What's "free" now may not be later:** It's common practice for businesses to entice customers with free services initially. But once they reach a certain number of customers, they could decide to start charging a fee for those same services. At that point, it may be too much of a hassle to change, especially if your business has found some success with the website, so you'll probably just pay up.

10. **No ownership:** Ultimately, the only thing you own is your content, and even that may be used, moved, altered, and deleted by the company at their discretion. Even if you upgraded and got all of the premium features, this is no different than leasing a website except that you took your valuable time to build it.

Once you start adding content to a free website you will find yourself needing to make a big decision. Do you take what you have and restart with more design options, functionality, and flexibility, or pay a premium price to unlock the features you need to get the most out of your "free website."

In my opinion, it is best to not use free websites because their limitations are already known. The ideal solution that offers the most control and flexibility over the look and functionality is building your site using WordPress.

4.8 What Is WordPress and Why Is It So Popular?

WordPress is a content management system (CMS) that lets you publish, edit, modify, organize, delete and maintain content from a single central online interface. The content you manage can be text, images, videos or audio files. That content can then be displayed and formatted in any way that you want.

The program's ability to store and manipulate information is fantastic, and what it does really well is displaying your information on the web in a way that allows you to create attractive and functional websites.

Why is it so popular?

WordPress is not just another plain publishing program that only shows what you type on the screen. With so many features available, many large websites such Whitehouse.gov, Sony Music, and IBM all use WordPress.

Here are 8 reasons why so many businesses choose WordPress:

1. **Customizable:** WordPress is open source; this means the source code is downloadable and editable by anyone, for free, for business or for personal use. It's flexible enough to use for a personal blog or a massive news site or social network, and you can make it look and behave however you would like.

2. **Easy to learn:** Anyone can learn to use WordPress. It requires almost no technical skills or special training.

3. **Easy to manage:** Any time software needs to be updated to remain secure, WordPress has a built-in updater that notifies you whenever there are updates available for your themes and plugins.

4. **Search engine-friendly:** Web pages created with WordPress can easily be optimized for search engines to get them indexed faster and ranked higher.

5. **Expandable:** There are thousands of free and paid plugins that can be used with WordPress to increase its capabilities. Plugins can do things like put a map of your business location on a web page or show your social media posts.

6. **Access:** If you have internet access, you can make changes to your website from anywhere in the world. You can add, edit, or delete content easily using a web browser. There are even mobile apps for smartphones and tablets.

7. **Automation:** With WordPress, you can schedule your content to appear on your website at whatever time best suits you and your customers. For example, if you know that most of your website traffic comes on weekdays

between 11 a.m. to 12 p.m., you could schedule your content to post around that time.

8. **Lots of support:** WordPress is a highly supported program with an extensive community of developers and users that can assist with any question or concern you may have.

4.9 What's the Difference Between Using Themes and Getting a Custom Design?

Themes offer businesses pre-designed websites. Many business owners hear this and wonder why they would want anything else. After all, if someone has already done the hard work, why spend the time, energy, or money on it yourself? But as convenient as they are, there's one drawback to think about.

The biggest problem with themes is that a lot of people use them. This means that your website may end up looking exactly like another one your customers may have visited. This is not a good look. A custom design on the other hand is just that. It's customized to exactly what you want depending on your own preferences and how you need your website to function. You'll get a website that is fully flexible in its design, function, and scalability, and one that really stands out from the crowd.

4.10 12 Essential Features Your Website Needs

When it comes to websites the biggest mistake that business owners make is building the website they want and not the website they need. Your website should provide a smooth user experience for visitors where it easy for them to discover the information they're looking for quickly. This is called usability, and it makes a person stay on your website longer so they keep exploring your products and services.

Here are 12 essential features to include on your website to keep visitors interested.:

1. **Visible Contact Information:** Don't make it hard for people to find your contact details. Have your phone number, email, address, and a contact form visible and easily accessible on every page. Web surfers are often looking for a specific solution and have little patience, and there's nothing more frustrating than not being able to get in touch with a business directly.

2. **A Call to Action:** A clear call to action is extremely important for your website. If your goal is to increase sales, then use eye-catching graphics to announce discounts and other incentives. "Buy Now!" "Click Here!" and "Learn More!" buttons are all calls to action, also known as CTAs. If you want to build a relationship with a prospect, offer them something for free in exchange for their email address (see #3). A strong call to action appears "above the fold." This is the top part of your website that people see before they scroll down. Design your website to make sure that the most important content is at the top of the page. If people do not see what they want before they have to scroll down, you risk losing their interest and their business. Don't be part of the 70% of small businesses that have no call to action on their websites.

3. **An Opt-In Form:** When a visitor comes to your website for the first time, they probably won't make a purchase. However, there was something good that you did to get them to come to your website in the first place. They're at least curious about what you have to offer. If a sale is not going to be made, then you must make a strong effort to pursue a relationship with these potential customers. Adding an opt-in form to your website allows you to collect information about them, such as their name, email, and phone number. You get their information by offering something in exchange like a free report or phone consultation. Once you've delivered what you promised you can begin to send them updates and information. This is where you start to build your relationship with them, so they can begin to trust you enough to buy from you. Make sure to read Chapter 11.6 for ideas on what to use to engage prospects.

4. **Easy Navigation:** The ability to get to different areas and pages of your website starts with how your navigation is set up. Typically, it's a menu at the top of every page. Your visitors should be able to find what they are looking for quickly and easily. If you have information that is important, place it on multiple pages. Make sure you have a search function on your website if you have a lot of pages (i.e., product pages). If your navigation is clear, visitors will stay on your website, and that leads to more sales for you.

5. **Professional Design:** A well-designed website will have an attractive layout that's easy on the eyes. It will be professional and modern with an intuitive layout. The colors should contrast well, and the text size should be easily readable. Too much text can overwhelm a visitor so make sure to break text into chunks to make it more scannable. Make sure design elements such

as images have a purpose and don't distract from the website's usability. Avoid a flashy and overcrowded design.

6. **Good Content:** Besides an outstanding presentation and layout, you want to make sure you are providing equally outstanding information. Make it interesting, accurate, and fresh. If you have content on your site that is no longer relevant or accurate, remove it or update it so that it is up to date. Make sure your content holds value for your visitors or they will get bored quickly. In Chapter 6.4 you will discover how to create compelling content that keeps website visitors coming back.

7. **A Blog:** Once a prospect comes to your website and sees your offerings, there really isn't a reason to come back unless they are ready to spend money. With a blog on your website, you can provide free useful content to your visitors, while also building a fan base of readers. You see, each piece of content you publish on your blog creates another page on your website that can get indexed in the search engines. This gives your website more opportunities to be found by people looking for what you offer. See Chapter 6.5.1 for more information on why your business needs a blog.

8. **A FAQ Page:** What are the most common questions that your customers ask? Take the time to answers those questions thoroughly and put them on a page on your website called FAQ (Frequently Asked Questions). This allows your visitors to immediately find answers to the questions they may have before considering buying your product or service. This will also cut down on the number of individual responses you'll need to make.

9. **Mobile Compatibility:** The amount of web traffic from mobile devices is increasing every year. If your website can't easily be seen on a person's mobile device, they're going to move onto another website to look for a better browsing experience. Google is also going to penalize your website in search results if it's not mobile-friendly. Read Chapter 10.3 to learn more about mobile websites.

10. **Social Media Integration:** Including social media integration on your website will increase your search engine ranking, give visitors a way to subscribe to your updates without supplying their email addresses—by following you on social networks, and give people the opportunity to share photos and posts about your business. You should include links to the social media profiles created for your business, place social sharing buttons on your blog posts to make sharing your content easier, and add

status and update feeds from your social media accounts so the latest comments and conversations are visible. If you are active on social media, this will automatically add fresh content to your website easily. Read Chapter 12 to find out the importance of social media for your business.

11. **Trust Signals:** A customer won't do business with you if they don't trust your website. Trust signals are things that are displayed on your website that give customers the confidence to buy from you. Some signals that visitors look out for when determining the credibility of a business include:

   • **Using a registered domain name:** Your domain name should be easy to read, type and remember. It should reflect your business (see Chapter 3.3).

   • **Displaying reviews and testimonials:** Customers are happy about what you do, right? Let everyone know what people think about your business (see Chapter 9.4.3).

   • **A professional logo:** An identifiable logo is a reassuring symbol for customers and an element of trust for your business.

   • **A toll-free or local phone number:** If your website isn't proof enough then all they have to do is call you with any questions or concerns.

12. **Media Appearances:** Make sure to mention and list any media appearances that you've made. Post videos and links to podcasts. If you've made several appearances, then make a dedicated webpage showcasing that.

These trust signals show that you are invested in what you do and gives the visitor confidence in spending their money with you. Read Chapter 16 to find out three powerful ways to increase your credibility online and off.

4.11 What Is a Lead Generation Website?

Whether online or offline, every business needs to get good at generating leads and converting those leads into customers. To get leads, you have to find a way to make your business stand out from your competition. Having a dedicated lead generation website (aka "lead gen site") is one of the best tools to do that. To be clear, a lead gen site is intended to be a simple, standalone website separate from your main company website (though perhaps on the same domain) which focuses on one product or service, or one type of customer. Instead of paying for internet ads to send people to your main website, you may send specific people to specific lead gen sites they are likely to be interested in. There are many cases to be made for having an entire website designed for lead generation rather than just relying on using your current website.

Let's say your business is diversified and offers many types of products and services, you may want a lead generation site dedicated to just one of those products or services—tailored to the appropriate customer base.

A lead gen site is also helpful because you can gauge and test the effectiveness of your lead generation tactics. When everything is on the same site, you can see how many visitors you've had to your site, but you won't know if this is their first time on the site, what exactly they are looking for, and if they found the information they needed. Having a lead gen site allows you to compare just one set of data.

Lastly, you never want to try lead generation as an afterthought. Like anything else in your business, you'll get out of it whatever you put into it. If you take the time and energy to create an entire lead generation website, you'll be more likely to get higher-quality leads, and probably a higher quantity of them too. If you simply post a form in the corner or to the side of your website and expect it to generate lots of leads, it could work but will not be as effective.

To learn more about getting leads and building a list of prospects read Chapter 11.

"Ecommerce isn't the cherry on the cake, it's the new cake."

– Jean Paul Ago, CEO of L'Oréal

5. Increasing Your Sales by Selling Online

5.1 What Is E-Commerce and How Does It Work?

E-commerce is any transaction involving the buying and selling of products or services on the internet. Online shopping has made it very convenient for customers to buy any time of the day or night from anywhere they have internet access.

The transactions can be business to consumer (B2C) or business to business (B2B).

The most basic e-commerce transaction works like this:

1. Consumers visit a website that offers something they want to buy or where they can make some type of financial transaction.

2. Consumers provide their contact details if necessary and send money electronically on the website using their credit or debit card, a bank transfer, or using a third-party payment processor such as PayPal.

3. The website owner receives the payment via one of the sources above. Depending on the transaction it will be fulfilled via the delivery of physical products, via a download for digital products, and via a confirmation email and follow-up of some kind for services.

5.2 10 Reasons Why You Should Consider E-Commerce for Your Business

Whether you're a small, local business that sells products, a professional that offers services, or just an entrepreneur with an idea, using e-commerce should be an integral part of your online marketing plan.

A survey conducted by Pew Research Center concluded that 8 in 10 Americans are online shoppers and 15% shop online weekly. As internet access expands to more areas, data transfer speeds increase, and mobile device usage continues to grow, customers are expecting businesses to sell online.

The popularity of e-commerce is expanding tremendously because of the range of benefits it offers to both businesses and consumers. If it isn't clear to you already, here are the main reasons why e-commerce is so important for businesses to take seriously.

1. Online Customers Are a Desirable Demographic

According to a survey of online shoppers conducted by the National Retail Federation (NRF), 49% are 18–34 years old, 53% earn more than $75,000 a year, and 53% live in a city.

Online shopping appeals to a younger customer audience, with a higher than average income, and living in cities with populations of 50,000 or more. If your target audience fits any of these descriptions, then you definitely need to incorporate e-commerce into your business.

2. Increase Your Exposure

If your business offers several products or services, each product or service can have its own web page on your website. These pages can be optimized for targeted keywords, so they appear in search engines like Google. When more pages from your website get indexed in search engines there are more and better chances for your business and products to get discovered by customers. This increases your online presence and puts more information about your business in places it can be found.

You can also sell your products on marketplace websites like Amazon and eBay. Having your products available for sale on these high traffic websites will give you exposure to a larger customer base. This will be discussed later in Chapter 5.5.

3. Increased Sales

When you incorporate e-commerce into your business, the potential for sales increases because it makes it a lot easier for customers to do business with you. When you add the ability to process payments online customers can buy from you without having to travel to a physical location.

You can list all of your inventory or services on your website so they can see everything you have to offer. Customers can discover things they didn't know you offered and make an impulse purchase. When you have "Buy Now" buttons, a phone number to call, or other call to action triggers on web pages with your products and services, it can help with the increase of sales as well.

4. Low Cost to Enter the Market

If you are just starting your business and want to make most of your sales via the internet, you are on the right path. E-commerce allows you to set up an online store without having to make a huge investment in inventory, infrastructure, utilities or other expenses traditional businesses have. You can add e-commerce functions to an existing website or have them incorporated into a new website. Both options are significantly less costly than getting a physical retail space.

5. Ease of Getting Up and Running

Nowadays setting up and managing e-commerce has become a whole lot easier than it ever was in the past. From how to list your offers, to where you can list them, and how to process payments for them, even business owners with a small budget can get started quickly. The biggest challenge will be deciding what to sell.

Content management systems have made it easy to add pictures, detailed descriptions, and payment links to pages for your products and services. So, technical skills or programming knowledge are not required.

6. Serve Your Customers 24/7

One of the most important benefits of e-commerce is that customers can pay for products, services, or make other types of financial transactions anytime, day or night. This is especially valuable if what you offer can be sold internationally. While you are sleeping, many people around the world are shopping on the internet.

7. Scalability

Once you start making a profit from online sales, you'll be in a position to make some decisions on how to expand your business and ramp things up. Your sales will reveal which products and services sell best so you can focus on promoting those more.

Scalability means you can address specific business needs as they arise. With the right e-commerce setup, you can easily grow and scale your business to handle increased sales, customer demands, industry changes, and more. It will open up new markets for your business giving it a national presence and even an international one if that is your preference.

8. Easier to Get Customer Data

One of the best advantages of e-commerce is that you can easily access your customer's data. New leads are often reluctant to give full and accurate contact details such as their mailing address and phone number. But e-commerce customers are inclined to provide complete contact details and other requested information because they want to make sure no errors occur with their transaction. Once you have their contact details you will have multiple ways you can market to them in the future with a better understanding of who they are and what they are looking for.

Depending on what you are selling you can obtain valuable information like their income, gender, birthday, education level, hobbies, clothing size, details about family members, and much more.

9. Ability to Track Customer Behavior Patterns

Once a customer does a transaction with you using e-commerce a record of that activity will be stored in a database. You can review these records at any time to see if there is a particular pattern or behavior relating to a specific customer or group of customers. You can identify buying behaviors like:

- What types of products or services are they likely to buy?
- How often do they make purchases?
- Do they spend a lot of money or a little?

When you add traffic monitoring software to your website like Google Analytics you can even learn and acquire more details about customers and prospects, such as:

- Which pages did they visit?
- How many pages on your website did each person visit?
- How much time did they spend looking at a specific product or service?

- How did they arrive on a specific web page?
- How many people stopped short of completing a transaction? (This is called shopping cart abandonment.)

With this information, you can make better decisions about your business and the customers you target.

10. Improves Customers Buying Experience

Customers are more likely to return and buy more when you make it easy for them. Some of the ways you can improve your customer's buying experience with e-commerce are:

- Having the ability to create an account that:
    - Has all of the details for their contact, shipping, and preferred method of payments. When they are ready to buy all of their information is available making transactions quicker.
    - Let's them save items in a favorites section in their account so they can easily find and buy the items at a later time.
- Showing recommended and complementary products and services to customers so they can learn about them immediately.
- Allowing customers to see if a product is low in stock or out of stock. Also, letting them know the backorder date.
- Showing them the anticipated delivery times for items based on the delivery methods they select.
- Providing more choices when they're placing orders such as size, color, quantity, installment payments, etc.

5.3 How to Get Started with E-Commerce?

How you start with e-commerce will depend on your existing business setup, resources, and desired goals. Answer the following questions to help you evaluate your current situation and what you might need to get things started.

What Are Your Objectives?

- What do you want to achieve by using e-commerce in your business?
- Do your business and marketing plans include your online sales goals?
- When do you plan on adding this component to your existing business?
  - If your business has not started yet, when will it launch?
- What percentage of your total sales do you want to come from online purchases?
- What is your budget for using e-commerce in your business?

How Is Your Business Operating?

- How large is your business?
- Do you have a website already?
  - Do you have someone to manage your website?
- Do you currently offer any products and services offline?
  - If you sell products do you offer mail orders?
  - Do you plan on using a drop shipper?
  - If you are currently not selling anything, do you know what you want to sell?
- If you have an offline business how much revenue does it make annually?
- Who will manage your e-commerce operation?

What Are Your Opportunities?

- Are you going to offer only one product for sale or multiple products?
- Do you plan to sell to customers in other countries?
  - Will your website be multilingual?
- Do you plan on making some, or all of your products available for sale online?

- Are there certain features and functions you want available to customers?
- Are you going to use incentives to encourage customers to buy online?
- Do you plan on consolidating your offline and online customer data?

There are so many variables to consider when getting started in e-commerce that are beyond the scope of this book. However, your answers to the questions above will give you an idea of what you will need to focus on initially and where you need help. As you continue to read this chapter, you will gain more insights to help you make the best decisions possible for your e-commerce endeavors.

5.4 How to Decide What You Want to Sell Online

When you decide you want to have an online business or use e-commerce in your existing business, you need to know what you want to sell. If this is your first business, then figuring that out will be one of your biggest challenges. Before making your decision, you'll need to consider factors such as:

- Should you sell only one product initially or multiple products?
- Should your product be mainstream or niche?
- What does your competition look like?
- What is the demand for the product?

The initial product you offer may not be original or unique, but there are still opportunities for you to be successful.

If you are still unsure about what to sell online there are ways to get ideas for products. Even if you already know what you want to sell, continue to read as you may discover new things you can offer your customers.

5.4.1 What Types of Products Are Being Sold Online?

Products and services sold online are usually organized into different categories. It's good to have an idea of what some of these categories are for two reasons:

1. To get inspiration for what you may want to offer initially if you don't already know.

2. To see what category your existing product, service, or idea would fit in.

Below is a general list of some common product categories and subcategories used in e-commerce.

Categories	Subcategories
Apparel and Fashion	Sportswear, lingerie, shoes, children's wear, ladies' wear, menswear, maternity wear
Automotive	Vehicles, accessories
Baby Care	Clothes, toys
Bridal and Weddings	Cakes, gowns, photography
Cell Phones and Mobile Devices	Smartphones, activation plans, accessories, tablets
Computers and Accessories	Software, laptops, monitors
Consumer Electronics	Home audio, cameras, security
Entertainment	Books, movies, music, video games, apps, gambling
Event Tickets	Concerts, sporting events, theater, movies
Finance	Banking, insurance, stocks, credit reporting, mortgage
Flowers and Greetings	Greeting cards, gift baskets
Food and Beverage	Snacks, alcohol, catering
Handmade and Custom Products	Jewelry, tee shirts
Health and Beauty	Supplements, cosmetics, fragrances
Home and Garden	Furniture, tools, appliances, paint, wallpaper
Information Products and Online Education	Online classes, e-books, courses,
Jewelry & Watches	Rings, bracelets, necklaces
Office Supplies	Printing, paper, pens, writing materials, furniture
Offline Education, Lessons, and Training	Dancing, cooking, learn a language
Pet Supplies	Pet food
Sports and Fitness	Exercise equipment, outdoors, jerseys, memorabilia
Toys and Hobbies	Drones, board games, dolls, collectibles
Travel-related Products and Services	Reservations, luggage, lodging, transportation

If you don't see a category in the list above that fits your product, service or idea, don't worry. Depending on where you plan to sell your product, you'll be able to search for and choose the best category for it.

5.4.2 11 Ways to Find a Product to Sell

Ideas and inspiration for products to sell can be found everywhere. You want to be proactive when you're searching for products, but it's easy to waste a lot of time when you don't have a clue of where to start. So how can you avoid this? You must become aware of the different ways to discover ideas and opportunities for products customers want or need.

In this section, we will highlight the strategies to use and places to visit to begin your search that will help guide you in choosing the right product.

1. **Solve a Problem:** You or someone you know may have a problem that many other people have. Create a product or service that solves this problem.

2. **Follow Trends:** Create or find a product to sell that is related to a hot trend. You can follow trends by watching television, using social media, browsing the internet, reading magazines, and visiting stores. To further investigate consumer demands you can use Google Trends (trends.gooogle.com) to see if interest in your idea is trending up or down.

3. **Improve an Existing Product:** Visit and read the reviews for products sold online. Take advantage of this information so you can get an idea of the level of satisfaction that customers have with the product. Then determine how to meet their needs with your improved version. Start with product review websites like TestFreaks.com and ConsumerSearch.com. Also, visit consumer marketplaces like eBay and Amazon.

4. **Bundle Products:** You can take existing products that are related and package them together to create a new product offer. For example, you might bundle a cell phone case with a charger and tripod.

5. **Create Your Own Niche:** Take the time to determine who you want your target audience to be and offer something that your competition does not have. You can offer a version of an existing product that could be stronger, faster, more affordable, or more functional than your competitors.

6. Get Ideas from Your Customers: Ask your existing customers what products or services they would like to see available. You can ask them to submit their ideas via email or you can create a web survey using SurveyMonkey.com to get more specific feedback.

7. Resell Public Domain Products: Content that is not protected by any copyright law or other restriction is considered public domain. This content may be freely copied, shared, altered and republished, and sold by anyone. Examples of public domain items are music, films, literature, images, software, patents of a certain age. Just make sure to check that you have the rights to distribute and profit from the materials. You can repackage, bundle or combine any of these works to create a new product.

8. Buy a Product Idea: Some very bright people have amazing ideas, but they don't have the resources to sell them on their own. Just do a search for "buy a product idea" in a search engine and you'll see web pages where you can buy products, ideas, and patents from their creators.

9. Sell White Label or Private Label Products: A white label product is a generic product or service made by a company that you can repackage, market, and sell as your own. Similarly, a private label product is one that is offered by a company but can be sold under the name of your business. Private label goods and services are available in a wide range of industries including food, cosmetics, web hosting, and many more.

10. Visit Wholesale Marketplaces: Wholesale B2B websites like Alibaba.com and GlobalSources.com have thousands of product ideas for you to choose from. It can be easy to get overwhelmed with the number of choices, so be focused and deliberate when you are searching.

11. Keyword Searches: Go to Google and enter the keyword for the product or idea you are interested in. If the search engine results page (SERP) has advertisements on it, that is an indication of an active market of interested customers, and your potential competition. The more advertisers you see on the SERP, the more competitive that market will be. Using Google's Keyword Planner, you can get an estimate of how much competitors are willing to pay per each click they get from people clicking on their ads. If a competitor is spending at least $2 for each click, then they are probably having success selling that product. https://ads.google.com/home/tools/keyword-planner. We will look at Pay Per Click Advertising in Chapter 14.5.

5.5 Where Can You Sell Your Products Online?

Another important decision that you'll need to make is the platform where you are going to sell your products. There are many options for you to choose from. You can use one or a combination of them depending on your product, your goals, and your budget. Your first question should be whether you want to create your own website store or use an online marketplace.

An online marketplace is a type of e-commerce website where products and services from multiple vendors are available for sale and they usually handle payment processing and sometimes even fulfillment. Marketplaces such as Amazon, eBay, and Etsy act as the middleman. They provide a way for your product to get more exposure by making it available to their customers.

Let's examine the choices of using your own website or a marketplace, and the pros and cons of each so you know which one works best for you.

5.5.1 What Are the Pros and Cons of Selling from an Online Marketplace?

Pros of Using an Online Marketplace

- **Sales Potential:** Online marketplaces have a large online presence. They get a lot of web traffic daily because their customer base is huge. Marketplaces will make your product available to more potential customers.

- **Convenience:** Marketplaces make it simple for sellers to add products and easy for customers to make purchases because their contact and payment information is often already saved.

- **Credibility:** These websites have been established for many years and they've invested a lot into marketing—as well as vetting vendors—so customers visit and buy from the site with confidence.

- **Lower Upfront Cost:** You won't have to pay to have anything developed, but you may need to pay a fee to get your product listed or to get premium placement on a web page.

- **Promote Your Business:** While you won't be able to change the appearance of the page your product is on; you may be able to add additional information about your business including your website. Take advantage of this to drive traffic to your website.

Cons of Using an Online Marketplace:

• **Marketplace Fees:** Marketplaces charge different fees for different things. Most charge a fee for each sale you make by taking a percentage of the revenue. Some websites charge you for listing your product and where it is placed on their website. Make sure you check and compare the various fees you may be subject to.

• **Crowded Market:** It is easy for your product to get overlooked on a marketplace website. The ease of listing a product has made it a very competitive place to sell.

• **Marketing Helps Competitors:** Any marketing you do to bring traffic to your marketplace product page will also benefit the other products that appear on the same page as yours.

• **No Branding:** You will not be able to make your business stand out from your competitors. Marketplaces focus on the products they sell and establishing their own brand.

• **Can't Acquire Customers:** Depending on what you sell and where you sell it, you may not get access to relevant customer details and the permission that would allow you to market additional products to them.

5.5.2 Should You Use Your Own Website to Sell Your Products?

Having your own website gives you complete control over everything and can make you stand out from your competition. However, this freedom comes with a cost in both time and money.

Pros of Using Your Own Website:

• More Control: You control the appearance of your products and the navigation of your content. You can create a unique buying experience for your customers.

• Marketing Freedom: There will be no restrictions on how you can market your website.

• Access to Customer Information: You will be able to get personal information from customer sales. This will give you the ability to communicate with them, build trust, and make additional offers to them in the future.

• Keep More Revenue: You won't have to pay fees when you list or sell products.

Cons of Using Your Own Website:

• Takes Longer to Set Up: It is more time-consuming because you will need to plan for how your website will look. You will also need to consider security, maintenance, customer service and a customer payment system if you are going to use e-commerce.

• Higher Cost: The upfront cost to develop your own website can be expensive if you plan on hiring someone to do the job. Necessary things such as web hosting and e-commerce software usually have a recurring cost.

• Needs Web Traffic: You will start at ground zero with no traffic coming in. This can take a while to get going depending on your web marketing strategy.

Think of this decision as choosing between taking the bus or buying a car. When you take the bus you pay a fare to get on, but you will only travel when the bus is scheduled to run. You can't change the route it takes, but there is also no desire to actually own the bus. You don't have to worry about maintenance or learning how to drive. This is the marketplace option.

If you decide to buy a car to travel, you can drive it when you want, listen to the music you want, and go wherever you want to go. But you'll have to buy the car upfront and maintain it. This is the having your own website option.

There are no rules that say that you can only use one method of selling, a multichannel sales strategy—i.e., using both a marketplace and a custom website—is an effective way to have more people see your product. But don't overextend yourself. Select the method that is best for you to start with and then gradually try out other methods.

5.6 What Are the 10 Components Every E-Commerce Website Must Have to Be Effective?

Having high-quality products will not guarantee success. Also, other factors influence how well your business performs such as the design of your website and how you market it.

Certain features can be very helpful on an e-commerce website that will make it easier for you to manage and make it more user-friendly to your customers. Below is a list of the components that you will want to have if you are building a new site or redesigning your current one:

1. **Product Pages:** They should provide a detailed description of your product so the shopper can easily see the functionality and the details of the product.

2. **Personalization:** If you sell multiple products or one that you anticipate being reordered then your e-commerce website should allow customers to create personalized profiles so their preferences are stored, and they can place their orders a lot quicker.

3. **Inventory Tracking:** When you are running low on a product you and your customer should be aware that the inventory for a particular product is running low. That may encourage them to buy sooner, and remind you to reorder the product.

4. **An Easy Checkout Process:** Customers should be able to see what they ordered. The option to change or add to order needs to be available as well.

5. **Fulfillment Explanation:** Customers need to know how they will receive what they will be ordering from you and when to expect it.

6. **Payment Processing:** You will need an online payment service in order to receive payments from your customers. Some of the companies that provide this service include:

- Authorize.net
- 2Checkout.com
- PayPal.com
- SquareUp.com
- Stripe.com

If you currently have a merchant account for an offline business, you can find out if that company offers online payment processing.

7. **Mobile-Friendly Design:** Having a mobile-enabled website has become mandatory for e-commerce. More people are using their mobile devices to shop online. With a mobile-friendly website, you are ensuring that your visitors will be able to see your content clearly and navigate easily. Learn more about mobile websites in Chapter 10.3.

8. **Social Media Integration:** More people are influenced by social media more than ever before. They read and share reviews to discuss their experiences with products and services. Adding social media buttons to your product pages makes it easy for people to share online and can increase traffic to your website and awareness of your offers.

9. **Security:** Your customers want to know that when they enter their personal information on your website that it's going to be secure. Any data you collect from them should not be shared with or exposed to an unauthorized third party. One of the ways you can demonstrate your commitment to keeping their data secure is to get an SSL (Secure Sockets Layer) certificate for your website. SSL is the security technology for establishing an encrypted link between a web server and a browser. It can encrypt sensitive data like credit card numbers and personal information. Most web hosting companies offer SSL certificates, but in time will be replaced by a newer technology called Transport Layer Security (TLS).

10. **Customer Service:** If a customer has a problem or a question, they should be able to reach you, or someone that you hired to handle support. Your phone number and hours of operation need to be easily found on your website. Using online chat is another way to offer customer support especially if you are going to outsource this function.

In addition to these components remember to include what you read in Chapter 4.10 (12 Essential Features Your Website Needs).

5.7 What E-Commerce Platforms Are Available for Selling from Your Own Website?

An e-commerce platform is a software that allows you to build an online web store or sell items from an existing website. If you've made the decision to start selling your products from your own website, then there are a couple of options available you should know about.

1. **Cloud-Hosted:** Cloud-hosted platforms—also called SaaS (software as a service)— consist of an e-commerce program, web hosting, and other functions being provided by a third-party company.

2. **Self-Hosted:** In this case, self-hosted means that you will be choosing the e-commerce program you want to use, providing your own web hosting, and adding whatever functions and features you think you'll need.
Each choice has advantages and disadvantages so let's find out what they are.

5.7.1 What Makes Cloud-Hosted E-Commerce Platforms Appealing?

This platform is appealing if you plan to sell your products online exclusively or you have an offline business with several products you want to sell online.

One of the main benefits is that many of the best practices you need to succeed are implemented automatically; you won't have to do a lot in order to start selling.

Pros of Cloud-Hosted Platforms:

- **Affordable:** Most companies offer different plans for you to choose from that will fit most budgets. There is usually no setup fee and payments are made monthly. Plan prices can
be based on how many products you want in your store in addition to different features you want your website to have.

- **Easy to Use:** It will not take long to create an online store and get your products online. No software needs to be installed and configured. You'll only need to focus on entering the details about your products. If you don't want to get bogged down with the task of designing the look of your online store, you'll be able to choose from a selection of premade templates to use.

- **Essential Components Are Included:** Almost all of the elements listed in Chapter 5.6 are included. So, once your store is set up, you can begin to focus on marketing it.

• **Software Support:** When any upgrades need to be made to the software they will be done automatically. If there are any problems with the software, they will be corrected as they are discovered or reported.

• **Maintaining Your Store:** The responsibility of making sure your website does not experience any downtime, processes payments, and remains secure is handled by the company providing the service.

Cons of Cloud-Hosted Platforms:

• **Limited Customization:** You may have a few free templates or store layouts to choose from. This makes it more challenging to be unique and stand out as competitors will be using the same platforms. Additional templates may be available but will need to be purchased.

• **Transaction Fees:** In addition to any monthly fees that you'll pay, there are transaction fees some companies charge for processing the payment for your orders. The amount of the fee is usually a small percentage of the sale price plus a flat fee. There may be additional fees so make sure to read all of the details before you make any decisions about which company or platform to use.

• **Lack of Ownership:** Since you are leasing the software, you do not own the website created by it. The cost and conditions for using the software can change at any time and you will be subject to those changes or you will risk losing your store.

• **No Custom Domain at Checkout:** Even if you are using your own domain for your e-commerce website when it is time to place an order, some cloud-hosted platforms will redirect your customers to a checkout page on their domain that uses their own SSL certificate.

Example:
Your customers see this: https://yourbusinessdomain.com/shoppingcart
When they click the checkout button, they may see something like this:
https://yourbusinessname.cloudhostdomain.com

This can confuse some of your customers and cause them to abandon the sale because the domain name used on the checkout page is different. The complexities of using your own domain on cloud-hosted checkout pages have been overcome for some companies. However, this feature is available to customers willing to pay for high-end service plans.

List of Cloud-Hosted Platforms

- BigCartel.com
- BigCommerce.com
- Shopify.com
- UltraCart.com
- Volusion.com

There are some limitations that you may not want to trade off for the convenience of using this option. Before you commit to a specific hosted platform, make sure you can migrate the data from your existing store to another platform if necessary.

5.7.2 Why Should You Consider Using a Self-Hosted E-Commerce Platform?

With a self-hosted e-commerce website, you will have control over how it looks and functions. While that may sound good there is a lot of responsibility and commitment that comes with this option. To get started, you'll need to have the following:

- **E-commerce Software:** Each piece of e-commerce software has its own requirements. Decide which software you want to use then you can make decisions about other requirements you'll need. Some popular self-hosted software options are listed below.

- **Domain Name:** You should already have this. If you still need to get one read Chapter 3.2.

- **Web Hosting:** Check to see if your e-commerce software has any special requirements.

- **SSL Certificate:** Needed to ensure that information that's submitted to your website is done so securely.

- **Payment Processing Company:** Find out which companies are supported by the software you want to use before you sign up with one.

• **Someone to Set Things Up:** You can research about items yourself or invest in a web marketing consultant that will guide you in the right direction for the best steps to take.

Here's what you need to consider if you are thinking about going with a self-hosted e-commerce platform.

Pros of Self-Hosted E-Commerce Platforms:

• **Customization:** You will be free to focus on and make changes to any aspect of your website to create a unique customer experience. You'll have control over your call to action messages, what customers see, when they will see it, and more.

• **More Integration Options:** You will have access to a wider variety of apps, plugins, and extensions to optimize your website with even more functionality. You can gain a competitive advantage by improving specific aspects of your e-commerce website such as the shopping cart and checkout process.

• **Ownership:** Everything related to your online store is owned by you. You won't have to worry about policies changing without your knowledge or consent.

• **No Monthly Fees:** Once your website is set up there will not be any monthly fees other than the cost of web hosting which is very affordable.

Cons of Self-Hosted E-Commerce Platforms:

• **Higher Setup Cost:** You will need to invest more upfront to ensure that you have all of the components needed to create your e-commerce website, beginning with getting it designed. Expect to invest more money if you want things set up quickly and correctly.

• **Longer Setup Time:** Since you are starting from scratch, the setup time will be longer and there may be some unanticipated delays that could influence your launch date.

• **Configuration:** The software needed to create and manage your e-commerce website must be installed and configured by someone experienced to make sure everything will work as intended.

- **Maintenance and Monitoring:** You will be responsible for ensuring that your website is always online and secure. If you have an issue that you can't fix, you'll need to hire a professional to correct the problem.

- **Various Tech Support Needed:** Your support needs will be spread out in multiple areas such as e-commerce software, website, payment processing, and web hosting/SSL issues.

Self-hosting your own website can be very time-consuming. This effort can be manageable if you have the budget to delegate maintenance and customer support tasks.

Self-hosting may take your attention away from your primary task: marketing your business. You'll need to have vision and some expertise to execute this plan. You might decide to hire a web marketing consultant who will bring this expertise into your business.

Some popular self-hosted e-commerce platforms include:

- Magento.com (aka Adobe Commerce)
- OpenCart.com
- PrestaShop.com
- WooCommerce.com

Using another analogy, think of the difference between cloud-hosted and self-hosted e-commerce platforms as buying and renting a house. When renting a house (cloud-hosted) you are subject to the terms of your lease. You can live there, but probably won't be able to make major physical changes. You may be able to make some cosmetic changes (changing the theme). But if the property owner decides to sell the house or raise the rent, you may be forced to leave and even lose access to your possessions (customer data, traffic). However, the benefits of renting a house are that you get to try things out before you decide to buy. You are not committed and can try out different houses with minimal cost. In comparison, owning your own home (self-hosted) means you have the freedom of making your house look the way you want, choosing where it is located, and deciding how fast you want to expand it. However, owning your own home is expensive and with that comes the responsibility for making improvements and fixing repairs.

5.8 What Is Affiliate Marketing and How Can You Benefit from It?

It's important to explore all of the options available to you for promoting your business. If you knew there was a way for you to get a salesforce the size of a small army to promote your offers, would you do it? Certainly, since more sales mean more revenue.

In addition to doing your own marketing, you can add some additional support to increase your sales. This is made possible with affiliate marketing.

Affiliate marketing is when a person or even another business promotes your products or services by sending customers to your website using their own marketing abilities. They would place ads, banners, or some other information on websites—including their own—about your business and what you are selling. Depending on what your objective is, you would compensate them for every lead, referral, or sale they are responsible for.

Using performance-based marketing is an effective way to promote your business because you can enlist third parties (known as affiliates) to reach untapped markets, drive sales, and then you simply pay them a commission. The affiliate does all the work required to get you potential customers and they are not paid unless they deliver results.

Some businesses are better suited for having an affiliate program than others. For example:

- If you sell digital products such as software, e-books, specialized information, and mobile apps.

- Your business is not location-specific like an e-commerce store and you offer multiple products.

- You have subscription-based offers (i.e., cloud software, nutritional supplements, food, or cosmetics).

- You are trying to capture leads for a high-value service (i.e., consulting, medical and health services, any type of repairing services).

- Your offer has high margins that make promoting your offer worth it to you and your affiliates.

- You have an acceptable sales conversion rate for your offer. Each industry has a target rate, but you should not start a program if the rate is less than 3%.

If your business offers any of these then you need to consider starting an affiliate program. If it doesn't make sense now, don't worry, you can always reevaluate the idea after some time when your business grows.

5.8.1 Where Do You Find Affiliates to Promote Your Products and Services?

To find affiliate marketers, you can either join a marketing program that helps you connect with affiliates or promote to affiliates on your site or in an email. Let's take a closer look at both of these options.

Affiliate Networks

The business model of these types of websites is only to promote the products and services of other businesses. They provide the technical infrastructure for business owners to have affiliate programs. They are also responsible for:

- Acting as the mediators between affiliates and advertisers (the business owners).

- Tracking all affiliate-generated traffic and sales activity.

- Making sure affiliates are paid.

- Providing affiliates with marketing resources to promote your business (i.e., unique affiliate hyperlinks, banners, etc.) and training.

When you register your business with an affiliate network some of them charge a setup fee and take a percentage of any of the affiliate commissions you pay. Some also charge an annual fee in addition to requiring a deposit that will be used to make the initial payments to your affiliates.

Affiliate networks help advertisers by recruiting new affiliates and listing their business in a directory that they can search. Affiliates can then choose products and services among the list of merchants they would like to promote. Their selection is usually based on how much commission is paid by the merchant. Once the affiliate decides which products to promote, they get the resources they need and begin their marketing.

If you are curious about affiliate networks, you can start your research with these:

- **CJ.com:** formerly known as Commission Junction, CJ Affiliate is considered the biggest affiliate network online. Most of the major retailers use them for their affiliate programs.

- **ClickBank.com:** sells physical and digital products worldwide created by entrepreneurs. From advice for getting in shape to healthy cooking recipes and dating advice, ClickBank delivers digital lifestyle products to customers in 190 countries.

- **CommissionFactory.com:** makes performance-based marketing available to everyone and does not require a steep learning curve in order to get involved and be successful.

- **RakutenMarketing.com:** formerly known as LinkShare, this company connects advertisers with publishers to reach new audiences and influence repeat purchases.

- **ShareASale.com:** one of the largest affiliate networks and has about 4,000 merchants listed.

5.8.2 Five Steps to Starting Your Own Affiliate Program

The alternative to using affiliate networks is to set up your own affiliate program. The nuances for setting up, growing and maintaining an affiliate program go beyond the scope of this book. However, you can begin to understand what is involved by knowing the five steps involved in starting your own affiliate marketing program.

1. Choose Your Affiliate Marketing Software: You will need a way to manage your affiliates in order to:

- Track how many clicks and sales each affiliate was responsible for.

- Calculate how much each affiliate needs to be paid.

- Make affiliate links and marketing resources available to affiliates.

- Generate reports to get details about the performance of your affiliate program.

Here is some software that you can review to see if any meets your needs:

- AffTrack.com
- EverFlow.io
- HitPath.com
- Impact.com
- LinkTrust.com
- PostAffiliatePro.com
- Refersion.com
- TapAffiliate.com

2. **Create the Terms of Your Program:** Clearly lay out the most important details about your program. Make sure you include important points like:

- Your Commission Structure;

- How will affiliates get paid? Per click, per lead, or per sale.
    - Will the commission you pay be a flat fee or percentage of each sale?
    - How often will payments be made?
    - How will payments be made? (direct deposit, check, etc.)

- What type of marketing will be allowed? Will affiliates be prohibited from using certain methods? (i.e., no spam emails)

- How long will affiliates be eligible for commission after one of their links is used?

3. **Provide Marketing Resources:** The easier you make it for affiliates to promote for you, the more likely they are to do it. Create online marketing materials they can use such as:

- Different sized banner ads and graphics they can put on their websites.

- Pre-written content like articles, emails, and Pay Per Click (PPC) ads.

- Special offers that are available only to them.
- Suggested keywords they could use.

4. **Recruit Affiliates into Your Program:** Your program will be useless and a waste of resources if you don't have any affiliates. So, here are a few ways you can target potential affiliates:

- Reach out to bloggers and website owners in your niche. Let them know about your business and find out if they would be interested in joining your program.
- Run PPC ads online that target niches related to yours.
- Use affiliate recruiting websites such as AffiliateRecruitment.com and Mgecom.com.
- Attend affiliate events that are held all around the world and introduce your program to attendees.
- Put a link on your own website that leads to a landing page that highlights all of the benefits of your affiliate program. Give clear and easy instructions on how to join.
- Stay competitive by knowing how much your competitors are paying their affiliates and becoming familiar with the marketing resource they have available in their program. Try to match or exceed what the competition is offering.

5. **Keep Your Affiliates Happy:** Retaining active affiliates is hard if they are not having much success. You'll need to engage with them and keep them encouraged. Try the following:

- Communicate with them often by email letting them know about new things happening in your business and the program. Keep them informed about which strategies are working best. Tell them how they can help themselves.
- Continue to make new marketing resources available and put a solid training system in place on how to use them.

• Offer incentives and reward top-performing affiliates with a bonus, gift, or increase in commission when they are performing well. This gesture will go a long way and increase their loyalty to your business.

• Always pay on time. Do this and affiliates will faithfully promote your business.

Some or all of these steps may seem daunting, but you don't have to do any of this by yourself. Some experts specialize in setting up and running affiliate programs for businesses and entrepreneurs. Affiliate managers can do all the work needed and keep you from making mistakes that will cost you. A good affiliate manager is an advocate for you and your affiliates. Their primary focus is to show affiliates how to promote your offers to increase your sales.

If you are thinking about hiring an affiliate manager, you'll want to take the following steps:

• Identify what you'll need so you can communicate what you expect them to do.

• Find out if they are familiar with the affiliate software you want to use.

• Make sure they are familiar with your products or services.

• Determine how much and how they will be paid. Will it be a salary or percentage of all affiliate sales?

Don't rush this process. If you need assistance a digital marketing consultant can help you find the right person for your business.

5.8.3 What Are the Pitfalls of Using Affiliate Marketing in Your Business?

With so many ways to market online, you want to use the best strategy for your business at the right time. There are many opinions in favor of using affiliate marketing, however, there are some arguments on why it can be a problem. Here are some of the challenges you could experience using affiliate marketing to promote your business:

• You will be competing with your own affiliate marketers for top space in the search engines, pay per click positions, on social media, and other websites.

• If you have a lot of affiliates promoting for you, it will be difficult to monitor every place your business is being promoted. Your products may appear next to some less desirable content or be marketed in a way that doesn't match your brand.

• Affiliates can easily get away with spamming people or using dishonest practices to try to sell your product. Based on the CAN-SPAM Act of 2003, you can be held legally responsible for the actions of your affiliates that send out junk mail associated with your offer. In any case, the customer could assume you were responsible for deceptive and unsolicited marketing tactics which could damage your reputation.

• Some affiliates can also scam you. For instance, if they purchase an item from you as an average person, you give them the commission, then they return the item as that average person. You have to be on the lookout for any shady affiliate behavior like that.

• Some affiliates can be fickle. They may have a great deal of enthusiasm for your offer, but if they are not having any success getting sales or their earnings are low, they will be off to the next business to promote.

• You can become dependent on affiliates. It is a good feeling to make a lot of sales when other people are doing the work. But if you become too dependent on affiliates, you may see your sales disappear overnight as they can stop promoting your product at any time without giving you a reason.

5.8.4 Five Practical Affiliate Marketing Tips

1. The following conditions can limit the effectiveness of an affiliate program:

• Your product or service is for a very niche and narrow market.

• You have only one product or service to offer.

• Your offer is limited to a specific local area or region.

• The profit margins for your offer is low.

2. Having more affiliates is not always better. Trying to manage and monitor a bunch of underperforming affiliates can be time-consuming. So always choose quality affiliates over quantity.

3. Some hosted e-commerce platforms already have the ability to set up an affiliate program built into the software. This can make this process a lot easier to set up and manage.

4. When it comes to building and running your own program consider hiring an affiliate manager that will be responsible for all aspects of the process.

5. Nothing is stopping you from becoming an affiliate of a product or service that is complementary to your own. If the offer is good and you feel the company making the offer is trustworthy, then you can make some additional revenue for your business.

Affiliate marketing is just another strategy to add to your arsenal. If your business is not ready for it, keep using other online marketing techniques until you are ready.

Step 3: Strategies

Use The Most Effective Digital Marketing Channels

The internet is an exciting place to market and sell things, but just building a website will not be enough to find success online. You will need to use one or more digital marketing strategies to bring attention to your offers.

The chapters in this section discuss 9 types of digital marketing channels and how each is used to generate more sales, attract more leads for your business, and position you as an authority in your industry.

"Explore your own innermost thoughts to create content that will evoke deeply relatable emotions and passion in others."

– Ken Poirot, author of "Go Viral"

6. Creating Content That Sells

6.1 What Is Content Marketing and Why Do You Need It?

In the early days of internet marketing, many entrepreneurs thought giving away free information would result in losing customers as soon as they learned what they needed to know. That has proven to be untrue, especially if their content is actually helpful. The most successful businesses give away a lot of free information and they are still able to charge a significant amount for their products and services.

Content marketing is defined as the consistent creation and distribution of free, high-quality content relevant to what you offer. This content is used to attract and build a loyal audience of customers. It's an umbrella term that encompasses many of the online marketing strategies covered in this book where some information is used to entertain, educate, persuade and/or sell.

Committing to regularly produce beneficial content positions you and your business against your competition. Over time, this tactic brings new members to your tribe, builds your audience's confidence in you, and ultimately builds your own confidence.

As you attract more people that resonate with your message and style use your content to establish who your customers are, what you offer them, and how you do it differently than others.

Once you establish your position in this way, all of your marketing efforts will be amplified.

6.2 What Are the Benefits of Successful Content Marketing?

Without a content strategy, there will be little to no beneficial information about your business online. If there is any info out there, it may be incomplete, ineffective, or worse, negative. It's difficult to market your business effectively no matter which online strategy you use if you have no content, or the content you do have is not current, relevant, or valuable to your target audience.

Everyone who uses the internet is looking for some form of content. It can be to get information, seek entertainment, or something in between. If someone happens to discover any content you may have, and doesn't find what they're looking for, they will not be going back to wherever they saw it posted. You would've missed out on a chance to gain customers. That's why you need a content strategy that identifies ways to engage people, helps them, and keeps them coming back until they become customers.

When you take the time to develop, implement and analyze your content marketing strategy here are some of the benefits you'll experience:

- **Increased Online Visibility:** When you put content on your own website and on popular social media websites like LinkedIn, YouTube and others, it has an opportunity to be seen by your target audience. The more exposure you give your content, the more likely it's going to be found by search engines and people which expands your online presence.

- **Larger Audience and Stronger Connections:** When you are consistently creating new content that people enjoy, and you continue to put it in the same place such as social media or your website, it gives them a reason to come back for more. Even when you take just a moment to answer a question or reply to a comment, people take notice and appreciate it. If someone found your content to be valuable, they can share it with the people they're connected to online. Over time, this ongoing engagement will grow your audience, build your reputation, and strengthen your connection with them.

- **Increased Credibility and Trust:** As you're growing your audience, you want to make sure that the content you put out positions you as an authority in your industry. This is how to demonstrate what you know, and what separates you from your competitors. Content that's authoritative, confirmable, and helpful to your audience will earn their trust. So, when you do decide to promote a product or service, they will be more receptive and less defensive toward your offer.

- **Attention from Your Ideal Buyers:** Customers these days are doing tons of online research to help them make better purchasing decisions. They have little interest in information that comes across as too "salesy." If you can support them in making choices they're satisfied with, they'll be more likely to do business with you.

That's why—after you have built trust with your audience—it makes sense to create content that shows how your products and services can help them solve a problem, reach a goal, or fulfill a desire. Based on their questions and feedback, combined with the relationship you have built with them, you can begin to create and strategically embed stronger call-to-actions in your future messages.

When done correctly, those messages can drive web traffic anywhere you want it to go such as a lead generation page or a sales page with one of your offers. Focusing on the group that has shown the most interest in your content will convert them from being casual followers to paying customers.

- **Longevity:** While they are effective, some online marketing strategies stop working immediately or shortly after you stop using them. A good content strategy takes this into consideration and uses long-term and short-term goals to identify which strategies to use and when to use them.

To give your content longevity, start creating evergreen content that remains relevant over a long period of time. The true effectiveness of content marketing is realized when people are viewing evergreen content that you created in the past and they're still getting value from it regardless of when they see it. Examples of evergreen content include research, statistics, case studies, how-to information, and a list of resources.

6.3 Five Reasons Why People Ignore Content

Before you invest any time into content marketing, you need to know the pitfalls that most business owners are making so you won't repeat them. To ensure you get the reaction you expected from your content, pay attention to these reasons that turn people off.

1. **Repeating the Same Message:** While you want to make sure as many people see your content as possible, your followers won't be able to see every post. You don't want to annoy the people who have already seen it by posting the same thing multiple times. Focus on creating new content and ways to attract new followers.

2. **Too Sales Oriented:** 71% of buyers say they had a negative impression with content that seems like a sales pitch. People who look at content regularly are not doing it because they want to buy something. If they want to buy something they probably already know where to go and how to do that. Realize that followers want to engage with you so don't miss an opportunity to connect with them and use less aggressive methods to convert them to customers.

3. **Too Self-centered:** There are other things to talk about other than your business, products and services. Even if you are not trying to sell, this can turn away followers just as fast.

4. **Too Much Content:** You may think this is not a bad thing, but it is possible to create too much content to the point where people start to tune out your messages. With so many voices on the internet, your followers may just skip over your content to see what someone else is talking about. Work on improving the quality of your articles so you can spend time elaborating on your ideas instead of having to constantly come up with new ones.

5. **Content is Redundant:** When a person follows you on multiple social media platforms, it is quite understandable that they ignore your content if they have already seen it somewhere else. The same goes for reusing content across different online marketing channels. Example: Don't send an email with the same content used in a Facebook and LinkedIn post. It's okay to have duplicate content occasionally, but you usually want your content to be tailored to the style of the platform or channel you're using.

Content marketing is not about creating content for the sake of it. You will need to put some thought into this strategy because it does impact all of the other strategies in this book. So, let's look at how to create content that gets people's attention.

6.4 How to Create Compelling Content That Your Customers Will Look Forward to Seeing

Every business using e-commerce wants the same thing for people to buy their products. With so much competition online, you have to not only differentiate yourself from direct competitors but indirect competitors as well. There is only so much content a potential customer can take in and consume every day, and you've got to compete to make it on that list.

Remember, your main goal is to create content that attracts loyal customers using free content people see value in. When you create low-value content that can't keep a person's interest, you are at risk of losing a potential customer or even an existing one.

The more compelling your content is the more time people will spend looking at it and wanting more.

6.4.1 10 Different Ways to Present Your Content Online

When thinking about using a content marketing strategy to grow your business, it can be difficult to know where to start when you don't know what your options are. There are several different mediums you can use, some—like blog posts—are inexpensive and easy to create, others—like videos—can be work-intensive and require a serious budget.

Here's a list of the various types of content you can create for your audience.

1. **Articles:** Writing articles does not require technical know-how, but you do need to know how to put words and ideas together to keep your readers interested in what you write.

2. **Audio Recording:** Original and pre-recorded content that can be downloaded or streamed from the internet. For example, podcasts, audiobooks, teleseminars, internet radio, interviews, etc.

3. **E-Books:** Digital versions of books that contain text, images, or both. They can be read online or downloaded to computers and mobile devices. They're a good way to take long content and break it down into easier to read chapters.

4. **E-Course/Online Courses:** An e-course is training or lessons sent by email over a set period of time. An online course is web-based training where participants enroll to learn a skill and/or meet requirements needed to achieve a level of certified proficiency on a topic. A curriculum is used and training is can be self-paced or conducted live via the web.

5. **Images:** Visual content that is used alone or combined with text to express

ideas. Examples include animated gifs, infographics, cartoons, comics, drawings, memes, photos, screenshots, etc.

6. **Presentations:** Creating or repurposing your content into presentation form is another way to get it in front of your target audience.

7. **Press Releases:** Similar to the ones created offline, online press releases are used to promote something newsworthy. The big difference is the information stays on the internet creating another way for people to find out about your business.

8. **Special Report/White Paper:** Special reports are short documents that contain introductory and "how-to" information on a topic. White papers are authoritative and persuasive reports that explain the benefits to prospects about a specific process, product or service you offer. Usually made available for download, these types of content are great for lead generation because they assert your authority and show your seriousness about your industry.

9. **Video:** Videos are becoming an increasingly popular way to teach, communicate ideas, and engage people. Details about video marketing will be covered in Chapter 13.

10. **Webinars:** Webinars are seminars conducted online. Also referred to as webcasts these events can be live or prerecorded. Presentation slides are usually shown on participant's screens while the presenter goes over their content. Webinars are very popular right now as they involve video and real-time interaction with participants. They can be used as a promotional tool or be sold just like a product.

Keep in mind different people prefer some types of content over others. Using various types of content in your strategy allows you to engage with people in a way that they prefer and are most likely to pay attention to. Make it a point to learn which types of content your audience responds to most and focus on those.

6.4.2 Choosing Topics to Share with Your Audience

Something that can impact your ability to create content is the belief that you don't have anything to talk about. That belief may come from having a lack of confidence in your process or when you try to create something you experience some type of creative block. Either reason would certainly slow down or stop the creation of content.

But creating content is how you attract new customers to your business so it must be done. Great content does more than sell, it shows customers why they should do business with you.

So, if you have ever had challenges thinking about what to talk about with your audience, or this is your first time trying and you're short on ideas, here are some topics that will engage potential customers and help build your relationship with them.

If You Want Help Creating Your Content

- Ask your audience a series of questions or one major question and use their feedback as your content.

- Share customer success stories. When you get a testimonial, ask for permission to use it in your marketing content.

- Interview customers, employees, and experts in your industry on a range of topics affecting your business and industry.

- Create a contest where audience participation serves as both the entry into the contest as well as content. For example: Ask customers to share a quick thought about their experience with your business in order to participate.

- Become a human web browser by researching, compiling, referencing, and summarizing interesting topics from various sources to share with your audience. This process is called content curation and it's explained further in Chapter 6.7.

If You Want to Educate and Train Your Audience

- Answer a frequently asked question that you get.

- Create informational and how-to content for solving problems. Incorporate your products and services as part of the solution.

- Make a list of people, places, websites, items, or whatever your customers may need that you can compile in one place for their convenience.

- Describe some of the common complaints that people have in your industry and how your business resolves them.

- Create a checklist of things for your audience to complete in order to accomplish something.

- Create a series where you take a complex topic you want to teach, and you break it down into several parts you make available over a period of time. This will give people a reason to come back repeatedly to your content.

If You Want to Build Credibility and Establish Your Authority

- Talk about trends in your industry.

- Give a report on an event or conference you attended.

- Make a prediction about what will happen in your industry.

- Review a book or magazine article you have read that your audience would benefit from.

- Explain a law, regulation, or policy that could impact your audience.

- Share your most favorite tool or resource that makes your life easier.

- Are there any myths or misconceptions about your industry that you can dispel?

If You Want to Gain the Trust of Your Audience and Build a Relationship with Them

- Share the story of how you got started in your business.

- Explain what you have gained or lost by deciding to start your business.

- Talk about the mistakes you have made and how you overcame them.

• Do you have any horror stories or "close calls" you can talk about?

• Reveal what lessons have you learned after ____ years in business.

• Mention any milestones you've reached or any recognition you or your business received.

• Reveal any future plans you may have for your business.

• Give a behind-the-scenes look at your business. Talk about who's involved and what needs to happen to keep the business going.

• Describe what a typical day in your business looks like.

• Explain some of your business processes like a unique way you make a product or what can be expected from your customer service.

• Highlight the professional and personal aspects of a staff member to your audience.

• Talk about a charity you support. Discuss why it's important to you and how you have been involved.

Don't let thoughts of people being critical of your content keep you from creating it. Follow these four guiding principles and you'll create content that will attract your ideal audience.

1. **Show Your Passion:** Get passionate about your content. Show your audience why you are excited about your industry, your business, and your life. If you're truly excited to talk to them, let them know.

2. **Share Your Vision:** Tell them where you want to take your business and how you plan to bring them along.

3. **Be Inspiring:** Everyone can use a little "pick me up" occasionally. Your inspiring words can be just what someone needed at that time. Whenever you feel inspired, share the moment.

4. **Enjoy the Process:** Have fun when you're creating your content. If you have a good sense of humor, share it. Don't be afraid to tell funny stories. They are a way to bring you and your audience closer together.

6.4.3 What Is the C.U.R.V.E. Method and How to Use It for Your Content Creation

Originally developed for writing email subject lines, the C.U.R.V.E. method consists of five elements that make content more interesting and engaging.

Curiosity: You want to create a strong desire for your audience to know what your content is about. Use catchy headlines, eye-catching images, and start your content with interesting hooks.

Urgency: Is there something you need your audience to take swift action on? The most obvious way to create a sense of urgency is to create a deadline along with a call to action. But this can become ineffective over time if it's used too much. Tell your audience what would happen if they don't follow your tips. Stressing the importance of something shows that you are looking out for them.

Relevance: Why is your content important to your audience? How will it help them? Structure your content around the answer to those two questions. Keep in mind that what is relevant today may not be relevant tomorrow.

Value: This is not referring to monetary value. What impact is your content having on the lives of your audience? Does it solve problems, make them smarter, feel safer, or more loved? Does it improve their relationship with others? You want to be seen as a difference maker in people's life. Stand out and be different with what you create, don't just regurgitate what everyone already knows.

Emotion: You want your content to evoke certain emotions in your audience. Decide what exactly that emotion is and do your best to create content that inspires the intended feeling.

You're almost ready to take your content creation to a whole new level. You have plenty of options for the type of content you want to create and many topics to choose from. Now is the time to put everything together using the C.U.R.V.E. method.

While ideally, every piece of content will have every element in C.U.R.V.E., to start, you should aim to have at least two of the five elements taken care of, and at least one of those two elements used should be R, relevance, or V, value. It's also important you never use clickbait to create curiosity. Clickbait is the deliberate use of enticing titles to get attention, but the content has no value and does not deliver what was promised. This will leave people feeling hoodwinked.

6.4.4 How to Measure the Effectiveness of Your Content

Did your content serve the purpose it was created for? Complete your content creation process by measuring its effectiveness. Here are nine metrics that can be tracked and measured:

1. **Audience Feedback:** Are you getting a good number of comments, direct messages, emails, phone calls, reviews, and tweets? More than just a simple "like" this feedback is more engaging and strengthens the connection between you and your followers. No one tool can measure these different types of feedback. Identify the metric that is most important and research a tool that can track it.

2. **Click-Through Rate (CTR):** You will see this term mentioned many times throughout this book. It is a measurement of the percentage of people that take action (i.e., click on a link) associated with an offer or call to action. If your content has a call to action some of your audience may respond to it and you will see an increase in your click-through rate (CTR). Google Analytics can measure CTR for pages on your website, each web strategy have their own way of reporting analytics, so you'll need to research how they report CTR.

3. **Lead Generation:** How many prospects submitted their contact details to receive your content? If you're going to be using email marketing, then the software you choose to handle your communications will provide analytics you can check. See Chapter 11.5.

4. **Sales:** If the purpose of your content is to generate revenue, then track which piece of content was seen before the sale was made. Use Google Analytics to set up a sales goal and monitor your sales cycle.

5. **Search Engine Rankings:** See if the page on your site where your content has been posted got indexed in Google. If it has, then check where it ranks among competing web pages and what search terms are people using to find it. To do this for free, use Google Search Console located at http://g.co/searchconsole.

6. **Social Media Follower Growth:** When you share a link to your content or post it directly on a social media platform, track how many new followers, fans, and subscribers you get afterwards.

7. **Social Media Share and Reactions:** If your audience found your content useful, they will show their approval and share it with their connections. Measure how your audience feels about what you shared. Count the number of likes, retweets, thumbs-ups, and other forms of approval.

8. **Time Spent Viewing Content:** For your website, you can find out the average time visitors stayed on each page using Google Analytics. A high average time means people are paying more attention to the content. If you created a video, the website where it's hosted can provide details such as the percent of people that watched the video and at what point viewers stopped watching.

9. **Website Traffic:** Use Google Analytics to see how many people are going to the page on your website that your content appears on. You'll be able to see where that traffic came from.

Use these metrics to learn what type of content people prefer so you know what to create in the future. See Chapter 12.7 for tools to use for measuring social media metrics. Checking your metrics before you distribute your content is recommended so you have an idea of where you are starting from.

6.5 12 Ways to Distribute and Promote Your Content

Content marketing is more than just creating good content, part of your strategy is planning where you are going to submit it when it's ready. The type of content you created will determine what distribution choices you have, and it's important for you to know the best venues to distribute different types of content.

There are also tactics you can implement that will bring more attention to your content and make your distribution efforts more productive. Let's review the methods of distribution and promotion available to you.

1. **App Stores:** If you have created an app for mobile devices, the operating system it was developed for will determine where you submit it. The top two places to publish your app are Apple's App Store and Google Play. Another option is the Microsoft Store.

2. **Author Bio and Signature File:** An author bio box is a short biography of the content creator that usually appears underneath a written blog post or

article. A signature file (aka sig file) is a short amount of text you set up to appear at the end of your email messages or posts you make on online forums. Both are important because unless you are a household name, this is how people will learn about you. When using them make sure to include links to your website, social media profiles, or links used to promote other content you've created.

3. **Email:** If you have built a list of leads, you can send your content directly to them using email or send a link where it can be seen. Read Chapter 11 where this is covered in more detail.

4. **Guest Posting:** Guest posting is writing content that will appear on a blog or website owned by someone else who already reaches your target audience. The benefits to doing this include:

- Increased online presence
- New targeted traffic to your website and other content
- Opportunity for your content to be shared by more people
- More followers on social media
- Increased authority and influence
- More sales leads
- More links back to your website which helps with Search Engine Optimization.

5. **How-to Websites:** If you're looking to share your expertise on how to do something then submit your content where people can learn from your expertise. If they want to learn more about you, they can always click on the link leading back to your website. The following websites have how-to content on various subjects:

- eHow.com
- Instructables.com
- WikiHow.com

6. **Online Learning Websites:** If you have an online course you want to offer for free or get paid for, there are many choices available. Here's a list of popular websites where you can offer your lessons:

- 360training.com
- Alison.com
- SkillShare.com

- SkillSuccess.com
- Udemy.com

7. **Online Profiles:** Business-oriented websites where you must create a user profile must be utilized to the fullest, especially if you have a local business. Most profile pages allow you to add links to your websites and social media profiles. You can upload pictures and videos too so definitely take advantage of this. Profiles can be completed on social media sites and local business directories. A list of directories can be found in Chapter 8.6.1.

8. **Opt-In Forms:** This is an online form that appears on a webpage that's used to get contact information from visitors in exchange for some form of valuable content. Usually, the exchange is for their name and email address so they can get access to eBooks, special reports, videos, webinars, newsletters, etc. Opt-in forms are very effective in getting attention and increasing opt-in conversions.

9. **Paid Online Advertising:** If you want to expose your content to a wider target audience in the shortest amount of time, then consider using paid online advertising. This option is especially effective if you created the content to sell a solution to a problem people are experiencing. Learn more about paid online advertising in Chapter 14.

10. **Social Media:** The most common way to distribute and promote your content is using social media. Facebook, Twitter, LinkedIn, and others make sharing your content with a large audience very easy. Find out more about using Social media in Chapter 12.

11. **Websites and Directories for Specific Forms of Content:** Some websites were created specifically to distribute one type of content only.

    - Articles Directories: EzineArticles.com, HubPages.com, SelfGrowth.com
    - Infographics: DailyInfographic.com, Graphs.net, InfographicBee.com
    - Podcast: Apple Podcasts, Google Play, Spotify.com, Libsyn.com
    - Presentations Slides: AuthorStream.com, SlideShare.net, SpeakerDeck.com
    - Videos: Facebook Watch, Vimeo.com, YouTube.com

12. **Your Own Blog:** The primary option for distributing your content should be the blog connected to your website. This should be the central hub for all of your content marketing and the place where your expertise and

authority are highlighted. If you don't have a blog or you are not using the one you have, the next section will explain why having one is important.

6.5.1 Why Your Business Website Needs a Blog

A blog is like an online journal where one or more writers publish articles about a specific topic, product, or industry. Blogs make money for businesses by attracting an audience that comes to read free content. Once a visitor comes to your website your job is to get them on your email list in order to build trust, and offer products and services that the audience you've targeted truly want and need.

If you want to get more prospects and make more sales, you need to understand how this tool supports your content marketing. Let's go over different reasons why a blog is important for your website.

Control of Your Content Distribution:

The most important reason to have a blog on your website is to have control over your content. You'll be able to post as much content as you want, whenever you want to. This matters because placing your content on websites owned by someone else makes it subject to their rules and guidelines. If you break a rule or create content that violates their terms of service in some way, your account on that website can be suspended or worse, you may get banned. There is also the chance a website where you put your content can lose its popularity or gets shut down for whatever reason. In all of these scenarios, access to your content is in the hands of someone else who will determine if and when it will not be available for people to see.

Helps with Search Engine Optimization

When you initially publish your main website and describe your products and services, the details usually don't change that often. The content on your website remains static and won't benefit your SEO efforts after search engines have initially discovered it.

However, posting to your blog regularly makes your website more dynamic and relevant to search engines that are always looking for new content. They will treat your website differently by checking it more often and indexing your new blog posts faster. That may explain why websites with a blog tend to have 434% more indexed pages.

Using proven SEO strategies, your pages will get ranked higher making them easier to be found by people who may be looking for something your offer.

Increases Traffic to Your Websites

Having people find your blog post on search engines is one way to get more traffic to your website. Another is to post links to your content using social media. Instead of always posting your content in its entirety on social media websites, try posting a title or brief description about your content along with a link. You want to begin training your social media followers to come to your blog to see your content.

Provides a Direct Way to Engage with Customers and Prospects

The same way people can leave comments about your content on your social media posts, they can leave comments on your blog posts too. When people leave either comments or questions, you need to respond in order to keep the conversation going and keep the page active for new visitors.

These conversations are social proof that your content is interesting, that people are looking at it, and they're engaging with you. As prospects see you interacting with your customers it begins to build their trust in your business and moves them closer to buying something from you.

Creates a Platform to Show Your Expertise

When you're producing content on a regular basis that is valuable to your audience it shows that you have knowledge on the topic. As you increase the amount of content you post your credibility increases. And when you respond to comments from your audience that conversation becomes a unique form of content that's exclusive to your website—making it a place to visit frequently for information about your market and industry from your perspective.

6.6 How Often Should You Create New Content?

If you don't have enough content posted on your blog or social media pages, it might look like you don't care about your business or customers. If you post too much, you'll overwhelm your audience with information. They'll eventually start ignoring you, or just stop following you by unsubscribing from your messages.

How often you create content depends on these three things:

1. What is the purpose of the content?
2. What type of content do you want to create?
3. Where do you plan on distributing it?

Every situation is different, so your best course of action is to learn about the various online marketing strategies and how they work. Find out what's involved in creating a specific type of content (i.e., video) and determine if you have the required resources to implement the strategy.

No matter what type of content is going to be created you should always focus on quality over quantity. You need to find the balance between posting just enough to keep things interesting and posting so much you turn people off. You will be better off creating one piece of great content and spending your time promoting it rather than creating multiple pieces of average content that very few people will see and pay attention to.

Use a Content Calendar

The use of a content calendar helps you with the planning and distributing of all of your content across the different online marketing channels. It will keep your ideas organized and remind you when and where you need to post new content. You can create a simple content schedule using a spreadsheet or use software that manages the process for you. See Chapter 12.7 for a list of automated solutions.

6.7 What Content Curation Is and How to Get Started Doing It

No matter which industry you're in there is already a large amount of information about it available on the internet. But you can save your audience time and possibly money by becoming a human web browser and curating content for them. Content curation is basically identifying pieces of existing content that you come across, that are relevant to a particular topic or area of interest and compiling it to share with your followers in an organized way.

Rather than having to scour the internet themselves for the information they need about your industry, business, or businesses like yours, now they can go to your blog where all of that information is in one place. The benefit to them is they won't have to process masses of blog posts, search engine results, social media updates, and videos to get good content. You already did all of the hard work.

By curating content, you are borrowing the ideas and expertise of others and leveraging it to build your credibility and position you as an expert. One survey found 85% of curators said establishing thought leadership is their main objective. As you introduce your audience to more things they probably would not have discovered on their own, they will start to rely on you over time and your following will grow as your content gets discovered.

Here are the steps involved in curating content:

1. Identify a theme or subject that your audience has an interest in. Find out what they care about, what they are searching for most, and what they like to see.

2. Determine how much content you want to curate. There are varying opinions among digital marketing experts on how much curated content should be used. Some are fine using 100%. Some feel there should be a mix of curated and original content. I say test and see what your audience prefers:

   a. mostly curated
   b. ½ curated, ½ original content
   c. partially curated

3. Gather content from reputable sources:

   - Search for ideas from various sources—search engine results and social media for different types of content like blog posts, tweets, infographics, videos, and so on.

   - Set up systems to alert you when new content is available such as Google Alerts or subscribing to an email newsletter that targets the same audience you have.

   - Use software that can help you find and follow news stories:

     - **Buzzsumo.com:** Analyzes what content performs best for any topic or competitor.

- **Feedly.com:** An RSS news aggregator application for various web browsers and mobile devices. It tracks news feeds from a variety of online sources that can be customized and shared with others.

Make sure the content you curate matches the image of your business. You don't want to use anything from a source that is questionable or controversial.

4. Compile and publish the best information into a blog post or social media post. Once you have decided what you want to curate, summarize the content and include hyperlinks back to the source. Embed video, social media posts, and any other type of relevant content you want.

5. Check your statistics. No different than creating original content, you want to know the effectiveness of each piece of content, and what goals were achieved by creating and distributing it.

Curating content can be a lot faster than creating original content, but it still takes time. The process can be sped up by using software that curates for you. Here is some more software to look into:

- **ContentGems.com:** A content discovery engine that scans hundreds of thousands of articles from the best online sources and provides you a stream of relevant and timely content.

- **ContentStudio.io:** Get trending content before it's trending and fill your social channels or blogs with interesting articles, videos, images, GIFs and quotes—in any industry or niche.

- **Flockler.com:** Combine all your content, including what your fans say about you, into one social hub.

- **Scoop.it:** Publish topic pages with curated content in minutes. Share them with your networks to build your professional brand

"SEO is a marketing function for sure, but it needs to be baked into a product, not slapped on like icing after the cake is baked."

– Duane Forrester, author and Vice President of Industry Insights for Yext

7. Ranking Your Business Website on Top of Search Engines

7.1 What Is Search Engine Optimization?

Search Engine Optimization (aka SEO) is one of the most popular buzzwords in digital marketing, but most business owners do not know enough about it to make it work for them. But even people who are knowledgeable about SEO have difficulty executing the steps necessary to produce the desired results.

SEO is the only process that gets your web pages noticed through high-ranking placement in the 'free' or 'organic' searches on Google and search engines like it. Proper SEO strategy will result in increasing the quality and quantity of organic web traffic to your website(s) and social media. A well-coordinated SEO campaign uses a variety of tactics in tandem.

SEO was one of the original ways to promote a website on the internet and while it's becoming more integrated with other forms of online marketing like social media and video marketing, SEO should not be underestimated or overlooked.

Most internet users put a lot of value on the results of search engines and are likely to only visit high-ranking websites when they search for something online. If you're not showing up on the first or maybe second page, you might as well not show up at all. SEO is your way to get free advertising by showing up first on all relevant searches.

The top driver of traffic to web pages is organic search results, so any website owners who do not invest time into optimizing their websites are missing out on a great deal of potential web traffic.

7.2 How Do Search Engines Rank Websites?

The ultimate goal of a search engine is to provide the most relevant and informative web pages to internet users. Search results for different search engines may vary depending on the algorithm that they are using. An algorithm is a set of rules search engines use to rank websites. They are designed to determine which websites are most relevant for particular search terms (keywords).

While each search engine has its own ranking algorithm and criteria to determine the relevance of web pages, there are certain key standards that all search engines focus on. Search engine giants like Google, Yahoo and Bing use crawlers (automated software agents) that visit each website and read the information available to evaluate the relevance of the pages. Once the data is collected, the crawlers go back to a central depository to build the index of the web pages which are fed through the algorithm to match people's search queries. This entire process is repeated periodically to gather any changes made on websites.

7.2.1 Do Search Engines Change Their Rankings Often?

You might find that after pouring time and money into your SEO, your ranking fluctuates. One day you'll be on page one and the next day you'll be on page three. This can be really frustrating for people just entering the SEO landscape.

Search engines promise their users and customers to deliver the most relevant information, so it makes sense that they would constantly be crawling the internet and updating their results.

Most often, the reason a website loses its ranking is because it hasn't been regularly updated, or it was for a while and then stopped which signals to the search engine it has been abandoned or is no longer relevant.

7.3 What Are the Major Elements That Determine Where Your Website Ranks?

Now that you understand why search engine rankings are so important you might wonder how to achieve these rankings. Remember, search engines don't publish their algorithms and they're always changing and updating the way they analyze websites, so part of this is a guessing game. With that said, I will tell you about—in my experience—the tactics which I believe will improve your ranking.

The major elements you need to worry about fall into two types: on-page and off-page elements. Basically, on-page elements are those things that you can do to improve your ranking by modifying some aspects of your website. Off-page elements are things that you can do to influence your ranking that is done away from your website.

The upcoming subchapters are just guidelines for you to follow rather than definitive statements.

7.3.1 What Are the On-Page Elements That Affect SEO?

On-page optimization is a technique that helps the pages of your website become more relevant and search engine-friendly. These elements are controlled by the web designer, whoever maintains your website, and whoever adds content to your web pages.

Some essential checkpoints to cover when improving on-page optimization include architecture, web development, and content.

Architecture

Website architecture is about the structure of your site and making sure it provides the best experience for its users. In order to do that ensure that all of the following are optimized:

- **Mobile Friendly:** Your website must be mobile right now. If your site is not optimized for viewing on mobile devices, the search engines may rank your web pages lower or not index them at all. A survey revealed that websites that were not mobile-optimized experienced a 21% decrease in search engine rankings.

- **Page Load Speeds:** Having a website that loads slowly is bad for your users, and for SEO. You want it to be less than 10 seconds, if not about 3 seconds, but definitely faster than your competition's website. Avoid having anything on your web pages that keeps them from appearing fast. Test the speed of your web pages at: https://developers.google.com/speed or WebPageTest.org.

- **Meaningful Page URLs:** Adding a keyword in your web page URL will increase the weight of your web page for the search engines. You want the URL to say what's on that page. Rather than saying page 1 or page 2, make sure it says "about your business" or "take a course" so that people and search engines know what will be on the page. For example; www.yoursitename.com/what-your-business-sells.

- **Avoid Duplicate Content:** This occurs when similar content appears on different web pages. This creates confusion for the search engines as they are unsure of which version to show when searches are being done. This can have a negative impact on web pages. To be sure, check any content you put on your website with Copyscape.com or Grammarly.com or another plagiarism checker. Even if you didn't purposely plagiarize, you want everything to be unique on your site.

- **Site Map:** A site map is a list of the web pages, videos, and other files on your site. Search engines send their crawlers to read the information on site maps in order to discover your content, the way your site is designed, and how everything is related. A site map tells search engines what information you think is important and what content is most current.

- **Internal Linking:** What helps a search engine identify the relevance of your website content is the site structure and internal linking. Always link to other pages of your website in a logical way. This allows for easier navigation for the users while giving search engine crawlers the ease to flow from one page to another.

- **Broken Links:** Broken links give a bad impression of your website to users and search engines. Although you have no control over third-party websites functioning properly, checking on outgoing links regularly will help avoid linking to non-working websites.

- **Security:** If you sell anything on your website, having an SSL certificate is important not just to people using the site but Google ranks secure sites higher than ones that are not. Ask your web host for information about this.

How your site is arranged and whether or not your audience can find what they want on your page is imperative for good SEO.

Web Development

Your next priority should be to make sure the web developer or software you use to build your site employs best HTML practices to improve your search engine rankings. Some of these details and best practices include:

- **Headline Tags:** Headline tags differentiate the headings and subheadings of a web page from the rest of the content. All the headline tags from H1,

H2, all the way to H6, must include keywords. This lets search engines know what that particular web page is about so they can direct the right traffic to you.

• **Meta Tags:** Meta tags are bits of code that tell search engines what's inside your web page. This information is located at the top portion of each web page called the header and includes tags for the page title, keywords used and description of the content.

• **Bold & Italic Tags:** There is a debate on whether these tags are still effective for SEO. It can't hurt to use them to help draw the reader's attention to important parts of your content. Only use bold or italic tags to highlight important keywords or phrases and never use them for the full copy of your content.

• **Image Names & Alt Attributes Tags:** Instead of keeping default image file names like 'IMG_278.jpg,' rename them using relevant keywords like 'Baby-Strollers.jpg.' An alt attributes tag (aka alt descriptions tag) is an HTML code attribute applied to image tags to provide a text alternative for search engines in case the image does not appear in a web browser. Add a keyword or two in the alt attributes tag of each image to rank your website in Google Image search and increase the keyword relevancy on your web pages.

• **Valid CSS (Cascading Style Sheets) & HTML:** The programming code used to create your website must be free of errors. CSS works within HTML to control the layout and appearance of multiple web pages all at once. Sloppy HTML or CSS codes will do your website no good. They don't only diminish your chances of ranking in the search engines but also ensure a low-quality user experience.

• **Canonical Tag:** This tag helps eliminate the duplicate content issue on a website. If you have several versions of your Home page URL indexed in Google like, www.homepage.com, homepage.com and www.homepage.com/home, Google will consider them 3 different pages with duplicate content. Using the rel="canonical" attribute will solve this issue for you.

If you hire a web designer, make sure that they'll help you with these integral items. If you are doing it yourself, learn all you can, and use a content management system like WordPress which makes doing many of the above items easier.

Content

Anything you put on your website that is meant to give information to your audience such as blog posts, reviews, product descriptions, images, and graphics is considered content. You want to have different types of content on your web pages for maximum SEO value.

- **Blogging:** Search engines are constantly looking for unique content and blogging only improves your chances of being found. Offer your audience tutorials, "how-tos" and top lists in your blog post.

- **Quality vs. Quantity:** While it's true that you want to put up a lot of content for your audience it's more important that it is high quality. You want to put up content more than once a month, but you don't need to add it daily if it's going to compromise the quality of the information you already have available for your audience.

- **Freshness:** Creating content that focuses on hot topics and trends of the day makes it relevant to search engines and interesting to readers.

- **Authoritative:** In fact, the word count for the average web pages that appear on the first page of Google is 1,890. While it may be attractive to have a simple modern website, it's equally important to have detailed information to establish your website as a credible and useful.

- **Keyword Research:** You should research the relevant keywords of the day or around a topic before adding new content, and then make sure that your new content includes those keywords. While people think this is optional, it shouldn't be. What's the point of putting time into content if you're not going to do your best to make sure it's effective? How to research and select keywords for your content is discussed in Chapter 7.4.

- **Video Marketing:** Video content has been becoming more and more popular in the last few years and it seems as if everyone is looking at YouTube to find the solutions to their problems. When used properly, video marketing can be used to gain traffic and potential customers. By adding video to their own web pages a business may experience an organic traffic increase of around 157%, a 105% increase in the time visitors spend on their site, and a doubling of conversions. If a business isn't using video as part of their content, then they are losing out on one of the best types of content to attract new clients to buy their products and services.

7.3.2 What Are the Off-Page Elements That Affect SEO?

Off-page SEO refers to all the activities you do away from your website, and which informs search engines what others think about your website. The quality of off-page elements is generally out of your control, but they are what search engines use to determine the overall relevancy of your website. That is, search engines like to see lots of other credible websites linking to yours because it "tells" the algorithm there is important and relevant information on your website. While many people associate off-page SEO with link building only, there are several other off-page elements including trust, backlinks, and social media.

Trust

There is almost nothing more important to your success than trust. If you lose the trust of your audience, you lose sales and any authority that you gained. But, if you do what you say you will do and don't disappear for long periods, you can build trust.

- **Credible Sources:** When you share anything, make sure that it comes from a reliable source if it's not from you. If it is from you, double-check your data to be sure that you are correct.

- **Available to Your Audience:** When you post anything anywhere, do you answer questions, share other things from your audience, and get involved? Don't forget that engagement helps build trust.

- **Reconsider Using Ads:** Depending on the type of site you have, pay attention to how your audience views ads on your website. Many people won't revisit sites that have lots of ads because they are too distracting and take the focus away from your own call to action.

- **Domain Age:** Some digital marketing experts believe that the length of time a domain name has been registered and active is a factor. It is assumed that search engines think if the domain was around for a long time the website must have something important, real, trustworthy, and relevant. Another assumption is if you register your domain name for a long period of time then you are committed to your venture, and search engines would reward that.

Backlinks

One way to build up traffic to your website is through link building. That means that there are web links going to your website from another website. For example, if you had a LinkedIn.com profile you could add a link to your website there. There are some important factors to consider before getting started with link building.

- **Link Building:** Link building is the art of trying to get as many links back to your website as possible. Whether this is on social media, affiliate sites, press coverage, indie blogs, or large news organizations, search engines reward websites that are linked to often.

- **High-Quality Links:** The links back to your website shouldn't come from sketchy websites or ad placement. The search algorithms take into account what they know about the site linking to yours; if it's a credible site, your website will have a better ranking, if it's a sketchy site, this might lower your ranking.

- **Keywords for Anchor Text:** Believe it or not, the text that makes up the link to your site matters. For instance, if you own a vacuum company, the search engines will consider a link to your website from a blog that reads "Click here for free money!" to be sketchy, and not a high-quality link. But if the link says, "Click here for quality vacuums," your link popularity will get a boost.

- **Guest Blogging:** Consider writing for other blogs as guest author on authority websites to gain quality backlinks to your website. Send an email or direct message to them with a post idea that you can write. Let them know when you'll send it from the time they agree and then stick to that.

- **Search Engine Submissions:** Search engines can find your website but sometimes it can take a while, so speed everything up by submitting your website to major search engines.

- **Online Local Business Directory Submissions:** Listing your business in places like Google My Business improves your ability to reach a targeted local audience. Most local business directories provide a free way to promote your business and make your website more credible in the eyes of the search engines. Learn more about submitting to these directories in Chapter 8.5.1 What Online Directories Should Your Business Be Listed In?

- **Link Baiting:** Controversy and disagreement are always popular, so also is novel information, online contests, giveaways, free access to software, or free materials. These sorts of content links are irresistible to internet users. Link bait is important because it shows search engines that your pages are interesting and authoritative which helps in improving rankings in SERPs.

- **Customer Reviews:** Websites like Yelp.com, and Angi.com allow users to give reviews about a business. Positive reviews improve your credibility which the search engines take into consideration when ranking web pages. Ask your customers to review your products or services. In turn, respond to reviews to show you value your customers and their feedback. Doing so may boost your visibility in some search engines. To learn how to respond to reviews read Chapter 9.4.2 How to Deal with Questions, Problems, Unhappy Customers and Fake Reviews.

For business owners new to online marketing, it's tempting to want to pay to get links to their websites. But it's important you do this as rarely as possible, if ever. Your online presence and your ranking on SERPs will benefit most from unpaid links—organic links—that won't be deemed sketchy by the search engine algorithms.

Social

This is by far one of the most important off-page SEO tactics. Using social media can effectively do wonders for your website traffic. But, you have to come up with a good plan of action and see it through rather than just getting on social media and posting random thoughts.

- **Get More Followers:** Understand your audience, produce valuable content, engage with them, and be consistent in order to gain more followers on the social media platform you're trying to promote and build.

- **Follow Influencers:** Find the influencers in your industry that you most want to mention your business, and then find a way to stand out from the crowd. Follow them, leave comments, and engage meaningfully with their posts.

- **Ask People to Share:** When you share something on social media that you think is really useful, add a call to action at the end of your content to encourage people to share it with others. If you don't ask, they may not do it on their own.

Social media is an amazing opportunity for all businesses. Make sure to stay active on other people's posts and that your own posts offer quality content and/or link back to your website. You want to give yourself as much visibility as possible in order to get more traffic to your site and pages, which will hopefully be converted into sales.

Taking SEO seriously can mean the difference between success and failure. Take the items in this chapter to be your checklist for success. While it's not guaranteed it will all work, I can guarantee without taking these steps, the journey to success will be a lot harder.

7.4 What Is the Importance of Keyword Research

Keywords are the words or phrases people often use on search engines. Researching the keywords relevant to your business is one of the most important things you need to do for SEO. For example, a business owner who is looking for someone to help them build a website might enter terms like 'website design' or 'small business website' into the search box. The search engines use those keywords to find 'relevant' web pages.

There are a lot of things that go into making a web page relevant to a particular search, but it is clear that the presence of related keywords on a web page creates a high degree of relevance.

7.4.1 What Is the Difference Between Short-Tail and Long-Tail Keywords?

When researching for the right keywords, you must know the differences between short-tail and long-tail keywords. The chart below highlights the outcomes of using one over the other.

	Short-Tail Keywords	Long-Tail Keywords
Word Count:	Has one to three words in a keyword phrase.	Has four or more words in a keyword phrase.
Focus:	They target a larger audience and less specific search engine searches.	They are a lot more targeted and not as broad.
Web Traffic:	Shorter keywords will bring more traffic to your website.	Traffic from long-tail keywords will be much lower.
Sales Conversion:	An increase in traffic won't automatically increase sales because the keyword is not targeted or too broad. Your business won't have what most visitors were looking for.	Since the keywords are more targeted, you will get more relevant traffic from people interested in what you are offering. Your sales conversion rate will be better.
Competition:	The competition is high for websites that try to get ranked for short-tail keywords.	The competition among other websites will be lower because you are being specific about what you are offering. Getting your website ranked will be easier.
Examples:	• Properties for sale • Carpet cleaning • DUI lawyer	• Pocono lakefront properties for sale • Chemical-free carpet cleaning companies • What can a lawyer do for a DUI

7.4.2 How to Choose Keywords for SEO

Selecting the proper keywords for your website is crucial to making sure your pages are returned when consumers are searching for the products, services, or information you are providing. To understand the value of keywords and to decide which ones to use, follow these steps:

1. Put yourself in your customer's shoes. Make a list of what phrases or words you think searchers would use to find your products or services.

2. Using this list, search for keywords or phrases in major search engines. Do a complete analysis and identify your competition. Visit their websites and see what keywords they are using.

3. Find out the popularity of the words on your list by using keyword suggestion tools:

   - Answer the Public: https://answerthepublic.com
   - Can I Rank: https://www.canirank.com
   - Google Ad Keyword Planner: https://ads.google.com/aw/keywordplanner
   - Google Trends: https://trends.google.com/trends
   - Keywords Everywhere: https://keywordseverywhere.com
   - Microsoft Advertising Intelligence: https://help.ads.microsoft.com/#apex/bai/en/ext00005
   - Wordtracker's Keyword Tool: https://www.wordtracker.com

4. Narrow your list down to just a few optimal words. Use all the collected data to determine which keywords to use for your website.

5. Update and manage your keywords list weekly to ensure the effectiveness of your keywords.

It can take a lot of time to narrow down your effective keyword list, but it's a good investment. If you rush through the process, you'll end up spending money and time focusing on keywords that won't work. Don't waste your time if you're not going to be meticulous.

Keyword selection is based off of data, but also how well you know your potential customers. Don't be afraid to test out some fringe or more detailed keywords, you might be surprised and find a niche!

7.5 How to Launch a Successful SEO Campaign

More often than not, the important aspects of launching a search engine optimization campaign tend to be ignored by people that want quick results, resulting in plenty of unsuccessful SEO campaigns. Before getting started on your SEO campaign, you need to know the fundamentals.

For the purpose of attracting the right customers to your web pages, you need a balanced combination of tactics. Follow these nine principles when launching an SEO campaign:

1. **Set Your Goals:** Establish some realistic but challenging SMART goals for your website. It will help in defining:
   - Why you want to do SEO
   - What actions you want to take
   - Identifying what kind of traffic do you want
   - What you want your visitors to focus on and do when they land on one of your web pages
2. **Know Your Budget:** How much are you willing to invest in SEO? Some tactics cost more than others.
3. **Assign Responsibility:** There are varying types of expertise needed to complete an SEO campaign—writers, developers, marketers—so make sure you know who is doing what and decide if you need to hire outside help.
4. **Know Your Audience:** Knowing who your audience is and getting a clear understanding of your industry, market, and niche will allow you to be more specific in your campaign.
5. **Study the Competition:** Frequent competitor analysis allows you to stay on top of what's trending and what's not.
6. **Test Keywords:** Conduct a thorough keyword research to target both long- and short-tail keywords. Keep an open mind regarding periodic keyword changes according to market trends.
7. **Conduct Audits:** Check your website analytics, on-page optimization and off-page optimization to see what elements you'll need to focus on.
8. **Establish a Content Strategy:** Narrow down and specify what exactly your potential customers want to learn about. Make a content strategy that

ensures you are creating high-quality content rather than low-quality content that then begs for sales. If your content offers value, then people will purchase your products or services because they know you offer value. Your content strategy needs to be customer-focused and optimized for the search engines.

9. **Build Links:** Apart from good keyword research, link building is an absolute must for the success of any website, and it is an ongoing process, so make sure you put some time aside for this.

7.5.1 How to Maintain an SEO Campaign

It's not enough to just build your website, review your SEO once, and then hope the results start pouring in. A successful SEO strategy requires evolving tactics and campaigns, and all of your content and settings will need to be maintained routinely to make sure they're still delivering your site to the highest search ranking possible. A few things to remember are:

Check your website's performance

- **Check on your pages regularly:** Make sure they're still listed in the SERPs. Your listings are the most important part of your SEO work. Whether the page is listed or not is vastly more important than what keywords you have. After all, if you aren't listed at all, what is the point of optimizing?

- **Monitor the listings:** Every week or two make sure your pages are displaying correctly and that there are no problems. While you're at it, see whether you've risen, dropped, or remained constant as far as listings go. Odds are that your position will not remain constant. If you do remain constant you should consider this a small victory as you have probably risen above some other web pages that were previously above you, but other pages from below you may have surpassed you.

- **Create monthly ranking reports on your site:**
See if any changes need to be made. Check out these tools that can create reports:

  - **AuthorityLabs.com:** automates your SEO monitoring.

  - **GoogleAnalytics.com:** free tool you need to analyze data for your business in one place.

- **Majestic.com:** audit websites and report on your successes.
- **PageModified.com:** get on-page technical insights quickly and track website changes automatically.
- **Woorank.com:** website review tool and SEO checker.

- **Watch for trouble and fix it quickly:** Don't think problems will correct themselves. Mistakes—typos, dead links, etc.—can be very costly if they are not dealt with in a timely fashion.

- **Resubmit your site if you make major changes:** The most important time to resubmit your site to search engines is if you have recently changed your titles. Titles are very important in SEO and allow you to update your content with a completely new set of quality keywords.

- **Keep growing your link popularity:** Continue to seek backlinks from authority websites, business directories, and other credible locations on the web.

- **Watch your competitors and the methods they use:** If they start trying to cheat by using spam, paid links or other bad practices, report them immediately. It gets them out of your way.

- **Write out an SEO maintenance plan:** Maintain a solid plan for dealing with your site's growth. Don't panic if you see a dip in key stats. If things change then make sure to set new goals and stick with them.

- **Stay up to date on the latest SEO information:** The more you know the better prepared you are for any changes in what's working in SEO.

7.5.2 How Do You Measure the Results of an SEO Campaign?

Measuring an SEO campaign can be a tricky business. Here are a few basic metrics that can give you a good start on measuring the success of an SEO campaign.

- **Organic Website Traffic:** One way to judge an SEO campaign is the increase of the website's organic traffic. Organic means the traffic didn't come from ads but instead from actual links around the internet, or people typing your domain name directly in their web browser.

- **Search Engine Rankings:** This is the simplest indicator of growth and can clearly help you determine what might or might not be working, and in what direction you need to take your campaign in the future.

- **Social Media Shares:** A higher number of social shares means more credibility of your web pages. This can lead to an increased search engine positioning.

- **Conversions and Leads:** The right SEO campaign will not only bring quality traffic to your web pages but also convince potential customers to buy. Track changes in your sales conversions and leads carefully.

- **Return on Investment:** An increased return on investment (ROI) is not something you might see immediately. There are several factors involved that add up to a reasonable approximation of ROI. Revenues may fluctuate initially which is why it is important to measure all the previous metrics before judging the results from the SEO campaign.

Bing Webmaster Tools (https://www.bing.com/toolbox/webmaster) allows you to review any improvement in visibility or page rankings. It'll show details about your website data to let you know if your campaign is working. The tools mentioned previously can also be used to measure the results of your campaign.

7.5.3 How Long Will It Take to See the Results of an SEO Campaign?

While there is no definitive answer to this question, most SEO campaigns show results towards the end of 4 to 6 months. Some campaigns get results much sooner, some later. Doing SEO takes time, so no matter what results you see early they are likely to get better over a period of time.

With any type of SEO campaign, you have to give it time to get going and the improvements will come. Business owners often think SEO is no good because they refuse to wait long enough to see any results. It all depends on how much is put into their SEO strategies. If a lot of effort is put forth, then the process will take less time to show good results.

Here are some factors to consider when determining how long it will take to see results.

- **Budget:** The amount of money you will invest in an SEO specialist plays a huge part in determining the results of your SEO campaign.

- **Competition:** If your business is in a competitive market, dominated by strong competitors, then making your way to the top won't be easy. It will be a slow and time-taking process.

- **Geography:** Targeting a local, national, or global audience will determine the amount of effort and time required.

- **Keywords:** Beware of keywords that are highly competitive and more generic. They are difficult to rank and take a longer time to show results.

- **Penalties:** Trying to trick the search engines by using shady SEO tactics to get a better ranking can get your website penalized. If you notice your web pages are no longer ranking well or your website no longer appears in a search engine, it may be penalized. It will take time to find and correct any problems.

- **Your Website:** A brand-new website, one with poor design, or an unfriendly SEO website is more likely to lose or not have search engine rankings or customers. Also, websites that are not mobile-ready are likely to rank poorly too. They will require more time and effort.

Attaining consistently targeted organic traffic to your website is a gradual and continuous process This is why you must have realistic expectations for your SEO campaign.

It is important to know what happens to your web pages when search engine optimization is stopped. Well, if any competitors are consistently doing SEO too, they will simply overtake you in the search engine rankings. Your listings will slide down the page and possibly onto the next page or further. Your hard work and progress will be lost and your web traffic, leads and sales may suffer. That is why you need to follow the procedures for maintaining an SEO campaign

7.6 Five Issues That Can Hurt Your Website's Ranking and How to Fix Them

There can be several reasons as to why your website is not ranking high. Here are some possibilities:

1. **Change in SE Algorithm:** Pay close attention to any changes in search engine algorithms. Google occasionally updates their process for determining what results they return. If any of your indexed web pages dropped in ranking, and you made no changes, that may be the reason. Stay updated on algorithm changes by visiting https://moz.com/google-algorithm-change and plan accordingly.

2. **Search Engine Penalty:** Violating the guidelines of search engines can lead to severe penalties and the removal of your website from searches altogether. This can happen due to duplicate content, hidden text, multiple domain names, links from non-reputable websites, excessive link exchange, and so on. Learn what the rules are and follow them. Here's a link to Google's Webmaster Guidelines: https://support.google.com/webmasters/answer/35769.

3. **Canonicalization Issues:** As discussed before, if the 'rel="canonical"' tag is not used, search engines might consider similar links of a single page as different pages with duplicate content. Your website can get penalized for this. Website creation software like WordPress makes it easy to take care of this.

4. **Broken Links:** An error in the internal linking of your website can lead to critical navigation issues. Outgoing links to other websites, if broken, can also make your website vulnerable to a drop in SERPs. Make sure all the links on your website work and go to active web pages.

5. **Server or Malware Issues:** If search engines have difficulty accessing your website because it is slow to respond you will see a drop in the SERPs. Do business with a reputable web host and upgrade to a VPS or dedicated server if necessary. Any detection of malware on your website and your ranking will drop. Keep any installed website programs updated along with any plugins you use to decrease vulnerabilities to hackers. Check with your web host or appropriate vendor and confirm all programs and applications are using the most updated versions. Protecting your business from cyber threats is covered in Chapter 9.6.

7.6.1 What Does Bounce Rate Mean and Does It Impact Where You Rank?

Bounce rate measures the percentage of visitors that arrived at one of the pages on your website and immediately left (bounced) without doing anything on the page like clicking on a link or navigating to another page. Bounce rate is a reflection of how "sticky" your website is. This means visitors stay on your page longer and take a look at other areas on your website. They're also more likely to come back if they find something they're interested in.

How to Find Your Website's Bounce Rate?

A website's bounce rate is calculated by dividing the number of single-page sessions by the number of total sessions on the site. For example, if 1,000 users land on your web pages (total sessions) and 400 of them exit without doing anything on the page they visited (single-page sessions), your website's bounce rate is 40%.

The easiest way to track, measure and review your website's bounce rate and other metrics is to use Google Analytics or a similar service that monitors website traffic. With Google Analytics you will need to have a Google account to log in and the ability to place a unique tracking code on all of your web pages. This is easy to do if your website was built using WordPress. Then you can use a plugin like Yoast (yoast.com) or All in One SEO Pack (aioseo.com) to add the tracking code to your pages.

What Is a Good Bounce Rate?

According to Semrush.com a bounce rate between 26% and 40% is considered good. The median range is between 41% to 55%, while 56% to 70% is considered to be high. Anything above 71% should be a concern and requires immediate action to be taken. If the rate is below 20% you would think it's a good thing, but it could be an indication that there's a problem with the implementation and/or the configuration used to capture your website data.

These statistics are only a benchmark. The type of website that you have will influence the rates you can expect. Here are the average bounce rate benchmarks for the most common kinds of websites:

52.5% for B2B websites
42.5% for e-commerce websites
75.0% for landing pages
57.5% for lead generation websites
47.5% for non-e-commerce content websites
77.5% for dictionaries, blogs, and news websites

The type of industry you're in will also play a part in your bounce rates.

What Causes High Bounce Rate?

There are many reasons that can cause a bounce rate to be high. Some of them include;

- Your web page takes too long to load and visitors leave your site.

- The information on your page is not what the visitor was looking for.

- The visitor may go to a page that no longer exists because you moved it somewhere else on your website or removed it.

- There may be a technical error causing your webpage to not appear.

- Web traffic from other sources may not be suited for what you offer.

- Your content is not good or optimized properly.

- The web design is bad and there may be too much going on like pop-up boxes and advertisements.

- Your site is not mobile-friendly which is not good for mobile phone visitors.

How to Lower Bounce Rate?

The first thing to do is investigate and address any of the issues I just listed. Use Google Analytics to identify which pages on your site have the highest bounce rate and make the necessary changes to fix them. To go even further take advantage of the ability to segment your bounce rate to find out specifically what is causing it to be high.

Here are some of the ways you can use segmentation to delve into your bounce rate.

- **Channel** – Visitors arrive to your website in various ways such as web links, social media, search engines, email, etc. Each channel will have its own bounce rate and will help determine which one you need to make a priority and which ones are unimportant.

• **Device** – The type of device a person uses does matter. Desktop and tablet users are different from mobile users who are more likely to be looking for specific information.

• **Location** – If you have a local business then you can expect visitors from outside of your area to leave your site quickly.

• **Visitor Type** – Another way would be to segment new vs. returning visitors. New visitors will have a higher bounce rate because they are not familiar with you or your business. You need new visitors—so create content that gets them to stay on your page longer, engage with your website, take some type of action (i.e., buy something), and come back again.

Does Bounce Rate Impact SEO?

Some SEO experts believe that bounce rate is a factor when ranking websites in search engines. However, Google Webmaster Trends Analyst Gary Illyes said, "Google does not use any of the data from Google Analytics in their search engine ranking algo[rithm]." I agree with that statement for these reasons.

1. Bounce rate does not accurately reflect the quality of a website. As I mentioned before, different types of websites will have varying bounce rates. A high bounce rate may be expected and is acceptable on certain types of websites.

2. Data can be manipulated. If search engines used bounce rate as a ranking factor, then it would be very easy to create web scripts or bots to simulate human traffic. The bounce rate could then be artificially deflated.

3. Every website does not use Google Analytics. One stat says only 54.7% of websites use it. It would not make any sense for search engines to rely on a stat for ranking websites that is not being measured on almost half of the websites online.

This does not mean bounce rate should be completely ignored. You should use it to see which web pages need your attention and can be improved upon.

7.7 What to Do If Your Web Pages Can't Move Up in The SERPs

If getting ranked in the search engine results pages are taking a bit of time and you want to see quick results, then opt for a few of the following strategies:

- **Try Paid Online Advertising:** Opt for online paid ads because it ensures search engine visibility for your website. You have control over how targeted you want your traffic. See Chapter 14 to learn more.

- **Submit to Online Business Directories:** Submit your website to popular online directories and get your local business added. Customers use these sites all the time while looking for solutions. This discussed in the next chapter.

- **Use Social Media:** Increase your social media activity. Create authentic profiles, engage with your online community, and improve your social media status. read Chapter 12 to learn about social media marketing.

- **Increase Offline Marketing:** Incorporate effective offline marketing strategies to engage your target audience and bring in leads. Chapter 16 explains which tactics to use.

- **Use Affiliate Marketing:** Starting your own affiliate program means affiliates will be sending traffic to your sales pages. Review Chapter 5.8 for an overview on affiliate marketing.

If you're still not seeing the results you'd like after a period of time, remember that search engine algorithms are always changing so you or your web marketing strategist may need to do some research on the latest Google, Bing, and Yahoo search engine news.

"You can say #SEO is even more important for local businesses as it makes you easier to find in your area."

– Larry Kim, CEO of MobileMonkey.com

8. How to Get More Local Customers to Visit Your Business

8.1 What Is Local Search Marketing?

Local search marketing is simply the process of making a broad search term used in search engines more specific by adding a location into the term. So instead of a user searching for "dental implants," they might search for "dental implants Springfield." This local search allows Google, Bing, and other search engines to deliver the most relevant results in the search engine results pages (SERPs) by showing that user the closest oral surgeon that performs dental implant surgery in Springfield.

This type of online marketing is primarily used by businesses that rely on most or all of their customers coming to them physically. The objective is to have details about the business appear on a customer's computer or mobile device at the time they are searching for services or products like theirs.

For customers that like to shop near their home, job or any place they plan to visit, local search marketing makes it easier for them to find nearby stores to buy from.

8.2 Eight Reasons Why Local Search Marketing Is So Important

According to Google 46% of searches now have a local intent. They also found out that 50% of smartphone users who conducted a local search visited a business within a day, and 34% who searched on their computer or tablet did the same. These kinds of searchers are qualified leads that are available now and they can be converted to customers when local search marketing is done correctly.

Here's a list of 8 reasons that emphasize why local search marketing is important.

1. **Targeted and Focused:** It allows your business to connect with potential customers just when they are looking for what you offer. Therefore, your business appears at the right place at the right time.

2. **Cost-Effective:** Local search marketing is a low-cost marketing method that allows you to market your business within a budget. In most cases, creating a dedicated business page and profiles that appear on a search engine or business directory is totally free.

3. **Offers a Better ROI:** Local search marketing yields a greater return on investment (ROI) because information about your business appears only when it is needed. Most of the people who are searching for local businesses are ready to make a purchasing decision. This makes the conversion rate higher than other digital and conventional marketing strategies.

4. **Competitors Are Lazy:** Local search marketing can turn out to be quite beneficial for you as many companies have not claimed their business pages in either search engines or business directories. Since this is an emerging form of marketing, you can take advantage by claiming your business and getting an edge over competitors that have not listed themselves. The biggest risk associated with not using local search is that competitors can get started at any time. And if new customers aren't finding a particular business because they can't be found within the search, the competitor that does have a page that's listed will get the business instead. So, when the competition isn't currently using local search marketing, that is all the more reason to get started doing it.

5. **Attract New Customers:** Do businesses still need to do local search marketing when their customers live close by? Yes. Even if they know most of their customers and they live within 10 miles, a business can still benefit from this strategy. Remember that local search marketing isn't necessarily used to attract current customers, but to gain potential new ones that maybe don't know about the business. While existing customers of course can benefit from it as well by easily finding the hours of operation on a particular day, the point of local search is really to promote the business to those that aren't aware that it's even there.

6. **Rapid Growth in Mobile Internet Usage:** People can search for anything through their devices whether at home, at a restaurant, at college or while traveling. This matters because more than half of consumers using mobile

to research want to purchase within the hour, and 83% want to purchase within a day.

7. **All Attention to the Internet:** Today's consumer follows the "Research Online, Buy Offline" (ROBO) behavioral pattern. After having researched the product or service they want, customers look for places offering that product/service nearest to them through the internet. As the number of online searches for nearby businesses increases, the need for your business to use local search marketing is mandatory if you want to be discovered when they start searching for products and services you offer.

8. **Local SEO:** Local search did begin with users simply trying to narrow down their search. Today, however, local search is an actual part of the search engine algorithms, and they will give websites that have been optimized for location better positions in their SERPs. Business owners now need to focus on optimizing their website for local search, and this very act is called Local SEO.

8.3 How Are People Using the Internet to Find Local Products and Services?

When a customer uses a search engine to find something they want to purchase locally, they type in the keyword for what they want along with a geographic modifier. Geographic modifiers better known as geotags or geo modifiers are location-specific keywords that help customers find businesses that are most convenient for them to get to. These include searches with certain location-based terms such as city, state, and zip code, as well as "near me" searches. These modifiers help search engines determine the "local intent" of the searcher so relevant search results are returned.

For instance:

Search Term	Geotag
yoga studio 10018	10018
car rentals Miami	Miami
pizza near me	near me

While geo modifiers are helpful for determining local intent, they aren't necessary when it comes to mobile searches. Smartphones have a location-based service (LBS) which is a software-level service that uses real-time geo data from the mobile device. This allows websites and mobile applications to determine the location of a person doing a web search from their smartphone.

Several factors determine if your business will appear at the right place and time when a local customer is looking for you. You may already have a head start as some search engines and local directories automatically list businesses without business owners having to lift a finger. If yours is one of them, it doesn't mean you should pause or stop your local search marketing efforts and skip the advice in this chapter.

8.4 What Are the Consequences of Having Incorrect Local Details about Your Business?

There's a good chance that customers are searching for your business but can't find it because of listing errors. Your business name, address, and phone number (NAP) are very important in local search marketing. It is critical to have a correct NAP in your business description because Google and other search engines use this data to link with geo modified search queries. To establish and maintain credibility, you must have a correct NAP on your website and on all other sites where your NAP appears throughout the web. You'll need to update your business information in case of any changes.

If you don't have the correct NAP, your business may suffer the following consequences:

- It can cause confusion and people won't be able to figure which one on the web is correct.

- An incorrect NAP could also make your business look shady, this, in turn, will give you a poor search engine ranking or no ranking at all.

- Customers will have a difficult time locating you and will eventually turn to competitors.

- The opportunity to get more local search web traffic will be limited.

- Precious time will be wasted in efforts to figure out the reason behind poor rankings and reduced traffic.

This is why it is crucial for you to carefully check that the correct NAP is being used all over the web.

8.4.1 How Does a Business NAP Become Inaccurate?

In order to provide users with the most relevant information, search engines and local business directories import details for businesses from data aggregators such as Acxiom, Infogroup, and Neustar/Localeze to use in their search results. Unfortunately, the data they use isn't always accurate.

If you ever see your business appear online on a web page with the wrong NAP here are some reasons how this could have happened:

- The data gathering companies have obtained incorrect data from you.
- There are variations of your business name.
- Your business moved to a new address.
- The business phone number you used locally has been changed.
- Your company's incorrect listing was passed along to other directory sites.

Examples of Correct and Incorrect NAP:

Correct **NAP**	Incorrect **NAP**
Boyce Web Consulting 555 Local Road New Haven, CT 06511 222-222-2222	Boyce Web **Services** 555 Local **Street** New Haven, **CO** 06511 222-222-**3333**

Due to any of these reasons or others, local businesses might fail to enjoy the perks of local search marketing.

8.4.2 What Are Citations and Why Are They Important?

Wherever there is a mention of your business NAP on any web page across the internet, it is referred to as a citation. Citations can be found on web pages, directories, social media profiles, and any other part of a company's online presence. If your business has a lot of citations around the internet, your search ranking will improve greatly.

Citations are more crucial for professionals in certain niches (i.e., electricians and plumbers) because many don't have websites. Therefore, search engines rely heavily on whatever information they can get since there is not much information available about these businesses. Accurate citations bring a drastic improvement in a company's local search engine ranking.

Additionally, citations validate a business because it's not easy to fake memberships in a chamber of commerce or local business association.

8.4.3 How to Audit and Clean Up Your Citations in Five Easy Steps

For all these reasons it's necessary to audit and clean up your citations. You can make use of the many online software options available on the internet, or you can choose to do it on your own. If you decide to do it yourself, here is a list of steps to ensure a thorough audit and cleanup.

1. Start by creating a spreadsheet to record all data you'll discover in this step and in the following steps. You will start by finding all of the places your business is cited online. Enter your business name, address, phone number, or web address in search engines, and you will be able to see the web pages where your business is cited. If your NAP is on a web page that is not indexed, you won't see it.

2. Check each citation that you find. Look for all possible NAP variations. Check to see that pages you found them on don't have the following:

   - A double listing of your business
   - An incorrect citation, or
   - Incomplete detail about your business.

3. Keep track of each citation found in your spreadsheet along with any errors they had.

4. Correct any issues you find. Start with fixing the ones in Google My Business, Bing Places for Business, and Yahoo Small Business. Then update

your information in the big three data aggregators. After that focus on cleaning up individual citation sources that need to be corrected.

5. Don't forget to follow up. Keep checking until all of the corrections have been made. Expect to make multiple requests for corrections until they are made.

It's essential that you keep checking for new citations to avoid any problems in the future. If you want to save some time, look into using software for cleaning and auditing citations. Here are a couple of options:

- moz.com/local/search
- brightlocal.com/local-seo-tools/citation-tracker/.

8.5 What Are Local Business Directories and The Benefits of Being Listed in Them?

Listing your business in online local directories offers many benefits to your bottom line. An online local directory is any website which aggregates and publicizes businesses in a certain locale. Oftentimes local newspapers have a section on their website where you can find and vet local businesses. Not only do these directories make it more likely that customers will be able to find and contact your business, but they are credible links to your business name and website that will give you credibility and boost your SEO ranking. You can also expect the following benefits:

- **Improved Traffic:** Expect more traffic because these local directories "vouch" for your business so Google and other search engines will be ranking you higher and sending more traffic to your site.

- **Strengthens your reputation:** The benefit of listing your business in an online directory cuts down all chances of your business being mistaken as a non-professional one. Having gone through the effort of getting yourself listed in an online directory itself shows professionalism and seriousness towards the business.

- **Better recognition:** The more directories you are listed in, the more recognition you will gain. Companies who make it a point to register themselves in all credible online directories become better known by people.

• **Increased customer interaction** - Being virtually present everywhere a customer may need a business is going to potentially bring more customer interaction for your business.

8.5.1 What Online Directories Should Your Business Be Listed In?

There are different types of directories, some take submissions, some are free, and some ask for a fee to include you. Most directories allow an upgraded membership to sponsor or promote your business in the directory. For high-quality, relevant directories, it's worth you paying to be listed because it can really make your investment worthwhile.

You should also consider The Chamber of Commerce and the Better Business Bureau which offer tools and resources for local business, including directories. Every locality in the US has one of these organizations and paying to get a listing is a wealth worth your time and money as it will give a lot of credibility to your business online and in the eyes of customers.

Here are the top 20 directories where you should list your local business:

1. **Alignable:** https://www.alignable.com
2. **Angi (formally Angie's List):** http://www.angi.com
3. **B2B Yellow Pages:** https://www.b2byellowpages.com
4. **Better Business Bureau:** https://www.bbb.org
5. **Bing Places:** https://www.bingplaces.com
6. **Brownbook:** http://www.brownbook.net
7. **Chamber of Commerce:** https://www.chamberofcommerce.com
8. **DexKnows:** https://www.dexknows.com
9. **eLocal:** https://www.elocal.com
10. **Foursquare:** http://business.foursquare.com
11. **Google My Business:** https://www.google.com/business
12. **HotFrog:** https://www.hotfrog.com
13. **Local:** https://www.local.com
14. **Manta:** https://www.manta.com
15. **Merchant Circle:** https://www.merchantcircle.com
16. **Superpages:** https://www.superpages.com

17. **Yahoo Small Business:** https://smallbusiness.yahoo.com/local
18. **Yellow Pages:** https://www.yellowpages.com
19. **Yellowbook:** https://www.yellowbook.com
20. **Yelp:** https://business.yelp.com

8.5.2 Use Your Competitors to Find More Directories

When conducting an analysis of the best and most impactful business directories, I suggest that you check on your competitor's listings. When you search the NAP of your competitors, you will discover the websites where they are cited. This will help you in getting yourself listed on those sites where your competitor is listed but you may have missed. If your better-rated competition is listed on the site, you should be as well. Any business can be found online easily if their NAP is on a web page that has been indexed by a search engine and the NAP is correct.

8.6 What Is the Process for Claiming Your Local Business Listings

Claiming your business listings gives you control over what information is being shared on those sites regarding your business. To claim your business listing you'll need to verify that you are the owner of the business. This would involve at a minimum following these steps:

- Many directories would ask about the existence of your business on their website. Search everything you can about your business on that site, including the name, phone number, fax number, email addresses, and anything else you can think of.

- If you do a search and see that your business is already listed in a business directory you need to claim it whether the NAP is correct or not. You will be asked to review your business details and make any edits that are needed.

- If after searching all of these you still don't come up with any results for your business, create a new listing then add your most current contact and business details to your profile.

- In either situation, you will be asked to verify the listing. The verification process can be through a phone call and pin number, a postal mail postcard and pin number or through email.

While you might hire a digital marketing expert to do all these tasks for you, it's important to remember that, oftentimes, you will still need to be part of the process. The directories want to know they are dealing with the owner or a representative of the business, rather than a contractor.

Many of the same types of software used to find and correct citation errors can be used to submit to local business directories—this will quicken the process.

8.6.1 How to Optimize Your Local Business Listings

After someone visits any business listing that you have claimed you want them to see more than just your NAP. Having a weak profile does nothing to encourage a potential customer to do business with you. When given the chance you want to provide as must detail about your business as possible.

Your profile creates the first impression of your business to your prospective clients, so you need to stand out. Here are a few tips on how to create an attractive and credible profile.

- **Contact Detail Consistency:** You must have a consistent contact for all of your profiles. If there is a difference in any of the details on different listings, it will create confusion and make you seem less credible. This applies to your NAP, website, and email.

- **Write a Meaningful Description:** You want to persuade your potential customer that your business has the solution to their problem. Don't just talk about what you offer. Explain what makes your business different. Create a short and long version of your description. Some directories prefer one version over the other.

- **Add Social Media Links:** In addition to your website make sure you add links to any social media profiles that you have. This gives potential customers more ways to learn about you.

- **Categorize Your Business:** Most directories give businesses the option to put themselves in a category to make listings more organized and relevant. Place yourself in a category that best describes your business.

- **Show Off Reviews:** People look for and rely on the ratings and reviews a business receives. Sometimes good businesses don't get picked as they don't have a record of all the good experiences their customers have had with them. It is important to have your business ratings and reviews on your profile. Get your good customers to leave reviews for you so that everyone can know how satisfied your customers are. Read Chapter 9.4.3 to learn how to get more reviews.

• **Use Plenty of Visuals:** Use attractive photos and videos to increase the number of clicks on your listing. If you have a logo, make sure to add it.

• **Appear Friendly:** Allow easy access on your profile for interested customers such as a "Contact us" area or any such option that presents you as a customer-friendly business.

• **Don't Forget Keywords:** Even directories will ask for basic keywords when listings are being created. Remember that the listings you're creating in various online local directories are a form of advertising. And any type of online advertising is dependent on the appropriate use of keywords.

• **Other Extras:** Here are some additional details you can add to your listing to help customers decide to do business with you.

Certifications/Licenses	Associations	Business Hours
Areas served	Prices	Forms of payment accepted

Having a profile that is better looking than your competitors and has content to discover will get more clicks and yield better results for you. Make sure you use the same information on all of your listings.

8.7 Four Ways to Improve Your Local Ranking in Search Engines

In Chapter 7 I talked about search engines having a set of rules known as their algorithm they use to rank websites. Part of that algorithms includes how they rank and display local businesses in search results. There are dozens of factors that are taken into consideration and they can change at any time. No one other than the programmers know exactly what the factors are, but some seem to remain important even when changes to the algorithm are made.

Here are four factors that have an influence on how local businesses are ranked in search engines:

1. **Google My Business:** Life will be a lot easier once you get your Google My Business listing set up. It's a free tool by Google to help businesses manage their online presence and how they show up in Google's search results.

2. **Relevance:** Relevance refers to how much of the information in your listing matches what someone is searching for. By making sure the details about your business are accurate and complete, search engines will be better able to show your listing when it is relevant to a user's search query. See Chapter 7.3.1 for ways to make your web pages more relevant.

3. **Distance:** How close is your business to the geo modifier used by the searcher? Search engines will direct users to a business nearest to them when the listing is more relevant, even if they have to travel a bit to get to the location. When a geo modifier is not used, search engines calculate the distance using any information they have about the location.

4. **Prominence:** This refers to how well-known your business is. Do people know your business, products and services by name? By making your business stand out from others it will become more prominent. Here are some ways to build and maintain your prominence online:

   - **Citations:** They must be complete and consistent. In the past, the number of citations was a benefit. Now the emphasis is to be in high-quality and trusted business directories.

   - **Reviews:** Reviews are becoming more relevant because customers are relying on them more to decide where to go and what to buy. Having more positive reviews and responding to them put you in a more favorable position on search engines.

   - **Personalization:** Provide as many details about your business as possible. Use the tips for optimizing your local business listing that was discussed previously.

   - **Backlinks:** Just like traditional SEO, backlinks are used as part of how search engines rank your site under a particular search. Links to your website from credible sites help your cause. See Chapter 7.3.2 What Are the Off-Page Elements That Affect SEO?

"It takes 20 years to build a reputation and five minutes to ruin it. If you think about that, you'll do things differently."

– Warren Buffett, American investor, business tycoon, and philanthropist

9. Protecting Your Online Reputation

9.1 Why Is Your Online Reputation So Important to Protect

Your business develops its own digital identity once details about it start to appear on the internet. This persona will not just be limited to your website, social media accounts or the content posted by you, but also by what others are posting about your business. Everything that has been said, in the form of posts, images, or videos about your business is attached to its persona and this is what creates your online reputation.

Reputation really does mean everything if you're in a customer-oriented business and suffering from a bad reputation is a huge obstacle in business. If customers had to choose between two businesses that sold the same products the one with the better reputation would always make more sales. Customers see a good reputation as good service, and this is what people are going to pay you money for. While a good reputation is something that's intangible it is an asset that can help you achieve your business goals.

Protecting your reputation is now more important than ever before because information about you or your business that finds its way online can remain there permanently. When you are unaware of what is being said online, you risk experiencing a slowdown in sales and the loss of customer trust. This is why you can't take your reputation for granted.

9.2 How Influential Are Customer Reviews?

When a customer uses or has had and an experience with a product or service, they may leave a review about it online. Getting reviews from customers gives insight into their level of satisfaction. Their feedback can be used as a measuring stick to see how good you are doing and help to identify what areas of your business need to be improved.

Those same reviews are seen by potential customers, and they're using them to decide if they should buy from you or not. No one wants to take a chance or second guess a purchase after it was made so they rely on the recommendation of other consumers in a similar situation to help validate their decisions. A study done by the Spiegel Research Center found nearly 95% of shoppers read online reviews before making a purchase.

Reviews are preferred 12 times more than descriptions because the reader wants to see objective information they can trust. It doesn't matter how honest you are, reviews provide social proof which is going to be more compelling. That's why positive reviews are so valuable to a business.

But even if the majority of feedback is positive it only takes a few negative comments to change a potential customer's perception of your business. In fact, a study revealed that businesses risk losing 22% of their sales if potential customers found at least one negative article when using a search engine to research a product they were interested in. The same study showed that up to 70% of business could be lost when four or more negative articles are found in search engine results. Negative feedback impacts your bottom line, and that's why there needs to be urgency in locating it so it can be addressed and any damage it may cause gets contained.

9.3 13 Ways to Damage Your Reputation Online

Failing to take the necessary steps to build a reputation for your business gives others the chance to do it for you, and you may not like the outcome. For this reason, it's essential that your business provides the best customer experience possible as a single bad review can tarnish your reputation in just a matter of seconds.

You also can't do anything that's going to sabotage how your business is perceived online. It is quite easy to do self-inflicted damage to your reputation when you are unaware of how it can be done. The following points expose some of the ways the online reputation of your business can be hurt:

1. **Ignoring Customer Questions or Complaints:** Dealing with customers is something you must be ready to do if you're going to be in business. Regardless of the size of your company, don't dismiss any questions or complaints a customer may have. Their message could be an email, direct message, or posted publicly online. A customer that feels like they've been

wronged and are being dismissed can become very irate and won't hesitate to let you and the public know about it.

2. **Deleting Negative Comments:** No one wants to see negative feedback posted about their business but deleting a post because you don't agree with it can make things go from bad to worse. The customer may become so enraged that they post their complaint all over the Internet in places where it will be difficult, if not impossible to remove. Things can get out of hand when customers feel you are not taking their issues concerning your business seriously.

3. **Responding to Complaints Defensively:** Getting into a war of words with a customer over their opinion of your business puts you in a no-win situation. Responding to a negative comment in a defensive and emotional way looks bad. Even if what they said was blatantly false, counterattacking could give people the idea that there is some truth to that customer's experience. Publicly putting the blame on customers for their lack of satisfaction with your product or service is arrogant and risky. You never know how the person you respond to could adversely impact how you do business.

   Never ask employees, family or friends to defend you online, watch the customer's other posts, or engage with other commenters.

4. **Bad Mouthing Customers:** Some customers can be frustrating to deal with, but it is never a good idea to bad mouth them—especially online. Comments like "Yesterday, I had a client that was so needy, they called me all day." This shows existing and potential customers that you can be disrespectful toward them. It doesn't matter how good your product or service is, if you do this you will turn some of them off. When you say something inappropriate about someone, even a competitor, it becomes part of your reputation.

5. **Lying or Being Deceptive:** There might be a situation where you think lying to a customer, employee, or colleague is acceptable or justified. It's especially easier and more tempting when it is done online. But you need to keep promises you make to your customers. Otherwise:

   - You will lose credibility.

- Your personal reputation and potentially your company's reputation will get damaged.

- Customers will no longer want to do business with you.

- The people you work with will no longer trust you.

- This is an embarrassing situation you do not want to find yourself in.

6. **Posting Fake Reviews:** Another mistake is to post fake reviews. It's true, the internet provides a certain level of anonymity, however, that does not mean it is to behave in an unethical way. It doesn't matter if the intention is to hurt the competition with negative reviews or boost your business with positive reviews, there are better ways to build your online reputation. To some this may not seem like a big deal but here's a list of reasons you should never write fake reviews or hire others to do it:

   - **Customer Backlash:** If customers find out your reviews are fake it will hurt your business. No one wants to buy from a dishonest business.

   - **It Devalues Real Reviews:** There are enough fake reviews out there and creating more just lessens the credibility of real reviews. Over time people will stop trusting them.

   - **Your Account Could Be Banned or Suspended:** Review websites could penalize your business and remove it from their listings or ban you from using their services.

   - **It Creates Unfair Competition:** If you are going to beat your competitors it needs to be done by providing better products and services. Besides, you wouldn't want anyone writing a negative fake review about your business.

   - **It's Illegal:** There have been cases where businesses that posted fake reviews about their competitors were fined or sued. Your misrepresentation can get you into legal trouble.

7. **Appearing in Embarrassing Photos or Videos:** Speaking of embarrassing situations, a photo or video posted of you behaving badly, out of character, or in a compromised position will definitely impact your reputation negatively. Even a recorded audio of you saying something inappropriate

will be held against you. Don't make the mistake of assuming no one will see or hear about these events or that it's not that big of a deal. When it comes to your business, perception is everything. Unprofessional, irresponsible, and shameful are not words you ever want associated with your reputation.

8. **Commenting on Hot Topic Issues:** Discussing your position on religion, politics, or other sensitive and controversial issues could turn off people you want to influence that hold opposing opinions. Unless the topic is relevant to your business it is not worth getting into a potential confrontation online. Other people will see this conflict and start making their own judgments about you at the time it happens and long after it occurred. Be careful to express your personal opinion whether it's on your real name or under one of your business profiles.

9. **Telling Jokes:** It seems like there is always a story in the news about someone who said something taken out of context or said in jest that gets them into a lot of trouble to where they lose their jobs, clients, and even their entire business. Jokes are funny at times but telling one that others think is offensive, insensitive, or blatantly disrespectful can instantly ruin your reputation. Everyone does not have the same sense of humor, and just because a joke may seem harmless doesn't mean you should repeat it—it might offend others.

   If the thought of posting a joke crosses your mind, remember what happened to comedian Roseanne Barr who posted an inappropriate joke that cost her dearly by the loss of her role in her own hit TV show.

10. **Being Inconsistent or Unavailable:** Building a good reputation online requires you to be consistent. Spending time and money to get customers and fans to follow you on social media, join your mailing list, or read your blog posts is useless if you're going to disappear for days or weeks on end. Making a bunch of posts in one day and then being silent for a few weeks is not a good example of consistency. Your audience followed you because they were expecting to get interesting and useful content regularly. Any online community you build will not manage itself. So, if you don't take time to routinely engage with your audience and be available to respond to their questions, comments or complaints, they will eventually stop paying attention to you. Some may even start talking negatively about you instead of trying to talk to you.

11. **Not Monitoring Your Blog Comments:** When you allow comments to be left on your blog it's a good way to let readers connect with you and it's a way to get ideas for future content. There is always a chance you may receive negative comments but the biggest problem you may face will be dealing with spam comments. These irrelevant comments are unsolicited advertisements in disguise and if left unchecked they will affect your reputation. As long as these comments remain visible it sends a message to visitors that you don't maintain your blog regularly. This can keep them from leaving comments or even stop reading your blog. There are plugins available for WordPress that can minimize the amount of spam comments you get on your website to make monitoring much easier.

12. **Having the Wrong Person Manage Your Online Presence:** There are many social media platforms and places online where a business may have an account and profile set up. It is crucial that if you are going to delegate the managing of these accounts that you choose the right person. This is a serious responsibility to give someone and if they put anything out on the internet that negatively characterizes the thoughts, opinions, and practices of your business the outcome could be disastrous.

13. **Not Respecting Your Employees:** If you have employees they must be treated respectfully. A lot of businesses don't do this as much as they should be, and this can have some consequences for them. If disgruntled employees start posting about their experience working for your online and you get a reputation for being a bad employer, you may lose customers.

Having a negative online reputation can impact you by giving the impression that anyone that wants to deal with you is taking a risk. This can keep you from establishing beneficial relationships and growing your business.

9.4 What Are the Three Steps Used in an Online Reputation Management Strategy?

In this digital era, consumers are very quick to share their opinions online. If one of them is determined to exaggerate a minor inconvenience into a major crisis just to tarnish your name, there are few obstacles to stop them. Dissatisfied consumers, disgruntled employers, desperate competitors, along with everyday internet trolls (haters) can derail your reputation if you don't actively protect it. This is why reputation management must be one of the online marketing strategies that you use.

Reputation management is the process of finding out how people feel about your business and what they are saying. Another component includes making negative search engine results containing reviews, posts, and comments less visible than all the good things that are being said about your business online. Your goal is to maintain a positive perception of your business and take the necessary steps to influence that perception at all times.

There's a three steps process used to effectively managing your reputation online:

1. **Review and Monitor:** Find out what people are saying about you, your business, products, and services online.

2. **Repair and Engage:** Address customers that had an unpleasant or negative experience immediately.

3. **Rebuild and Influence:** Creating content that guides the conversation about your business in a positive way.

Even if you are providing fantastic services and able to exceed customer expectations you must still manage and protect your online reputation. As the amount of competitors using online marketing increases, it is even more urgent to follow these steps if you want a reputation that will make more opportunities for growth available to your business. Let's take a closer look at the steps in the process.

9.4.1 Find Out What People Are Saying about Your Business

Step #1 Review and Monitor

The first thing you must do in order to protect your reputation is to proactively track what customers and competitors are saying about your business. If you don't, you're not going to see any complaints or negative comments that can damage your reputation until it is too late. Bad comments and reviews get indexed like any other content on the internet, so there is a chance these reviews are the first or the only thing potential customers will see about your business.

That puts your reputation in further jeopardy as potential customers will know what has been posted before you have a chance to manage the situation. Thankfully, there are ways for you to check what is being said about you online. Some ways require a little bit of work on your part, the others automate the process for you.

Examine Search Engine Pages: The first step is to find out what people are saying about your business online is to simply Google your business name and the names of your products and services.

Check to see what appears in the first position on the search engine result page (SERP). Is it a press release? Is it something you or your company created and published? If not, you may have your first problem with your online reputation.

Also, check for the following:

- How many times does your business/product name appear on the first page?

- What results do you get when you add the word "review" to your search?

- Do you have positive reviews or comments that appear after the first page? If you do, then using SEO strategies will help move them to the first page.

- If you see any negative feedback that appears on the first page, you'll learn the steps to take to manage them in the following subchapter.

It's important that you use a private browser window and sign out of your Google account if you have one when searching for yourself or your business. Google often tailors results specifically for you and your search history so you're not going to get an accurate view of your search results.

Monitor Social Media Accounts: Be sure to monitor social networks frequently. They play a big role in managing your online reputation so they must be watched over carefully.

Businesses that don't use social media have no clue about any ongoing conversations that are taking place about their business. Whether you use social media for your business or not, you need to use it to know who is talking about your business positively or negatively. If you are not part of the conversation you won't be able to thank loyal customers or resolve issues with any that are unhappy. Hashtags, @mentions, tweets, retweets and other social signals can be monitored so you won't be caught off guard by anything that is said about your business. See Chapter 12.7 for a list of tools available to use for this task.

If necessary, hire someone to manage your social media accounts in a professional manner. Remember that these pages are representative of you, and you want them to always have a positive impact.

Check Customer Review Websites: Depending on your type of business that you have there are different types of review sites that you may appear on.

- **Business Review Websites:** Some of these websites are the same business directories mentioned in Chapter 8.6.1. In addition to providing information about your business directories allow customers to leave reviews. Some industries like tourism and healthcare have dedicated review sites (i.e., TripAdvisor.com and Zocdoc.com).

- **Product Review Websites:** If you sell a product from your own website you may find it mentioned on a product review website. These websites can be one of the well-known ones like ConsumerReports.org or a small obscure independently run website. When you sell a product on one of the big e-commerce giants like Amazon reviews for your product can be found on its sales page.

Talk to Your Audience: To get a better insight into how your business is perceived reach out to your customers and social media fans and get their help. Ask your audience to take a quick poll or survey about your products, services, their experience using your website, customer services, and the other ways you engage them. Their feedback will provide a wealth of information.

Use Google Alerts: Have Google notify you whenever it discovers new content that contains the keywords or topics that you want to monitor. You can set alerts to track:

- Mentions of your name, business name, and product name
- Competitor's name and their product name
- Keywords for your industry and target market.

Your alerts can be filtered by delivery frequency, sources, language, region, and relevancy. Alerts can be deleted, and settings can be changed at any time. To get the most from Google Alerts use the following:

- Quotation Marks: Multiple words within a keyword search need to be surrounded by quotations if you want the results to match the exact phrase. For example, using the keywords "my business name" will return results with those specific keywords in the same order. Without the quotation marks, Google will send you alerts for any page that has those keywords, but they may not be in that exact order.

- Misspellings: Use common misspellings of your name and any keywords you are aware of.

- Create Multiple Alerts: You can create up to 1,000 alerts per Google account so be thorough and use multiple keyword combinations.

Reviewing and monitoring your company's online reputation is something that you will have to do constantly. But what do you do if you have an unhappy customer, or you find a bad review? Next, we are going to discuss how to resolve those issues.

9.4.2 How to Deal with Questions, Problems, Unhappy Customers, and Fake Reviews

Step #2 Repair and Engage

As your business grows, you'll receive more feedback from your customers. From time to time some of those messages may be complaints posted online that you'll need to address. The feedback may be one of the following types:

- Messages posted on social media where the customer needs assistance with an existing problem.

- A customer posted a comment venting their frustration about a recent experience they had, or they left negative feedback on a website that shows reviews.

- Fake reviews from haters and competitors who could care less about the success of your business or its reputation.

Whenever you see a question or negative comments about your business online act quickly. The longer you wait to respond, the more likely potential customers will see what was posted and believe the feedback is a true representation of your business. You also need to be proactive the moment you realize a problem that may have an impact on your customer's satisfaction. Let's take a look at how to handle each of these scenarios.

Scenario #1: Answering Customer Questions on Social Media– One survey revealed that more than three-quarters of people (76%) expect businesses to respond to comments on social media, and 83% expect them to respond to these comments within a day or less.

Follow these rules when answering questions that are meant for your business.

1. If the customer's question or problem has a simple solution answer it publicly.

2. If the solution is not simple and requires them to provide additional details such as an account number or other sensitive information, then request that they send a direct message or use whatever form of communication is appropriate.

Scenario #2: Dealing with Unhappy Customers That Leave Negative Feedback– When dealing with an unhappy customer there are three objectives you should try to achieve:

- They turn from unhappy and upset to happy and satisfied.

- They remove or change their negative remarks and post one that is positive.

- You discover something about your business that will help improve it and avoid getting negative reviews in the future.

Here are six steps to turn negative feedback into positive engagement:

1. **Investigate the complaint** to see where things went wrong while analyzing the situation from your customer or client's perspective. Actively read or listen to what they said. Empathy is a very powerful skill and being genuinely concerned with a customer's frustrations is a trait that every business owner should have. Remember **a complaint is not a personal attack against you, it's an expression of dissatisfaction with a product or service**.

2. Politely and respectfully respond publicly to their feedback.

    - If your business was obviously at fault, thank the customer for sharing their opinion, admit the mistake and briefly apologize. Possible situations would be where something was damaged, missing, mishandled, lost, ignored, delayed, etc.

• Sometimes, the customer expected too much for too little or they did not have the experience they imagined. Resist the temptation to call them unreasonable.

Instead, respond to them with something like this:

"Hi there, thank you for your feedback. Please contact us so we can resolve your issue and work together to find a solution. Thanks!"

If their complaint was legitimate, they may contact you, but if they were just griping, you probably won't get a response from them. Even if there was no error on your part realize that customers want to be heard, and want to air their grievances. At least you responded in a professional way and those who saw the feedback will hopefully see that you tried to be helpful and resolve the situation directly.

Your response may require a brief explanation of the policies, capabilities or limitations of your business and what you offer to clear things up. Take a look at the descriptions of your products and services making sure they describe everything before you make another sale. If you need more time to investigate let the customer know in addition to giving them a time frame for when they can expect to hear back from you.

Expectations will vary from one person to the next and you want to make things clear, so customers don't make any assumptions. If you allow them to there will always be a chance they'll be disappointed.

• Don't reply publicly more than twice after your initial response. The customer may continue to complain if you keep replying. When your first response is not satisfactory, use a follow-up response to invite them to send you a private message to resolve the issue.

3. Once you have sufficient details, **offer a resolution.**

• If you have an idea of what will satisfy the customer tell them and see if they accept it.

• If you're uncertain of what the customer would want, or they reject your suggestion, give them the opportunity to make their own. If it's reasonable, possible, and you agree with it, then make it happen. Otherwise, continue to negotiate until a solution is agreed upon.

• If part of your resolution to a complaint was something like offering a freebie or discount on a future purchase, make sure the word doesn't get out. You want to keep the details of what you offered to the customer private. It would be a mistake to post the details of how you have resolved a complaint, only to receive lots of complaints aimed at getting the same treatment from your business.

4. **Follow up with the customer** within a couple of days after the resolution was agreed upon. In urgent situations, you want to contact them much sooner. You want to make sure everything is going as discussed. Continue to follow up until your obligation is fulfilled and the customer is happy. In a situation where the outcome was not ideal for the customer, you want them to at least feel satisfied. In either case, you want to show you are committed to providing excellent service.

5. **Try to get bad feedback changed.** If the customer replies positively to your follow-up, but their negative comment or review is still showing online, ask them if they would be willing to update it. Request that they share how you took care of the problem. This should only be tried when you are absolutely sure the customer is positively satisfied.

6. **Learn from the experience.** Use the information you gathered from your investigation together with the customer's feedback to find the root cause of the issue and then correct it. Examine how you responded to the complaint and see if improvements can be made there too.

Scenario #3: Handling Fake Reviews– Fake negative reviews are written to damage the reputation of a business by trying to convince customers "not" to visit a business or buy whatever is being reviewed. In 2017 BrightLocal.com did a study and discovered 79% of consumers have read a fake review and 84% can't always spot them. This is troubling as many people rely on reviews to make purchasing decisions.

With online marketing being so competitive some business owners will do whatever it takes to make a sale including hiring people to write fake reviews to take out their competition. But fake reviews are also written by people who may have issues with some of the decisions that a business has made. They'll give negative feedback on things such as where a company gets its products from rather than discuss the quality of the product based on their own personal experience with it.

If you see a negative comment about your business your first impulse may be to respond immediately, especially if it is untrue. It is quite understandable if you get angry and want to defend your business, but this is not the way to handle this problem.

Follow this plan of action to minimize any damage caused by fake negative reviews:

1. **Don't respond right away.** Take time to gather your thoughts. The last thing you want to do is engage with the hater and start a war that there's really no way for you to win. Participating in any battle with a real or fake customer will make you look bad in the eyes of other customers. Even worse, continuing an online debate only continues to push that review to the top of the search engine ranks because you are adding fresh and relevant content to conversation.

2. **Determine if the review is fake.** You must be certain that you are not confusing a fake review with one that is honestly critical. Do your research and check the review for false statements and discrepancies, along with the profile of the reviewer.

   As you are investigating try to find out:

   - Are the statements made in the review true or false?

   - Was the review written by an actual customer or client of the business?

   - Does the profile of the reviewer look legitimate with identifiable information, or is it incomplete and anonymous?

   - Does the reviewer have a history of making reviews or is this the only review they've made?

   - Is the language in the review over the top, hostile, or full of insults? Does the reviewer sound like a customer or do they use terms like someone that works in your industry?

• Does the review discourage people from doing business with you and suggest another business, product, or service to use instead?

3. **Try to get the review removed.** Check the guidelines and terms of use of the website where the review is posted and see if it breaks any of the rules. When a review violates one of the website's policies it can be reported. Examples of violations include:

   • Inappropriate content, profanity and racial terms

   • Threats, harassment, bullying, discrimination, or defamation

   • Posting information that can be proven to be false

   • One person using multiple accounts to leave reviews on the same business

   • Reviews from current or former employees

   • Reviews not relevant to an actual experience or purchase

   • Copyright infringement

   • Inappropriate images.

   If you flag a review for a violation include as much evidence as possible to help moderators decide on how to handle the review.

4. **Consider Responding Publicly.** As you wait for the outcome of the flagged review the fake review will still be visible. Ignoring negative reviews, even fake ones, is not a good idea. But every situation is different. Someone leaving a fake 1-star review saying, "this business sucks!" would not be worth your time to respond to when you are getting a lot of reviews.

If you decide to respond:

• **Don't respond by saying the review or reviewer is fake.** It makes you look bad and may give unwanted credibility to the review.

- **Don't threaten with legal action.** Unless you can prove the review had a negative impact on your business this will be perceived as an empty threat that the public will see. If you feel you have grounds for legal action, then seek consultation and handle it offline.

- **Don't try to retaliate.** Seeking revenge against the person that left the review by slandering or threatening can get you in trouble and ruin the very reputation you are trying to protect.

- **Take the high ground.** Write a polite, professional response that focuses on the critiques mentioned in the review and offer to resolve the issue privately. Your objective is to show potential customers you are willing to engage with your harshest critics and win the battle of public opinion.

Keep in mind that responding to one negative review (real or not) and not others, may cause people to think the negative reviews without a response from you are true. Use your discretion when deciding whether or not to respond.

Scenario #4: Keeping Customers Informed About Problems – If you know that you are having a problem with one of your products or there is going to be a delay to any time commitments that you've made, don't cover it up. There is no sense in trying to fool your customers. Rather than ignoring the issue, take responsibility for it and try to quickly correct the mistake. People appreciate that type of honesty. Have a set of business principles that you live by. This means you need to deal honestly with customers and be willing to admit errors. Being transparent in your business transactions fosters a good reputation.

Taking the necessary steps to repair your reputation is vital to running your business. After you've dealt with any negative issues focus on engaging with your customers. Building strong relationships with your online community can take a while, but it will pay off and make your customers happier in the long run.

9.4.3 How to Build a Rock-Solid Reputation and Gain Customer Trust

Step #3 Rebuild and Influence

The last step is to build up your online reputation so it properly reflects your business. Once you have identified and addressed any negative comments, you need to start taking measures to influence the way people think about your business. Every situation is different, and the exact methods used will vary, but for the most part, the process will involve the creation of new content. Additionally, the quality of that content must be better than what is already available online in order for search engines to rank the new content over the old material.

Let's look at the approaches to take when building your online reputation:

Improve Your Website: Most business owners that have a website believe that it represents their business in the best possible way. After all, they put a great deal of thought into it when it was created. They may have even hired professionals to help them maintain that website, and it says everything they want it to say. That could all be true, yet their website still does not represent their business in the best possible way.

Maybe their website has straightforward basic information with little or no engaging content. Or perhaps it's missing information that the business owner didn't even think to include. A big mistake though, is often that the company's domain name doesn't directly mirror the actual business name, making it difficult for people (and search engines) to find it.

If your business name isn't the same as your domain, have no fear. You can take other steps to help it get found on search engines. Start by making sure your business name is placed in the headers and permalinks of all web pages where the name is mentioned. The same applies to images on your website. Add your business name to alt tags for relevant images. Another step is making sure any profile photo you use on your website matches the rest of your social media profile photos. As people see your photos in different places you will become more recognized.

Your website is the first line of defense when it comes to protecting your online reputation, so during any reputation management campaign, it must be looked at with a very critical eye. Make sure that it has high-quality content that includes not only promotional pages and material, but also helpful tips and news about your industry. A good website, complete with relevant keywords and SEO tactics is a strong remedy for negative content.

Build Your Online Reputation through Blogging: Blogging a few times a week is a good way to keep your business on the mind of readers. This is more content and more information that the search engines can pick up and place high in their search rankings. More significantly, it's information that you control, so it's going to impact your reputation positively. Blogs can be used to provide up-to-date information and current news. Your post doesn't have to be long or detailed in order to be effective. You just need to know the reason why you are writing that piece of content, and who it is for, so you choose topics that are relevant to your audience.

Besides creating content for your blog, you can create guest posts for other people's websites too. By becoming a guest author on blogs in your industry and related to your market, you can increase your exposure. Look for places where you can post your content on a monthly basis and strengthen your reputation by becoming a thought leader people will listen to.

Keep Up with Your Industry: Stay current on what is going on in your industry. Staying current ensures you are providing the best new information to all of your customers. You can also learn about things that have an effect on your business. Take five minutes out of your day to search for the newest facts about the industry you are in. Start with the following:

- Read industry publications, and websites.
- Join relevant forums and groups.
- Follow industry experts and influencers on social media.

When you have more time:

- Read books.
- Attend events, conferences, and seminars.
- Find mentors that can share new information and answer any questions that you have.

If you want to gain the reputation of a thought leader and excel at content marketing this is how you get started.

Have an Active Social Media Presence: Social media can't be ignored if you want to change and solidify your online reputation. Get started by answering these questions: How many social networks do you currently use? Do you have a separate profile for your business? Do you have any abandoned profiles that people might mistake for your main profile? Take stock of where you are then following these steps to get things in order:

- Clean Up Your Social Media Profiles

  • If you found abandoned profiles, delete or hide them.

  • Ensure that your profiles are all consistent across all accounts by using similar descriptions, pictures, links, and contact info.

  • Make sure your profiles and posts include keywords you want to have associated with your business.

  • Try to make your profile match your website's appearance by using graphics, colors, and information found on it.

  • Try to get the same name on all of the platforms to maintain consistency and prevent others from using the same name. That could confuse customers and search engines.

- Make Your Connections Meaningful

Posting social media messages is worthless if you don't communicate regularly and directly with your followers. Take the time to be active and build a community where you can share your content, leave comments and demonstrate your expertise to your audience. Make sure to link back to your website wherever possible.

Reply quickly because when you are more responsive than your competitors, customers will see that, and it makes you stand out. If you get asked a question and you don't know how to answer it, tell the person that you're working on finding the answer. Most companies aren't going to be as diligent as you, so this will give you an edge over them.

Register Your Business with Local Online Directories: Claiming the business name across the top online directories has two purposes. The first is that it appears in more places online that you can claim, and that helps you get higher visibility in the search engine results pages. It's also information that you control, which helps to build and protect your online reputation. This is important because when customers can't find anything about a business online, they become skeptical and are not likely to trust it. Registering with online directories is also good because you move a little closer to competitors that have already registered their business while gaining an advantage over your competitors that still have not done it. See Chapter 8.6 for more details about local directories.

Follow Up with Customers After Sales: Always stay in touch with your customers, particularly after they have done business with you. This is even more crucial if your business is large. They really want to feel like something other than a number. Following up with customers builds stronger customer relationships which are vital if you want them to continue to buy from you.

Some of the ways you can follow up with customers include:

- Email
- Postcard
- Text Messaging (SMS)
- Phone call

You can automate all of these processes to occur after customers have made their purchases, but for some businesses, a phone call from a live person is preferred.

Follow-up messages should have a purpose. Don't contact customers just to see how they are doing. Use social media for that type of conversation. Here are three types of messages that are typically sent to customers after they've made a purchase:

1. Thank you or Confirmation Message: Sent to show appreciation for the sale and will sometimes come with:
    - a set of instructions or list of items purchased
    - a confirmation for an appointment or reservation information.

2. Request for Review: Ask customers to give their feedback on the purchases they've made.

3. Upselling and Cross-Selling: Immediately or a few days after the initial sale customers are made aware of additional products and services that are available.

Following up with customers has the potential to positively influence their overall perception of your business and can impact the reviews that they leave online.

Become an Event Sponsor: By becoming an event sponsor you commit to providing financial support to an event in exchange for benefits such as attention and recognition for your business. It provides an opportunity to connect with customers and build long-lasting relationships with them due to your contribution and association with the event. As it turns out 91% of consumers have more favorable feelings about businesses that provide quality experiences at an event. Also, 85% admit they are more likely to buy after participating in an event.

Some of the other benefits that can come from being an event sponsor are:

- Gaining access to your target audience
- Getting the opportunity to make more sales
- Getting more leads and contacts
- Meeting potential business partners
- Receiving media coverage.

When considering what events to sponsor ask yourself the following questions:

- Who is my target audience at the event?
- Will I have access to the audience?
- What type of exposure will my business get?
- What will I gain from helping the person putting on the event?
- Are any of my competitors sponsoring the event?

Use these questions as the starting point to determine if you should sponsor a particular event. When customers see that you help others to reach their goals they will think positively about your business and it will do good for your reputation.

Use Online Press Releases: Press releases can be published and shared online very quickly. They give you an opportunity to tell your customers about major sales, new offers, and major news in your industry. A well-written press release contains carefully selected keywords that can get it ranked in search engine results pages and helps push down negative content. Just like all online content, press releases give your business another place in the search rankings, and it's a way you control what's being said.

Provide Excellent Customer Service: Since most negative feedback is related to poor customer service, make sure you pay attention to this part of your business. Not doing so may take the control of your reputation out of your hands.

Leverage your time by creating systems, automating routine tasks and outsourcing phone support in order to meet your customer's needs.

Respond to Positive Reviews: Part of building a relationship with your customers is being responsive to their needs, but equally important is responding to their praise. Dealing with negative reviews demands a lot of attention, but customers who give positive feedback deserve just as must attention since they took the time to let you and others know about their satisfaction. Responding does matter because 30% of customers name this as key when judging local businesses.

Before responding, verify positive comments as you would negative or fake ones to make sure the reviewer is genuine. After verification respond by expressing your gratitude, matching the reviewer's tone and echoing the details they shared. Customers pay attention to how you respond to feedback left by others. When they see you are responsive, they know you are listening and will be more likely to share their feedback.

The benefits of responding to enthusiastic customers are not just gaining their loyalty. Your responses increase your visibility adding more positive content for people to see. That engagement appears on web pages that search engines will find and take into consideration when ranking your web pages.

Get More Positive Reviews: Even when you do everything right a customer may not think of giving you a review on their own. It's ok to encourage customers to leave reviews when it's done politely and without any pressure put on them to agree. Here are some tips for getting more positive feedback:

- **Ask Customers to Give Them:** Ask customers to leave a review after each sale. Make the request verbally, put it on printed receipts, postcards, text messages, or include it in follow-up emails.

- **Set Up Accounts on Multiple Review Sites:** Create profiles on the review websites and online directories related to your business. Now customers have the option of leaving a review in places they may already visit.

- **Make It Easy to Leave Reviews:** Provide links in multiple places like your websites, emails, and newsletters for customers to easily submit their reviews. Consider providing instructions to make the process clearer.

- **Communicate the Importance of Reviews:** All of your employees should know how important reviews are. Make sure the ones that interact with customers ask them to leave a review.

- **Use Customer Review Software:** Try using software that allows interacting with customers and manages your reviews. Check out Podium.com and ReviewTrackers.com.

There are no shortcuts when it comes to building your reputation, but all of these tactics along with your planning, persistence and execution can protect one of your biggest assets. Use them to rebuild and influence customer confidence whenever there is damage caused to your reputation by mistakes.

9.5 How Long Does It Take for Reputation Management to Work?

Each business is unique, and so are their online reputations. That's why there is no way to accurately determine how long it will take to complete a reputation management campaign without doing a thorough assessment of their current online reputation. If you have little to no online reputation currently, it can take as little as just a few weeks to build up your reputation. However, if there is a lot of negative content out there about your business, it could take several months to as long as a year to repair and build your reputation.

While reputation management is essential, it's definitely not something that happens overnight. One of the reasons why a campaign may take longer than expected is simply because there's a lot of work to be done on different websites. You must visit all the different social media sites and set up profiles and pages for your business. If you have a local business you must also visit all the local online directories and claim your business on each of these, as well as set up a profile. You'll need to have an SEO-optimized website that's mobile-friendly along with a blog that needs to be maintained.

All of these components are needed to ensure that the content out there about your business is good, and more importantly, that it outweighs any negative content that may be out there. Putting in this kind of work simply takes time.

Another reason why it can take so long before you start seeing results from an online reputation campaign is because search engines don't rank new sites very high in their search results pages. So, if a blog or website has just been created, it's going to take time before the search engines give it a high ranking that's above any negative content visible on the first page. This is why search engine optimization is one of the strategies you must use as it plays a big role in managing your reputation.

9.6 How to Protect Your Online Reputation against Hackers and Cyber Attacks

There are a lot of internet-based components needed to market and sell online. Making sure those components are secure must be a priority if you don't want to be a victim of hackers. The size of your business does not matter when it comes to hacking. Data compiled from SCORE.org shows 43% of all cyber attacks are directed at small businesses, so this is not something to take lightly. If there is a breach in any of your online systems the result can be devastating, and you could lose the trust of your customers.

Here's a list of some of the online assets you need to keep an eye on:

- Domain name access
- Web hosting and website access
- Social media and online directories accounts
- Payment systems access and customer information
- Access to third-party cloud-based software and managed services used for e-commerce, email marketing, customer relationship management (CRM), etc.
- Sensitive data stored on computers for your business

Consequences of Being Hacked

There are so many different ways in which harm can be done to your reputation based on what systems could get compromised. For example:

- You can lose access to your domain name which is your primary online identifier. The hijacker can create a website that looks similar to yours and use it to collect visitor data for malicious use.

- Your website can be hijacked and used to spread viruses to anyone that goes to it.

  - Search engines could blacklist your website for posing a threat and lower your ranking on SERPs.

  - Web browsers will alert visitors that your website is dangerous and advise them not to visit it.

• If someone gets control of your email, they can send spam and links to malware to your contacts. This is also how access can be gained to all of your other accounts.

• Access to any system that deals with customer information puts that data at risk for fraud and ID theft.

• An emerging threat is ransomware which is a type of malicious software, or malware, that prevents you from accessing your computer files, systems, or networks and demands you pay a ransom for their return. Ransomware attacks can cause costly disruptions to operations and the loss of critical information and data. According to Purplesec.us small to mid-sized businesses make up 20% of ransomware victims.

Securing Your Online Assets

As long as hackers remain persistent in their desire to wreak havoc on businesses, you need to start taking the necessary steps to increase your protection against them. Follow the tips below for safeguarding your online assets from cyber attacks:

• **Be Careful What You Download:** You can unknowingly download malware or ransomware onto a computer by opening a file sent by email, clicking on an ad, following a link, or even visiting a website that's been infected with the malicious software. The best way to avoid being exposed to ransomware—or any type of malware—is to be a cautious and conscientious computer user.

• **Have a Password Strategy:** Your business passwords are the gateway to all of your sensitive data including financial information, proprietary information, as well as your customers' private information. Don't store your passwords as plaintext in files, use a password manager like LastPass (lastpass.com) or Dashlane (dashlane.com) to securely generate and manage all of your passwords. Do not reuse passwords or similar passwords on multiple sites, don't let your browser save passwords for you, and change your important passwords often. You could lose a lot of your credibility and even be legally liable if your data is hacked.

Every freelancer you work with is also a security risk. Be sure to only share files and folders that they need, and revoke access once the job is over. Make sure you are using cloud storage services so that you don't have to worry about everything being deleted.

• **Backup Your Data:** This includes computer files, software configurations, databases, or any information critical to running your business. Back up data regularly and double-check that those backups were completed. Secure your backups. Make sure they are not connected to the computers and networks they are backing up.

• **Keep WordPress Updated:** Make sure your WordPress install and plugins are kept up to date. This will ensure that any known security weaknesses are addressed and fixed. There are plugins available that can do this automatically or see if your web hosting account has a backup program.

• **Paid Themes Are Better than Free Themes:** As the saying goes, you get what you pay for. Free themes are often poorly developed and have security flaws you would never know about until it's too late. Always pick a theme that has several positive reviews. Paid themes are better because the developer's livelihood is tied to the success of the theme, so they usually want it to be as clean and secure as possible.

• **Use an SSL Certificate**: An SSL (aka Secure Socket Layer) certificate serve two important functions. First, they permit communication with a web server to be encrypted. Web servers commonly use encryption to protect private data, such as passwords. Second, SSL certificates allow visitors to validate the website they're communicating with is authentic (and not, for instance, a malicious copy intended to trick visitors into disclosing passwords). This adds an extra level of security when sensitive data is sent and received between users and websites. SSL Certificates can be acquired for your website from a domain registrar or web hosting company.

• **Use Premium Anti-Virus Protection:** If malware has allowed a key logger into your website, computer, or mobile device—that tracks when you type—it will be easy for even a great password to be compromised. It is a good investment to purchase premium upgrades to your favorite anti-virus program—especially if you often log into your sites using free Wi-Fi at public locations such as coffee shops.

• **Establish Cyber Security Rules:** Create a set of rules for employees to follow covering topics like handling sensitive data and password protocols.

You need to secure your online assets against cyber attacks by limiting access to them and putting measures in place to backup important data. Your best defense for fending off hackers is having a good offense. Stay on top of the latest types of cyber attacks and how to protect against them. Follow the tips suggested to give your business the best chance to keep your reputation out of harm's way.

"If your plans don't include mobile, your plans are not finished."

– Wendy Clark, former Coca-Cola Marketing Executive

10.Getting Started with Mobile Marketing

10.1 What Is Mobile Marketing?

Mobile marketing uses a combination of different online strategies where businesses promote, advertise, sell and engage with consumers through mobile devices.

More specifically, it is the process of making relevant content available whenever and wherever a customer needs it on their smartphone, tablet or any wireless handheld device they may use with internet access. In this case, relevant content can be described as information that is:

- **Personalized:** Suggested content that appears based on a user's online behavior and preferences.

- **Time Sensitive:** Messages sent to customers alerting them to sales, special offers and discounts taking place at a specific time.

- **Location Specific:** Marketing messages sent by local businesses to customers that shop locally.

By researching mobile user tendencies and positioning your business as one that is conscious of the needs of the mobile customers, you can make it more appealing, user-friendly, and helpful to that audience. Mobile users are motivated buyers so the sooner you start engaging with them, and providing solutions to their problems, the sooner you'll start to see more leads and sales.

10.2 Why You Should Not Underestimate the Importance of Mobile Marketing

Knowing how mobile marketing works will help you understand how different online strategies work together so you can have more control over all of your marketing. But a big challenge for small business owners with little to no online marketing experience is knowing how to reach and connect with potential customers that access the internet in so many different ways. Since more people are now using their mobile devices to get online, mobile internet usage has already exceeded desktop internet usage.

Let that statement sink in for a moment. Can you imagine spending your time and money creating online marketing campaigns targeted at customers using desktop and laptop computers only to find out they use their mobile devices more often? You probably wouldn't be too happy, but that's what most small business owners are doing.

If you are not taking the steps to prepare your business to be found by people using mobile devices or making sure your online presence can easily be seen on them, you're already behind your competitors. You'll need to reinvest in rebuilding your online presence, and the longer you delay the more missed sales opportunities you're going to have.

Mobile marketing is only going to get bigger and here are some more reasons you need to be doing it now rather than later.

Mobile Users and Device Usage Is Increasing: About three-quarters of U.S. adults (77%) say they own a smartphone. This is a broad audience that covers a wide range of demographics.

Mobile devices are not only popular communication tools they are becoming powerful all-purpose portable computers. U.S consumers are spending as much as five hours a day on their smartphones performing various tasks.

As technology improves and smartphones become more affordable these numbers will certainly continue to rise and so will your opportunity to connect with this audience.

Mobile E-Commerce Continues to Grow: The way consumers are making purchases online is changing. E-commerce sales are steadily increasing, but a large portion of those sales have been made using a mobile device. Over 40% of online transactions are now done on mobile. It is important to note the distinction because mobile commerce (or m-commerce) is about the ability to make purchases or conduct financial transactions at any time and from almost anywhere. The combination of convenience and secure transactions has influenced customer's shopping behavior to a point where they're starting to prefer buying from their smartphones.

Has a Positive Impact on Email Engagement: Email engagement is a measurement of what actions people take when they receive your emails. It is estimated that emails viewed on mobile devices will account for 22% to 77% of the email opened, depending on your target audience, what you are selling and the type of email you send. A survey showed that about 3 in 5 consumers check their email on the go and 75% of Americans say they use their smartphones most often to check email. These are encouraging statistics especially if you want to use email marketing as a complementary strategy with mobile to build a relationship with customers. This is significant because it gives you the ability to use email marketing in a way that is familiar yet different.

The Connection between Mobile and Social Media Can No Longer Be Ignored: Statistics indicate that 91% of people with social media accounts use mobile devices. If you are currently using social media marketing or have plans to in the future, then understanding how customers use it on their mobile devices is something you must know.

Social media is regularly used by consumers to find out what others are saying about something they have an interest in. They read comments and check reviews to assist them in making buying decisions.

The same benefits for using social media to connect with customers that have computers apply for users of mobile devices with a few extras:

- **More convenient:** People can access their accounts from anywhere as long as they have internet access. The ability for them to easily post, read, comment and share on social media from their mobile device has made this experience a part of their everyday lives.

- **Closer connection:** Mobile devices are personal items that their owners spend a lot of time with, so when they are used to communicate the conversation seems more personal.

- **Faster responses:** Whether it is liking, sharing or responding to a post or message, actions are done a lot faster because users receive notifications on their devices.

The opportunity to monetize social media and use it as a promotional tool will continue to exist. But it's the savvy business owner that has done their homework and understands the users of mobile social media that will have the advantage when it comes to connecting with that audience.

The Dawn of Micro-Moment Marketing: Marketers at Google define micro-moments as a situation where a customer reflexively reaches for a device (often their smartphone) to address an immediate need to . . .

- Learn something
- Watch something
- Find a place to go
- Find something to do
- Determine what to buy.

These are the moments when decisions are made, preferences are influenced, and customer expectations are at their highest. These actions by mobile users are not random or isolated. This is definitely a change in consumer behavior in terms of using mobile technology and the internet to meet their everyday needs.

Micro-moment marketing involves creating valuable content that is quick and easy to understand. The strategy takes into consideration that people are busy, don't have much time, and they have other types of content they want to consume. They won't always be ready to buy, but when your relevant content appears when they need it, they will remember you and come back. Over time these short interactions will add up and lead to more sales.

10.3 Why Your Small Business Needs a Mobile Friendly Website

Getting the most from mobile marketing starts with making sure you have a mobile optimized website for your business. Traditional websites that have a lot of text and graphics were designed for viewing on desktop and laptop computer screens. When a mobile user tries to view these regular sites on their device it is almost impossible. You have to scroll all over the place just to find the information you're looking for due to the limited screen size.

Other problems users experience include:

- The content is too small and hard to see.
- It can be difficult navigating to different pages.
- Pages with a lot of graphics take longer to load.

Customers are more likely to stay longer on mobile friendly websites and revisit them more often compared to websites that aren't viewable on a mobile device. They are doing more product research and online shopping from mobile websites because it offers them content in a way that meets their needs in the moment.

A survey by Google found 48% of users say they feel frustrated and annoyed when they get to a site that's not mobile-friendly. The same amount of respondents believed that if a site didn't work well on their smartphones, the company probably didn't care about their business. You certainly don't want that to be the experience for anyone that visits your website.

Having a mobile optimized website is no longer optional because Google has adopted a mobile-first approach. In the past Google used the content from the pages of regular websites to determine if they were relevant to a person's search query. Now that most mobile users are performing web searches from their smartphones Google will predominantly use the mobile version of the content for indexing and ranking web pages on their search engine. This makes sense since Google is responsible for almost all smartphone search traffic. The main point is if you don't have a mobile optimized version of your regular website it may not rank well in on Google which will impact present and future Search Engine Optimization strategies.

10.3.1 Three Ways to Make a Mobile-Friendly Website

Now that we understand why having a mobile-ready website is so important, let's learn about the options for converting an existing website or what to do when building a new website.

But first, I suggest that if you currently have a website check and see if yours is optimized for mobile. Here are two websites that you can use to run a test:

- https://search.google.com/test/mobile-friendly
- https://ready.mobi

Both tools are free to use and will show you how a web page looks when it is viewed from a mobile device. If your web page passes the test for being mobile-friendly, then you are on the right track. If it did not pass, then here are three ways to fix it.

1. **Create a Separate Mobile Version of Your Current Website**
   If you have an older static website or one that was not built using a content management system (CMS) like WordPress then I suggest you think about getting a new website. If you are not ready to do that then you can use these services to create a mobile version of your existing website:

• MobilifyIt.com
• mobiSiteGalore.com
• Mofuse.com
• Winksite.com

Some of these services use the existing content from your website and attempt to make a mobile version that looks the same. You can make changes if you want and some companies offer assistance with setting things up. The process is quick, but the downside is you will need to maintain both versions of your website and may need a separate domain name for your mobile site. There are not too many companies left that provide this service as newer websites are already optimized for mobile.

2. **Use a Mobile Plugin**
Plugins are software programs that integrate with other software like CMS applications. Websites built using WordPress can be given additional functions with the use of plugins. So, if your website was built using WordPress you can use a plugin to make it mobile-friendly.

With this option, there are free and premium choices available.
• Any Mobile Theme Switcher: https://wordpress.org/plugins/any-mobile-theme-switcher
• WP Mobile Edition: https://wordpress.org/plugins/wp-mobile-edition
• WPtouch: https://wordpress.org/plugins/wptouch
• WPtouch Pro: https://www.wptouch.com.

Using one of these plugins will immediately make your website mobile-ready. You can modify settings for your mobile version without affecting your regular website theme. However, since the plugin is an add-on the appearance of your website (i.e., color scheme, available content) may not be consistent when viewed on different devices.

3. **Use a Responsive Website Theme**
When building a website with a CMS you're able to quickly create good-looking, well-designed web pages using themes. Now that mobile web design has become so important, "responsive" themes have been created to make it easier to have a mobile-friendly website.

A responsive theme is one that responds to the dimensions of the screen size, no matter which device it is viewed on. The layout of the web pages will adjust to fit the viewable area of the device accordingly. Other benefits include:

• **Usability:** It offers better readability and usability for viewers with smaller screens which provides a more positive user experience.

• **Appearance:** You won't have to worry about appearance and consistency issues since you will be working with only one website.

• **Improved SEO:** Search engines prefer a responsive website over the use of a separate mobile website. The reason is to avoid having duplicate content on different websites which has a negative impact on SEO. Also, a mobile website will have a different web address than that desktop version and will require a separate SEO strategy.
If you plan on investing in a new website or redesigning an existing one, make sure it is responsive.

10.3.2 10 Features Your Mobile Website Must Have

So, what makes your website mobile-friendly and always accessible to potential mobile customers? Here are 10 things it should have:

1. **Quick Loading Time:** Websites that take longer to load on a mobile device tend to lose customers. How fast your web pages load is determined by but limited to factors such as:

    • The speed of the server your website is hosted on

    • The file size of images, their quantity, and type of images used on your web pages.

    Improve your website's speed by optimizing your mobile website design.

2. **Clean Design:** Mobile users require web pages that have a simple design, plenty of white space, readable text, and a layout that is easy to navigate. Avoid the clutter and confusion that comes from too many graphics and posting unnecessary content.

3. **Availability of Relevant Information:** Think about what your potential customers might be looking for when they visit your website. Details about a product, service, or perhaps something about you. Make that

information easily available to them so they don't have to hunt around for it. They may not have time for detailed content, so at the very least have your business name, address, and phone number (NAP) located where it is easy to find.

4. **Ability to Enlarge Product Images:** If you sell products, customers should be able to click on your photos to enlarge and zoom in on them to get a better view.

5. **Limited or One Direction Scrolling:** Your mobile users would not want to scroll endlessly to find what they are looking for so keep relevant information near the top of the page to avoid unnecessary scrolling. Or edit the amount of content on the page to reduce the amount of scrolling needed.

6. **Multiple Browser and Device Compatibility:** To offer your users the best mobile experience, you will need a mobile version of your website which is compatible with the widest selection of internet browsers and mobile devices. Implement a device testing strategy to determine its compatibility.

7. **Large Mobile-Friendly Buttons:** Ensure that your mobile website has no usability issues and offers visitors large buttons that are easy to locate and link to relevant information.

8. **Mobile-Friendly Call to Action:** Use call to action buttons that visually stand out and succinctly describes what you want customers to do, or that hint at what they will get after they click the button. An example of this is having a click-to-call button so customers won't have to memorize and dial your phone number.

9. **Map and Directions:** If you have a local business, then adding a map to your website helps to quickly let people see where you are located and get directions from their current location at the click of a button. There are plenty of free and paid map plug-ins available for you to choose from.

10. **Links to Your Company's Social Profiles:** Always include social media icons that link to your company's profiles on the different social platforms to increase your online presence. Most users are in a hurry so make it easier for them to "Like," "Follow," or "Subscribe" via your mobile website so they can connect with you.

10.4 What Are the Six Channels That Make Up Mobile Marketing?

As mentioned earlier in the chapter mobile marketing is a mix of strategies that attempt to attract, engage, promote, and sell to a rapidly growing market or mobile device users. These channels can be used individually or combined for a more comprehensive strategy. Here's a summary of each channel.

1. **SMS Marketing:** SMS or Short Messaging Service marketing is a technique that uses permission-based text messaging to send quick promotional messages directly to the mobile phones of your target audience. In order to send these types of messages, you'll need to select a service provider that will handle the process for you. You can then provide instructions to your audience on how to sign up to receive messages from you. Once they've signed up, a confirmation message is usually sent along with instructions on how to unsubscribe from receiving messages.

   SMS marketing is similar to email marketing with one key distinction, you are sending messages to mobile devices instead of personal computers. The response rate for SMS is significantly higher than that of email because the messages received are more relevant. Almost all text messages are read within minutes of receiving them, so this is a good way to promote offers, deals, coupons and your business to customers.

   With SMS you are limited to 160 characters in your messages. If you wanted to send longer messages plus have the ability to add audio, video, and images then MMS (Multimedia Messaging Service) is an option you can look into.

2. **Digital Coupon Marketing:** A mobile coupon is a digital version of the ones found in printed newspapers and store circulars. However, there are four big advantages that mobile coupons have:

   • **Immediate Availability:** Links to coupons are sent to customers' smartphones via SMS or they can be found online. There is no waiting period before they can be redeemed.

   • **Easy to Use:** They are able to be used once they are retrieved and can be redeemed in stores or on websites.

• **Relevance to the Customer:** Customers can search for coupons that they want or sign up to have them sent to them. They won't have to sort through a bunch of coupons they're not interested in.

• **Portability:** Unlike paper coupons that can be lost, forgotten or get damaged from being handling, mobile coupons can be retrieved when needed on a smartphone.

Mobile coupons are distributed by the following methods:

Email	SMS / MMS	Social Media	Mobile Apps
Mobile Websites	QR Codes		

Customers love mobile coupons as they're convenient to use and offer them tangible benefits in the form of savings. Reports suggest that coupon users tend to decide to shop quicker, spend more time on a website, and will add more to their shopping cart as compared to users who don't have one.

Business owners love them for these reasons:

• They help build a contact list of customers that are interested in buying.

• They're easier to distribute than printed coupons.

• They have a higher rate of redemption than printed coupons since they are easier to claim.

• They increase sales.

• They increase traffic to brick and mortar stores and businesses that sell online.

Coupons are a fast-emerging trend and are worth looking into for businesses that want to increase their revenue through mobile marketing.

3. **Quick Response (QR) Codes:** A QR code is a two-dimensional patterned bar code originally created to keep track of auto parts in Japan. The codes have found a new purpose in the world of mobile marketing now by being used to store text Information about a business, link to a web page, or mobile app.

The embedded information can be retrieved by using a mobile app that can scan QR codes. Once the code is read, users are immediately sent to the URL of your choice. There are plenty of creative ways in which these codes can be used.

4. **Mobile App:** A mobile application is a software program that runs on smartphones, tablets, and other gadgets like smartwatches. Many apps come preinstalled on mobile devices or they can be downloaded from an online marketplace made available by the device's manufacturer. Apps serve many functions: they can send messages, play music, check the weather, search for information, be used for posting on social media, and much more.

   A misconception about mobile apps is that developing them is usually done by large companies. Another belief is that creating an app is expensive and they are not worth the investment. Those notions are false. A solid mobile strategy means looking at all available options regardless of the size of your business. Mobile apps have become a useful tool for small businesses that have identified the best way to use them.

   Here are four ways a mobile app can help your business.

   1. **Direct Marketing:** Depending on the purpose of your app you'll be able to provide instant access to whatever information, products, or services you want to promote. Some customers prefer this over having to follow the steps needed to visit a website and then having to look for what they want. If your app was not designed to specifically sell, you can make your promotions accessible in a not-so-obvious way so customers can get the intended benefits of the app and keep using it.

   2. **Engage with and Build Customer Base:** A mobile app offers a convenient way for customers to contact your business and give feedback without having to deal with the distractions that come with

other types of digital communication. If you personally respond to incoming messages, you'll have more opportunities to engage with customers and gain their loyalty.

3. **Gives a Competitive Advantage:** If your target audience is millennials (age 22 to 37), a mobile app will give them the impression that you are a tech savvy entrepreneur. You'll stand out from your competitors by having something to attract a young and growing audience that already has a mobile-first mentality.

4. **Ability to Sell Faster:** If you want to sell a particular product in a short period of time you can send a promotional message or notifications via your mobile app to your customers to encourage sales

Before you think about creating an app you need to keep in mind that its main purpose is to help you to serve your customers better. To generate interest, you must give people a reason to download it. Below are 5 tips to get you started on the right track:

1. **Develop a Plan to Be Prepared:** Take the time to create a plan for your mobile app. Research apps targeted to your market to see what is already available. Think outside the box and develop something that has multiple purposes. Depending on the type of business you have and the industry that you're in it may not make sense to have an app. Determine this quickly to save yourself time so you can move on to another strategy.

2. **Make Sure Your App Solves a Problem:** Good apps solve a problem or makes something easier to do. Create a list of problems that your app could solve for your target audience. Get your customers involved and ask them what type of app they would like to see available.

3. **Make Your App Visually Appealing:** The user interface of your app should be simple, intuitive, and have a nice color scheme. Just as important is the icon used to promote your app. Use unique shapes and vibrant colors to help your app stand out and get more downloads.

4. **Offer Special Promotions for App Users:** Your app should have a way to reward your users. Make discounts and freebies available so occasional buyers can become frequent buyers.

5. **Integrate Social Media with Your App:** If possible, find a way to take advantage of social media like sharing the content on your app. If your app requires users to log in let them use the ones from their social media accounts. This way you can benefit from having a way to build your following, increase engagement and promote your business.

   With proper planning and a clear purpose, you can hire a programmer to create your app or use a DIY app builder to bring your idea into existence in a matter of days. See Chapter 10.7 (Websites to Help You with Your Mobile Marketing) for a list of resources.

5. **Location-Based Marketing (LBM):** This strategy uses the location of a customer's mobile device to let them know about an offer that is available from a business that they are geographically close to. Customers find out about these offers by opting in to receive notifications via SMS messaging or installing an app developed by the business. The notification can be about a sale that is going on or a digital coupon that can be used for purchases.

   LBM is possible by the use of a method called geofencing. Geofencing is the use of GPS and RFID (radio frequency identification) to create a virtual perimeter that surrounds an actual physical area. When a person's mobile device enters or exits a pre-defined virtual boundary set up by a business they want information from, they'll be notified with a message or alert notification.

6. **Mobile Advertising:** Mobile advertising is a form of paid advertising that's specifically created to appear on mobile devices. Information such as customer shopping habits, past browsing history, and geographic location is used to identify what kind of ads a person is most likely to respond to. Advertisers use the collected data to determine what kind of ads to run and where to place them. Types of advertisements used range from SMS text to rich media (interactive) ads. Some of the places where you'll see mobile advertisements are text messages, mobile websites, and within apps.

   What makes mobile advertising effective is the fact that the ads that are sent to consumers are extremely targeted. With so many people using at least one type of mobile device the chance of someone seeing a mobile ad is much higher than other forms of advertisements. Learn more about how paid online advertising works in Chapter 14.

10.5 Seven Steps to Get Your Business Ready for Mobile Marketing

Capturing the interest of mobile prospects is a lot easier when you have a solid mobile presence and strategy for converting them into long-term customers. It's not too late to get on board with mobile marketing, but every day you delay you're missing out on your share of this rapidly growing market.

You want to be in a position to attract the right audience at the right time. So, when getting ready to plan a mobile marketing strategy follow these seven steps to ensure you're putting the right pieces in place to have a strong mobile presence.

1. **Identify Mobile Audience:** You can get clues on how many people are discovering and interacting with your business with their mobile device by using Google Analytics and other tools that track a customer's online journeys and habits. Find out:

    - What type of content are they viewing?
    - How long are they staying on a specific page?
    - How did they get to your website?

    With this information, you will get a better idea of what to focus on with your mobile marketing.

2. **Set Goals:** Mobile marketing is different from other types of online marketing in that goals for a mobile strategy focus on getting a response to a call to action targeted to mobile users. Examples of some goals would be:

    - Increase customer engagement by using text messaging.
    - Increase the amount of phone call inquiries from a business website.
    - Reaching a certain amount of app downloads per week or month.
    - Make a certain amount of sales from mobile advertising per week or month.
    - Make sure customers find your business when they search for whatever you offer.

3. **Have a Mobile-Ready Website:** A top priority is to have a mobile-friendly website. You want to make a good first impression using this. I recommend that you have a website that is responsive because it is easier to maintain, and all of your content will be available on both large and small screens.

4. **Optimize Content for Mobile:** If you have a local business make sure your web pages have accurate information about your physical location and how to contact you. Keep paragraphs on each page short and easy to read so site visitors don't become impatient.

5. **Choose a Mobile Marketing Channel:** Identify the mobile marketing channel you want to use from the ones listed in the last subchapter. Get the details you need to get started or find an expert or agency to help you create and execute a plan. Read Chapter 18 to learn find a consultant to work with.

6. **Connect with Social Media:** To get the most from mobile marketing having a social media strategy in effect is suggested. Use social media to let your audience know about what you have going on in the mobile world. Then ask anyone who finds you from your mobile marketing efforts to follow you on social media so you have multiple ways to contact them and grow your audience. Read Chapter 12.2 to find out how to grow your business using social media.

7. **Monitor Your Mobile Metrics:** Track everything from website visits to sales you've made. Every mobile marketing channel has data that is tracked and can be analyzed. Observe and learn how much impact customer mobile use is having on your business and adjust your strategies accordingly.

10.6 Websites to Help You with Your Mobile Marketing

Want your business to take complete advantage of mobile marketing? Here are a few websites that can help you get started right away:

SMS Marketing

- **EZTexting.com:** Send a text to your customers in 3 easy steps.

- **Mozeo.com:** Lets you create and send bulk SMSes to your targeted customers

- **SimpleTexting.com:** Makes sending text marketing campaigns as simple as starting one-on-one text message conversations.

- **SlickText.com:** Allows you to quickly and easily spread the word to your best customers with a simple text message.

Mobile Coupons

- **CouponTools.com:** One-stop solution for mobile couponing.

- **Koupon.com:** They provide businesses with flexible digital promotion technology to make launching digital campaigns easy.

- **Mezzofy.com:** All the nuts and bolts you need to create, distribute, redeem and manage for Digital Coupon, within one powerful platform on the cloud.

QR Codes

- **CodeQRCode.com:** More than a simple QR code generator service. For advanced users and small businesses.

- **Flowcode.com:** Connects your offline audience to all your online experiences.

- **QR-Code-Generator.com:** Create a QR code with logo and tracking.

- **QRStuff.com:** Create unlimited non-expiring free QR codes for free.

- **Wordpress Plugins:** Use plugins to create QR codes. https://wordpress.org/plugins/tags/qr-code/

Mobile Apps

- **AppNext.com:** Turn your app into a platform, becoming a trusted partner for apps your users discover and use throughout the day.

- **AppyPie.com:** Anyone can build a stunning app in 3 simple steps with Appy Pie's app builder.

- **Builder.ai:** Turn any idea into tailor-made apps, websites or wearables with our easy software builder.

- **GoCanvas.com:** Replace your paper forms with fully customized mobile apps that you design, deploy, and distribute.

- **Shoutem.com:** Build a native app for Android and iOS in 3 easy steps—without coding!

Location-Based Marketing

- **Nuviad.com:** A mobile marketing company that provides businesses the solutions they need to promote their products and services through hyper-local targeting.

- **ThumbVista.com:** Specializes in geofencing, advanced mobile advertising, mobile coupons, and location-based advertising.

Mobile Advertising

- **EZMob.com:** A self-serve programmatic advertising platform.

- **Google Ads:** Promote your app by running mobile ads across the entire Google network with Universal App Campaigns—no design experience required. https://ads.google.com/home/resources/mobile-advertising

- **LinkedIn Marketing Solutions:** Marketing on LinkedIn helps you engage a community of professionals to drive actions that are relevant to your business. https://business.linkedin.com/marketing-solutions

- **Waze Ads:** Advertise your business on the Waze map app. https://www.waze.com/business/#home

"Email is the lowest common denominator.
It's the way you get communications from one person to another.
There isn't really an alternative."

*– **Stewart Butterfield**, co-founder of Flickr and Slack*

11. Building Relationships with Your Customers Through Email

11.1 What Is Email Marketing?

Email marketing is the use of email to sustain engagement and build a relationship with your target audience so you can occasionally promote products and services to them. The strategy allows you to reach a wide audience in a short span of time, and costs less than traditional print mail marketing.

Email marketing is permission-based so once people agree to join and be part of your email list you have permission to start sending them both informational and promotional emails. Coupons, announcements, and other types of content can be distributed by email to educate customers and market your business.

11.2 Why Should You Use Email Marketing?

Contrary to what some experts may be saying, email marketing is not dead, declining, or losing its effectiveness. A survey revealed that 80% of business professionals believe that email marketing increases customer retention. By sending emails to customers and prospects, it helps you build loyalty with them and encourages new and repeat business.

Also, MarketingSherpa.com found that 72% of people that were surveyed prefer to receive promotional content through email compared to 17% who prefer social media. All of us are subscribed to some mailing lists that are bothersome and we will eventually unsubscribe from, but many of us remain subscribed to business newsletters because we like the business and/or the content provides value to our lives or work.

Here are some other reasons for using email marketing:

- Social media is great, but it doesn't account for everyone. While tons of people have social media accounts, all of those people plus a lot more have email addresses.

- Email marketing has a fantastic return on investment (ROI). Email's average ROI is 28.5% compared to 7% for direct mail according to ChiefMarketer.com. And CampaignMonitor.com states that email marketing drives $44 for every $1 spent. Yours probably could be higher if you're a solo entrepreneur with a smaller budget.

- Email is more personal. While you might send out one post on social media that thousands of people see and ignore, emails not only go directly to someone's inbox that they will check, but you're able to customize the email with the name and preferences of your subscriber.

- Increase sales. Sending your audience links to your website sales pages or affiliate offers in your messages can generate multiple sales that you otherwise may not have made.

- It creates instant traffic. An email list is great to promote new content because if you have a new blog post up and you share it in your email list, a percentage of your readers will click it and generate traffic to your site.

- Unlike most social media, you can track detailed activity in your email. The percentage of your readers that click a link on your email is called the click-through rate, and it's how online marketers measure the success of an email campaign. You can learn about each customer based on what links they click.

11.3 Why Is It Important to Generate Leads?

Business owners can't just sit around and wait for sales to come in, you've got to generate leads. Basically, leads are people or organizations who have expressed interest in your product, and lead generation is the process of giving potential customers as many opportunities as possible to express that interest, whether that is via downloading an e-book, signing up for a mailing list, or any other action which puts them on your radar. Leads can come from different sources such as social media, referrals, paid online advertising, live events, SEO, and other forms of online and offline marketing driven to one or more of your websites.

Remember in Chapter 4.3 where I stated that your website has two purposes; to sell, and capture leads? The need to capture leads is critical because so many people don't buy or call when they first visit your website. Did you know that around 98% of new traffic leaves websites without converting? People may have discovered your business online by your marketing efforts, but they'll most likely forget about it if you don't prompt them into taking an action and converting them into a lead. In fact, at this point, you should be offering them some type of opt-in offer because of where they are at in their buying process, and if your product or service is expensive.

An opt-in offer, sometimes called a lead magnet is an incentive that you offer prospects in exchange for their email address, or other types of contact information so they can join your list. Think of it as a trade. You will give them something free which asserts your authority in exchange for their contact info. An opt-in offer is usually a piece of digital content that can be downloaded such as a free whitepaper, e-book, report, checklist, video, etc. It's definitely worth having a good incentive because having the right people on your email list is the beginning to generating profits quickly and in the future.

Once you have their email address you need to have a tactic for how to convert them into a sale. All it takes is simple engagement through email to remind them about what you offer, so that when they do decide to make a purchase, they will have your business in mind, and would definitely check it out.

11.4 What Is Email List Building?

Email list building is the deliberate effort to create and grow a database of names and email addresses that are obtained from potential customers through some type of lead generation. These people have willingly joined your list which shows their level of interest in you and your business. From there, you can turn them into sales and even repeat business.

Your email list is one of your biggest business assets because you own it. With other marketing channels, more specifically social media, you are subject to rules and guidelines that can change at any time. When you are building an audience on another platform you are technically sharing it no matter how hard you worked to get your followers. If Facebook, Twitter or YouTube decided to shut down or changed their policies it could have a negative impact on your business. What would you do? That is why you need to build a list that you control so you always have a way to communicate with your audience, no matter what. In this chapter, we'll cover the eight steps to a successful email campaign: getting leads to sign up for your email list, getting those leads to open your emails, and getting those people to click the links in your emails.

11.5 What Are the Tools Needed to Capture Leads and Build Your Email List?

Whether you want 100 or 100,000 people on your email list you would not want to have to manually enter their contact details or communicate to each of them one at a time. To make list building more efficient for you, there are a few tools you're going to need that will automate the process of collecting contact details and distributing your messages. Here are some that are best suited for your email marketing needs.

Email Marketing Software

The most important component of your email marketing arsenal is the web-based application you choose to plan, implement, and monitor your email marketing campaigns.

There are plenty of email service providers (ESPs) to choose from, and perhaps hundreds more if you include all of the small providers and self-hosted software choices. It can be hard to choose which one to use, but it's better to go with one of the larger ones instead of a smaller one.

Established providers have strong relationships with the various internet service providers (ISPs), which helps ensure that the email deliverability rate remains higher. If your subscribers don't receive your emails because they're being sent to a spam filter, your results will be very poor, to say the least. Using one of the popular providers will ensure deliverability.

Pricing can vary considerably between different providers. Most of them base their price on how many people you have on your list. You'll need to anticipate how many people you will likely add to your list to decide which provider is the most affordable so you can start out small and expand as you need to.
Most email marketing software will have the following features:

• **Subscriber Management:** Build, track and manage your subscriber list. Create subscriber segments to send targeted emails and campaigns. Segmentation allows you to group subscribers and send them emails based on data collected from form submissions like their location, interest, purchase history, or actions they've taken with previous emails.

• **Email Automation:** This is the ability to select what email message you want to send, who will get the message, and when they will receive it. A type of automation you may already be familiar with is an autoresponder which is one or more automatic emails that will be sent in a sequence to a customer once they take a specific action like joining your email list.

• **Newsletter Creation:** Blurbs of your blog post and other content, along with a link to read them in their entirety can be sent to your subscribers in the form of an email newsletter.

• **Email Templates:** Use professional mobile-ready templates for sending your messages or create your own to match the look and style of your business.

• **Email Analytics:** Find out how many of your emails were delivered, read, and who clicked on the links in your messages.

• **Opt-in Forms:** Create mobile-responsive signup forms and pop-ups to use on your web pages to capture subscriber information and grow your list.

Email service providers you should consider are:

- ActiveCampaign.com
- Aweber.com
- ClickFunnels.com
- ConstantContact.com
- ConvertKit.com
- GetResponse.com
- MailChimp.com
- Mailerlite.com

Landing Page Builder

Also known as a squeeze page or lead capture page, a landing page is a promotional web page that is meant to sell something or generate a lead. Visitors can reach the page in one of the following ways:

- search engine results pages
- links posted on social media websites
- paid online advertising
- emails
- text messages
- links on other websites
- direct entry of the web address of the page in a web browser

A landing page can be a page on an existing website, or a standalone website (review Chapter 4.11). A dedicated landing page nets 220% more leads than call to actions located above the fold of website pages.

Should you use a dedicated website for your landing page, or use a product page on your current website? There are a few reasons why a standalone website is more beneficial:

1. You may offer different types of products or services; multiple lead generation sites allow you to only target one type of customer and give them a tailored experience.

2. It's easier to analyze which ads and lead generators are most successful, and then you can further optimize your marketing to maximize your conversion rate.

3. There will be more space to use for more compelling content that will get visitors more interested in your offer. Your call to actions can be visually bigger and bolder.

Your landing pages can be short or long, but each should focus on one topic, solution, and offer. Design the page to introduce the freebie you're giving away and provide details about the offer's benefits. Include an opt-in form on the landing page to collect the name and email address where the offer will be delivered.

Here are some solutions for creating landing pages:

- Carrd.com
- Landingi.com

- Leadpages.com
- Kickofflabs.com
- OptimizePress.com
- Unbounce.com

Best practices for using landing pages will be covered in Chapter 11.10.

Opt-in Form Builder

An opt-in form builder is software that creates the forms used to capture contact details of the prospects that visit your web pages. The forms can appear on web pages in a variety of ways such as pop-up boxes and lightboxes that bring attention to your incentives. They are specifically designed to get your website visitors to take action.

Opt-in form builders are available as plugins for WordPress and they're also included with most email marketing software. Some website themes come with the ability to make opt-in forms, but they are not as dynamic.

Here are some options you can learn more about:

- Bloom: https://www.elegantthemes.com/plugins/bloom
- ConvertPro.net
- OptinMonster.com
- Thrive Leads: https://thrivethemes.com/leads

11.6 How to Launch Your First Email Marketing Campaign in Eight Steps

Email marketing campaigns are just like any other advertising campaign. In this case, it would be a series of emails that are sent out to a large number of people automatically and instantaneously. In order to build and maintain a solid, targeted email list there are several steps you must take.

Step #1: Determine Your Goal: No marketing campaign should ever be started without it having a clear goal. If you want to be successful take the time to think about what you want to achieve. For example:

- Are you trying to get people to call you? Then your messages will have that call to action.

- If you have an online store your messages will have links to specific products you are trying to sell.

- If you are looking to build your credibility, then you will give your subscribers beneficial content that will also show how much you know.

When you know your goals, it makes it a lot easier to present the best content for the intended purpose.

Step #2: Know Your Audience: You need to narrow down who your target audience is. Sometimes you can do this by writing up three fictional "ideal customers" to understand what your demographic is. What keeps your potential customers up at night and how will your products or services help them sleep peacefully?

Step #3: Know Your Products & Services: If you want customers and potential customers to trust you, you have to show you're dedicated and focused. If your products and services are all over the place, lack clarity, or are confusing, people will lose interest.

Step #4 Provide a Compelling Opt-in Offer: Your opt-in offer should be related to the reason people are on your site and provide specific benefits to the subscriber. It's important that your offer catches the reader's attention and provides exceptional value. Offer a much-needed solution or group of solutions, which they are convinced will make their lives easier in some way. Show them what realistic benefits they can expect from your lead magnet. Use wording that motivates them emotionally and compels them to opt in. Review Chapter 6.4.1 for more information on planning and writing compelling content.

There are many different opt-in incentives you can use. It's a matter of choosing the one right for your business. Here are a few lead magnet content formats that are used widely and successfully to provide readers with solutions, info, and items they want and need most.

Apps, Plugins, Software	Free Graphics	Spreadsheets
Blueprints	Free Trials	Step-By-Step Guides
Cheat Sheets	Quizzes	Templates
Checklists	Resource Lists	Webinars
E-courses	Short Reports	Whitepapers

Step #5: Create Effective Follow Up Strategies: Soon after people subscribe, when you and your business are still fresh in their minds, you've got to give them a tailored and organized stream of content to their inboxes. Think of it as striking while the iron is hot. You don't want people to subscribe and then not get any interesting content until you decide to send out a campaign several weeks later.

- **Say Thank You:** Send them a thank you email, a link to a free download, and a bit of information about what they can expect from future emails.

- **Have a Short-Term Plan:** Write a series of 7–10 emails to be sent out sequentially over a month or so. Make sure the emails provide information that is useful to your customers and slowly builds up towards a call to action to sell your products and/or services.

- **Keep It Up:** As you learn more about your subscribers, you can tailor your messages and have them sent at the right time, with the right offers which will provide the best results. Make sure to constantly be linking to your blog posts and social media updates to lead them back to your content. It's also useful to ask for feedback and encourage interaction with your audience to begin building trust and relationships with them through conversation, and giving them a chance to express their opinions.

- **Make Sure Mobile Users Have a Great Experience:** As you know by now, everyone is on their smartphones. It's important you test your emails on a variety of devices and email apps to ensure that everyone can click the links and interact how you expect them to.

- **Make It Easy for Them to Unsubscribe:** Any email list which does not include easy unsubscribe links is technically violating the CAN-SPAM Act signed into law by the U.S. Congress in 2003. You could be legally/financially liable. Furthermore, you will gain trust from your readers because maybe they are not unsubscribing for a bad reason. Maybe they just want to follow your social media content instead.

Step #6: Location Location Location: You want to give your website visitors as many opportunities as possible to engage with your content. There should be forms or interactive elements before or after blog posts, in the sidebar of your website, on your custom landing pages, in the footer of your website, and in pop-ups when visitors first come to the site.

The internet happens fast, you have very little time to grab your visitors' information and attention, so make sure to entice them with numerous freebies and opportunities to engage.

Step #7: Review, Revise, Repeat: Keep a close eye on your email marketing analytics. Is your open rate rapidly declining? Why is that? Have you done split testing in your campaigns to see which subject line works better? Make sure you're testing out different formats and text link descriptions to see which produce the best results, and then constantly make sure results are improving.

Step #8: Don't Let Up: You should constantly be both learning more about your current subscribers and adding new subscribers to your list. Your email list should be in a constant state of growth and intelligence gathering.

11.7 How to Write Subject Lines That Get People to Open Your Emails

There are three simple actions that make email marketing work: people subscribe to your list, they open your email, and they click a link in the email. But, if step two doesn't happen, and nobody opens your email, then all the work you did to get their information and all the work you did to create the email and the content it links to will go to waste. You need to think hard about and really explore the right subject lines which entice your audience to open the email.

Don't try and be clever or mysterious, a good subject line tells people what to expect when they open the email. Over the years, I have learned a couple of useful tricks:

- Make your message seem exciting and urgent.
- Keep the subject line short and simple.
- Use numbers where possible.
- Avoid the word "free."
- Focus on a customer pain point the email will solve.

Refer to Chapter 6.4.3 where the C.U.R.V.E. method for writing subject lines was explained.

11.7.1 How to Write More Effective Email Messages When Talking to Your Audience

If you want to make money from your emails, people have got to enjoy them, and for people to enjoy them, they have to provide value over and above what your product or service could offer them. Show them the value you and your business offer, and they will be eager to get more of it.

- **Trust Through Relevancy:** People will trust you and open your emails if the subject line immediately refers to the email. If the email says, "Click here for free money," but your email says nothing about free money, then you will have lost subscribers who want to trust you but felt gypped. Make sure the first couple of lines of your email refer to the subject line, so people know to trust your emails in the future.

- **Less Is More:** Don't make your emails long, they should be short and to the point. You should make sure that people don't have to scroll too much and just get enough information to click through to the content or products you're promoting.

- **1st & 2nd Person Only:** Remember your emails are most likely going into people's personal inboxes, so the emails should be personable. They shouldn't be in the third person, but rather written to somebody. Feel free to refer to "I," "My," "Our," or "We." You can also refer to the reader as "You," so they are reading a letter written to them versus some generic marketing copy.

- **Find Your Voice:** Give readers the feeling they are getting to know you. Show your personality, find your business's voice and stick to it.

- **Sell Benefits Not Products:** Instead of focusing on the features of the product and why they should buy it, focus on the benefits the products or services will bring to their lives.

- **Keep Your Enemies Closer:** It's important you're well versed in your competition's products, services, and marketing tactics. That way, you can consider these details when writing your email and make sure to take advantage of your competition's known weaknesses.

- **Call People to Action:** You should always make it clear to your readers why you are emailing them and exactly what you want them to do. This is covered in the following subchapter.

Writing compelling emails takes practice, testing, and some prep work but it's not difficult. Make sure that each email has a purpose, uses the words your audience understands, and lets them know what's in it for them. If you need some ideas on what content to send to your subscribers review Chapter 6.4.2.

11.7.2 Creating Dynamic Calls to Action That Get Responses

While most business owners understand that marketing emails need some sort of call to action (CTA), oftentimes they aren't making the calls dynamic. Think "Begin your new life today!" instead of "Call now."

You want the call to action to be compelling, have some pizzazz, and be tailored to your product or service. Your call to action needs to encourage or convince rather than command your readers. They should be short (around 30 characters), use strong action words like "buy," "download," or "subscribe."

Much like in subject lines, exclamation points really do help! They make everything seem exciting! If you're careful, negative calls to action work as well. Such as, "Stop relying on crappy home security systems today." Finally, FOMO (fear of missing out) also works. You can say things like "Join the 10,000 other members."

There are two distinct types of CTAs you can use in emails. The first is hyperlinked text, and the second is an image. You should probably use both types. Your images should always be linked to a destination of some kind, but some email providers block linked images so always make sure to have a text hyperlink call to action as well.

11.7.3 Don't End Up in a Spam Folder

It's nearly impossible to know if your emails are ending up in peoples' spam folders. With that said, there are various precautions you can make to bypass spam filters responsibly.

The first way to avoid your messages going into readers' spam folders is to not buy email lists. While it seems nice and easy to pay and get a bunch of email addresses, it's a horrible idea. Using their various security measures, if an Internet Service Provider realizes you purchased an email list, they could blacklist your email address ensuring that your emails won't get delivered. Many spam filters look for words like "free" or "sale" and automatically put them in the spam folder.

Don't try and trick the spam filters, just don't do anything spammy! Some people add "Re:" to the subject line to make it look like a response, but tricks like this no longer work, and will be detrimental to your online reputation, for both subscribers and service providers. Furthermore, make sure your email address is legit. If it's i34hr734fwl@website.com, it will likely be flagged as spam. But if it's info@yourwebsite.com, it's likely to be seen as legit mail.

Finally, within moderation, send emails fairly often. The more a customer interacts with the emails you send, the more the spam filter will understand it's email they actually want to receive. But don't send too many emails! That in itself is spam. The rule of thumb in terms of frequency is to not campaign for the sake of campaigning; only write to your list when you have something of value to offer them. This will also ensure you stay out of their spam folder.

11.8 What Is Lead Nurturing and How to Do It

Lead nurturing is the idea of humanizing your leads. Instead of just aiming for tons of email subscribers, aim to have good relationships with your subscribers. Look into your most active subscribers. Do they have a family? Is price a priority for them? What sort of thing do they post about on social media?

Use this information to understand the personas that really resonate with your marketing and your business. Engage with them on social media, respond to the inquiries quickly and thoughtfully, and really maintain a holistic view of your marketing so that every interaction people have with your business is meaningful and friendly versus stressful and pushy.

Nurturing leads is all about personalization. When sending out emails personalize it with the customer's name. For example, say: "Dear Darrell," instead of "Dear Customer." It's the little touches like this that will make a big difference in nurturing a good relationship with your leads.

Finally, speed is of the essence. Whether on email, social media, or your support portal, your response time should never be more than 24 hours. Quick and efficient communication will go a long way towards turning your leads into lifelong customers.

11.9 Five Ways to Tell If Your Email Marketing Is Working and What to Do If It's Not

If you want to know how well your email marketing campaigns are performing, then there are some vital metrics you should be tracking and measuring regularly. Paying attention to the right metrics will help you understand and improve your email campaigns.

Let's review what these metrics are:

#1 Open Rate

This metric indicates the percentage of recipients that actually opened your email. It's important to track because it can reveal problems with your subject line, email delivery software, or your email campaign overall. Usually, the subject line is the issue. It is, after all, the first thing the subscriber sees and the main thing determining if they'll actually open the email. Use the C.U.R.V.E. method to make your subject lines more compelling.

The calculation for open rate is . . .

$$\text{Email Open Rate} = \frac{\text{Emails Opened}}{\text{Emails Sent} - \text{Bounced (undelivered) Emails}} \times 100$$

The average open rate typically falls between 15 and 25 percent of marketing emails opened.

#2 Click-Through Rate

Another metric to check is the click-through rate (CTR). This metric measures what percentage of readers clicked on a link in the email. If you have a really high open rate but a low CTR, it means your subject line is great but your content and your call to action are lacking. Start by changing the calls to action first and see if that helps it at all.

The calculation for click-through rate is as follows:

$$\text{CTR} = \frac{\text{\# of click-throughs}}{\text{\# of messages delivered}} \times 100$$

The average click-through rate for email campaigns is between 1 and 5 percent.

#3 Conversion Rate

The most important metric to track and measure is the conversion rate. This is the percentage of people who purchased something, watched a video, downloaded a book, or did whatever action you wanted them to after opening your email. Conversion is the end goal and this metric reveals how successful your campaigns are doing.

If you want to improve your conversion rate, your first step should be to improve your click-through rate, since people can't convert if they haven't hit your landing page. After that, you should focus on your landing page, obviously, its design or content isn't helping improve conversions.

This is the calculation for finding your conversion rate:

$$\text{Conversion Rate} = \frac{\text{\# of conversions}}{\text{\# of delivered email}} \times 100$$

According to digital marketing experts, the average conversion rate for emails is about 2.5 percent.

#4 Unsubscribe Rate

The unsubscribe rate is the percentage of email users that have signed up for the campaign, but then later unsubscribed from receiving emails. It's understandable to be concerned about every person that unsubscribes from your list. But you shouldn't despair because customers come and go.

Maybe they would rather follow along on social media, maybe they have another email address subscribed, maybe they purchased and loved your product but don't need updates. In and of itself, an unsubscribe is not always a lost customer. However, if you want to decrease it, there are some things that can be done.

The first is to make sure that the content within the email is exceptional, compelling, and drives customers to not only remain subscribed but also take action.

If it's not content that you think is the problem, you should evaluate how often you're sending emails. Many customers unsubscribe simply because they're hearing from a business too much, and they simply want to quiet them for a little while. Reduce the number of emails you're sending, and see if that helps keep your current subscribers.

If you're really worried about your unsubscribe rate, consider providing a short form for customers to fill out when they unsubscribe. Don't make it long; it can be as simple as a multiple choice question about why they're unsubscribing. Based on the answers, you may be able to reduce your unsubscribe rate.
Use this formula to calculate your unsubscribe rate:

$$\text{Unsubscribe Rate} = \frac{\text{\# of unsubscribers}}{\text{\# of messages delivered}} \times 100$$

The average unsubscribe rate is between 0.2% and 0.5%. Unless the unsubscribe rate is mysteriously high for one email or campaign in specific, I wouldn't worry too much about it.

#5 Bounce Rate

In terms of email marketing bounce rate reflects the percent of emails that did not get delivered to your subscribers. This is different than a website's bounce rate. Bounce rate reveals the problems in the email list you are using. Emails bounce because of many reasons:

- Recipient's inbox is full
- Invalid email address
- Email server issues (i.e., overloaded, unavailable, blocking incoming email)
- Closed email address.

The use of a valid email list results in lowering the bounce rate.

You can remove the bounced email addresses manually or automatically through your email marketing software. A high bounce rate affects the reputation of your account which can lead to it being shut down, and you not being able to use the software.

Here's the formula for calculating your bounce rate:

$$\text{Bounce Rate} = \frac{\text{\# of bounced email}}{\text{\# of delivered email}} \times 100$$

A bounce rate that's under 2% is acceptable. If it's over 2% you need to start investigating the possible causes. Having a bounce rate that is 5% or higher means you have a problem that needs immediate attention.

Many variables have an influence on these metrics such as:

- the industry you are in
- your location (if your business is local)
- the type of emails you're are sending (i.e., newsletter, follow-up, inactive subscriber, abandoned shopping cart)
- the size and responsiveness of your list

Use the averages mentioned as a benchmark. Determine the rates that are best suited for the type of business that you have and the audience you are trying to reach.

11.10 Best Practices for Your Landing Pages

Every step of the conversion pipeline is important, but the landing page or your lead generation website is really where you turn up the heat. The subject line, the email content, the calls to action; all these elements keep your lead's interest, but the landing page is where you convert that interest into revenue and/or meaningful engagement.

Here are some elements you should consider for your landing pages:

- **Focus:** The whole point of having a landing page instead of sending people to your website is that it focuses on one product or service and doesn't distract people with the whole business.

- **Tailored:** You should consider having multiple versions of a landing page tailored to specific visitors. For instance, maybe you're marketing to a specific audience in their online forums, your landing page could include a reference to that forum, so they already feel like they are involved with your product/service.

• **Headlines:** Your headlines should use the slang, tone, and voice that they would be most comfortable and interested in. Don't be afraid to have personality, just make sure it matches your customers'.

• **Testimonials:** If you are asking for reviews and testimonials on your follow-up emails (you should be), then you can use these quotes to lend credibility to you and your company.

• **Images and Video Content:** Big buttons and enticing imagery and video content will go a long way towards helping with conversions. In addition to meaningful copywriting, the graphics will convey emotion and branding immediately.

• **Design:** You want the landing page to work more or less seamlessly with your website. So, make sure to use the colors and logos that they associate with you.

• **Mobile-Friendly:** Just like regular websites, landing pages must be mobile-ready to meet the needs of site visitors using mobile devices.

• **Scarcity:** It helps to give the sense that supplies for the product or service will not last. This adds urgency to your "ask" and will likely improve conversions.

• **Include Numbers:** Statistics and infographics go a long way towards adding weight and value to your landing page.

"Focus on how to be social, not how to do social."

– Jay Baer, Keynote Speaker and Host of The Social Pros Podcast

12. Engaging Your Audience on Social Media

12.1 What Is Social Media and How Is It Different from Social Networking?

The term social media has various definitions, but the descriptions have a common theme.

- First, social media is the use of electronic communications such as websites and applications to create and share information.

- It's also a broad term that's used to describe different types of online content, such as text, images, videos, blogs, infographics, etc.

- Another description would be social media is a place where people gather to talk about what's important to them, their interest, give their opinions, and exchange ideas.

Social media is the vehicle that makes it possible for people to share each other's content. But the act of sharing is what would be considered social networking. Social networking is the use of social media to create and maintain personal and professional relationships with other people. As a result of these connections, benefits can be gained such as revenue, exposure for your business, partnerships, and clients.

The two terms are often interchanged, however, the term social networking is used more when talking about the connections with others online (the who). While social media is more about the message (the what) and how it's communicated (the how).

The topic of social media is very large so my goal is to give you a general overview so you know where to start and decide which tactic may be best for you.

12.2 Seven Ways Using Social Media Helps to Grow Your Business

Savvy business owners understand the value of going to where their most profitable audience is located online. Using social media is the easiest way to access your target audience and make yourself available to them. However, planning and execution are necessary to ensure you get the good outcome you hear people talking about, and avoiding the poor results most businesses experience. If you are new to social media, or you've been just dabbling with it, then now is the time to take a look at the numerous advantages it offers.
Let's look at seven ways social media can grow your business:

1. **Increases Exposure for Your Business:** Marketing your products and services becomes a lot easier when your business gains more exposure. Since so many people are using social media you can understand why businesses are trying to learn and leverage this online strategy. Here are a few tips on how you can use it to get discovered by more people.

    - **Chose the Right Channels:** There are many social media channels to choose from, but you don't need to be on all of them. Different platforms cater to different audiences so it is important to find the channels that are the best for your business and have the customers you are trying to target. A list of the most popular channels used by businesses will be covered in Chapter 12.3.

    - **Create Valuable Content:** When you take the time to create useful content people will be more likely to share it. As you add more content to your profile you create more opportunities for your business to be found, followed, and talked about.

    - **Be Consistent:** It's important to be consistent with social media marketing because it builds credibility. You don't want to be active for 5 consecutive days and then do nothing for two weeks. Remember there are competitors that want to talk to your audience too. Consistency also refers to the tone of your messaging and the look.

    - **Engage with Your Online Community:** Encourage your followers to take action, ask a question or leave feedback after they view your content. Respond to them so other people can see and join the conversation.

2. **Increases Traffic to Your Online Properties:** An additional benefit to getting increased exposure is getting more web traffic to places online where you want people to visit. You can drive traffic to your website, sales pages, landing pages, or your other social media pages by putting hyperlinks on your profile pages, in your content, and in your responses. People who want more information can click on the links and go to the web page you want them to go.

3. **Provides Insights to Your Target Market:** Social media is beneficial for marketing because the various platforms capture a lot of data about their users. Basic demographic information such as the user's name, age, sex, location, occupation, education, income, etc. is used to create a profile. The information that users choose to share publicly in their profile is called social data. Each platform also keeps track of their user's interests based on their interaction with the platform, and the advertisements users have looked at. This collected user data is available to you and here are some ways you can use it:

    - **Use Advertising Data:** An effective way of getting information about your primary audience is to choose a platform that caters to that group and use the advertising data they provide that targets their users with ads. This data shows customer behaviors and their interest.

    - **Keyword Research:** Another piece of valuable information you can acquire from social media is the keywords people use to search for their interests. You can explore how often was a keyword searched for and which ones are looked for most often. You'll get a better idea of how to create and deliver your messages by researching and identifying keywords.

    - **Social Monitoring & Social Listening**

        - Social monitoring is the process of searching and watching social media channels for individual conversations or mentions about your business, products, services, competitors, keywords, trends and topics relevant to your market. You can find out, what consumers are saying, who is doing the talking, and why are they saying it.

Monitoring is helpful for alerting you when a customer has a question, comment or problem so they can be addressed immediately.

• Social listening is taking a "big picture approach" to analyzing the insights you gathered from monitoring. After the data has been compiled and evaluated it can bring to light revelations like ways to differentiate your offers, marketing, and other aspects of your business.

- **Conduct Competitive Analysis:** Observing what your competitors are doing on social media can be very enlightening. You'll get an idea of what's working for them, and what's not. As you study your competitors keep these questions in mind:

  • Do they have a large social media presence?

  • What type of content are they posting? How often are they posting?

  • What features and benefits of their products and services are they highlighting? Price, convenience, guarantees, etc.?

  • Are they using paid online advertising?

  • What is the tone of their content? Fun, serious, or a bit of both?

  How does their strategy compare to yours? Pay close attention and look for what they are doing well. Notice how their audience is responding. If their strategies are getting results you don't want to just copy them. You will want to create or adjust your own game plan accordingly.

4. **It Provides a Platform:** The ability to talk directly to your target audience means you have control over the impression you make on them. Even if you are just starting out in your business, it's possible to build a loyal base of followers that will look to you for information and guidance. Follow these steps to get started:

   - **Establish Your Voice:** Voice refers to the style of your messaging and how you deliver it. Based on your industry you need to decide on how to present yourself and your business.

What type of voice will you have?

- Will you be easygoing, serious, or somewhere in between?
- Will you use complex language and industry jargon, or keep it simple and fun?
- Are you going to educate, entertain, inform, or sell?

Choose a style and stick with it. Avoid being inconsistent as this can make it harder for people to get to know you.

- **Become a Thought Leader:** Show your audience and peers that you have an understanding of your industry by giving advice. Become the go-to source by keeping up with news and information about your niche. Think of yourself as a "human web browser." As you come across relevant and useful information share it along with your perspective. Over time your credibility increases and so will your ability to influence.

- **Join Existing Communities:** Contribute to discussions by joining the social media channels where your customers are most likely to be having conversations. Get personal and don't be afraid to share your opinions on a topic you are knowledgeable about. If you are going to commit to using social media, consider building your own community.

5. **Makes Lead Generation Easier:** With social media, it does not take long to target and qualify people and businesses that fit the description of your ideal customer. In addition to providing good content, using paid online advertising and engaging your audience you can also get leads by looking for them.

   - **Search for Prospects:** Gather details about your leads so you can contact them. Some platforms are easier to get this information from than others. It may take some extra research, but it's better than using a list of untargeted leads.

6. **Build Relationships with Your Customers:** Customers are the heartbeat of all businesses, so being able to connect with them must be a top priority. Social media makes it easier to build a following for your business so you can interact with customers. Many benefits come from engaging with your customers online such as:

• Getting feedback about your current offers so you can make improvements.

• Getting suggestions for other products and services they may want so you can create new offers.

• Addressing customer service issues one-on-one (and sometimes publicly) so customers know how you take care of them. This is a major component to managing your online reputation discussed in Chapter 9.4.2.

• Providing your customers with information and resources that can be used to make informed decisions or solve a problem that they have.

• Letting them know when you have a new product or service available and the details about it.

• Discovering new places online where your target audience may visit and start a conversation with them.

• Showing appreciation to loyal customers who are advocates of your business and sharing your messages by giving them recognition, rewards, and discounts.

• Building a community where you can get a pulse of the interest of your target audience so you can serve them better.

7. **Increases Sales:** All or a combination of the benefits listed above will put you in a position to sell more using social media. Whether you target new or existing customers, when you gain the trust of your audience the opportunity to make more sales increases.

   Here are a few approaches you can take to increase your sales using social media:

• **Direct Selling:** Lead your fans, followers, and subscribers directly to your sales pages from your content (post, videos, etc.) or comments.

• **Use Paid Online Advertising:** Use this on social media websites that offer it so you can target people that are most likely to buy from you.

• **Promotional Marketing:** Depending on your offer and industry you can deliver promotional content around holidays, seasons of the year, and events (like the Super Bowl). These are good times to offer discounts.

• **Influencer Marketing:** Build authentic relationships with leaders in your industry that can affect how you and your business are perceived and help get your messages out to more people.

• **Social Selling:** Find prospects to engage with and take the time to understand their needs, build relationships, and answer questions. You want to establish top-of-mind awareness (TOMA) so you and your business are the ones that are initially thought of when the prospect is ready to buy.

12.3 Which Social Media Channels Should You Use for Your Business?

Before you identify which social media channels you want to explore, you must determine your objectives.

- Do you want more exposure for your business?
- Do you want to get more leads?
- Do you want to build a platform for you and your business?

Your chances of success with social media will greatly improve if you know the answers to these basic questions before taking any uncalculated actions. Once you are confident with your reasons for wanting to use social media next you must select one or more channels that you will use to reach your audience.

While dozens of social media websites exist, you don't have to be on all of them to boost your online presence. Each channel attracts different types of users with different interests, and every one of them won't be suitable for your business.

If you are going to commit to using a platform, then make sure it has the audience you are trying to reach and supports your overall marketing objectives. Let's examine some of the most popular social media sites for business.

Facebook

Depending on who you ask Facebook is one of the top two social media websites with over 1.4 billion active daily users worldwide. The demographics for the users are very diverse so it's more than likely you will be able to find and reach your target market.

The best way to promote your business is using a fan page which will have all the tools you need to promote your brand and content to the Facebook community. Facebook will allow your posts to spread like a wildfire if you play your cards right. Fan pages are best used with a well-planned advertising campaign using Facebook's built-in ad tools. Over 95% of social media marketers believe Facebook produces the best ROI.

Instagram

Instagram is a mobile app-based platform owned by Facebook whose primary users are teenagers and college students. Used by over 400 million daily active users it's a visual platform that encourages individuality with photos and videos.

This platform is good if you want to engage with your audience on a personal level. For example, showing what happens behind the scenes of your business. Post pictures and videos of your products, services, office, and employees.

By creating a business profile, users will know that you own a business and can contact you directly from the app. As a business user, you will be able to get customer insights from analytics that show their interaction with your content.

Since the company is owned by Facebook you can connect your fan page to your Instagram account and have the content posted automatically. Also, if you want to create ads on Instagram you can do that from Facebook's ad manager.

Engaged Instagram followers are worth more than those on Facebook, with an average order value of $65 versus $55.

LinkedIn

LinkedIn is the largest platform for business owners and professionals with over 546 million users. It's a place where you can make connections and get referrals you may not be able to through other channels like Facebook.

Over 60% of LinkedIn's users are between 25 and 54 years old. However, younger demographics are growing rapidly as college grads realize the usefulness of a professional social network.

LinkedIn isn't the best place to post all of your content and try and spread your brand, it is, however, a good place to share business-to-business information, find new team members, and keep track of your competition's activity. You likely won't find lots of customers there, unless you're a B2B (business to business) company, but it's still a great place to be present and relatively active in order to build your professional network. About 80 percent of B2B leads generated on social media come from LinkedIn.

It's an incredible tool for building credibility. You get to lay out all your accomplishments on one page, as well as receive recommendations from people in your network such as customers, employees, and associates. These recommendations can be made visible on your profile and increase your credibility because they highlight your specialties.

By creating a LinkedIn Company Page, you increase your exposure to potential customers as well as suppliers, distributors, and potential employees. Just like other platforms, you'll be able to feature your products or services and lead people back to your main website.

LinkedIn will enable you to see all of your connections in your network. You can, for instance, see who you have in common with someone you're interested in contacting, and then reach out for an introduction. Think of it as a 24/7 professional networking event.

You'll also want to search for user-created groups relevant to you where you can discuss what is going on in your industry with other business owners.

Pinterest

Pinterest is basically a mood board software where users can save photos to "pinboards" and curate them based on their interests. Users are called Pinners and the content they save is called Pins which can be categorized into different boards. As Pinners browse the internet, they can Pin the content they're interested in to one of their boards.

For example, if you're a graphic designer, you might create a board called "The Best Book Covers." When you're browsing books online, you can pin the covers you like to your board. Then, customers can come to you and request you design a cover similar to one of your pins. Users can also browse pins and "re-pin" your pins.

You can create your own Pins that highlight your products and increase sales. When somebody saves your Pin, their followers will see it as well, revealing it to more people with similar interests. Now your Pins will be seen by even more Pinners.

Connect with Pinners by sharing things that you find beautiful, interesting and actionable. Arrange your board by product category, interest or seasonal topic. If a Pinner sees something they like they can either save the Pin to one of their boards or click the Pin's URL to learn more, shop or make a purchase.

By setting up a business account you have the ability to promote Pins that can be seen by more people and get access to analytics.

Pinterest has over 200 million Pinners:

- 50% of its users reside outside of the United States.
- 70% of them are women.
- 80% of Pinners use the mobile app to access the platform.
- Especially popular with women between 18–49, and with companies who sell cookbooks, jewelry, and clothing.

If your demographics fall out of these criteria, it's probably best you don't waste time on Pinterest. If your demographic matches, it's a wealth of customers for you! About 90% of weekly Pinners use Pinterest to make purchase decisions.

Twitter

Twitter is an online news and micro-blogging platform where users post and interact with short messages known as "tweets." While messages are limited to 240 characters this is the platform most used by celebrities, athletes, politicians and corporations to interact with their audience. You connect with other users by following their Twitter feeds. When you click the follow button, anything that person or business posts will appear in your timeline.

Posts are shared by retweeting. When someone retweets your content, they're sharing your business with their networks and your reach can grow exponentially. Another way to get more people to see your tweets is to use

"Quick Promote." This is a paid way to get your best content in front of a larger audience quickly. This is useful for posts where you are at events or on the go. You can also grow your followers by doing a follower campaign. This type of promotion displays your profile on user's home "timelines", "who to follow" list, and in Twitter's search results.

For businesses, Twitter is useful for having conversations that support and educate customers. It's usually the first place customers go when they have a problem or complaint about a company. This is one reason why having a Twitter account for your business is strongly suggested.

Along with being important for customer service it also supports:

- Communicating with your audience individually or as a group.
- Generating leads by encouraging followers to find out more.
- Researching trends to discover what your audience is invested in.
- Getting feedback from your followers about your offers.

The platform has about 330 million monthly active users with 69 million living in the United States. Most users like to access the platform on the go using a mobile device with videos being the type of content that gets retweeted the most.

Twitter was the first social media platform to use hashtags which is simply the pound sign (#). To use hashtags effectively, they need to be placed before a keyword or phrase used to describe a topic or a theme. Using them helps people find your tweets.

Twitter found that over half of their users had taken an action after seeing a business mentioned in Tweets (this includes visiting their website, searching for the business online, or retweeting their content).

YouTube

Along with Facebook, YouTube is one of the biggest social media platforms with over 1.3 billion users that watch 1 billion hours of video every day. It reaches more 18-49-year-olds than any cable network in the US and half of the overall video views come from mobile devices.

YouTube is actually the 2nd largest search engine after Google with over 3 billion searches conducted per month. You can get a lot of traffic from YouTube by being deliberate about your approach. It's even possible to have your videos ranked in Google for targeted keywords. It's very easy to upload videos and embed them on your own website or share them on social media.

Most people prefer video over other types of content and YouTube is a trusted source of videos that people like to share. YouTube is owned by Google and integrates very well with other Google services.

If you decide to do video marketing, then being on YouTube makes sense for these reasons:

- You need a way to distribute the videos you create.

- It provides a cost-effective way to reach a large number of people that all have the potential of becoming prospective customers.

- You have a product or service you want to demonstrate.

- Your business is based on providing information you want people to know about.

- If you run a website based on entertainment, using YouTube is almost mandatory.

- You have a cause or mission that you are passionate about and you want to bring attention to it.

- You want to show your expertise with tutorials and tips to build your credibility.

- It offers a different way to get your content indexed in search engines.

- The platform makes it easy to share your videos on other social media platforms.

- You can create a channel that serves as your homepage on the site. You'll be able to provide a description of your business and organize all of the videos you uploaded on the platform. If people like what you are doing, they will subscribe to your channel.

- To increase sales and traffic to your website YouTube offers different advertising formats such as:

    - Video ads that can appear before or during videos created by other users.

    - Display ads that can appear on top of videos or somewhere on the YouTube page of a video your target audience may watch.

Most US Marketers are confident that video ad content on YouTube is useful when it comes to driving views (84%), engagements (81%) and making sales (79%).

To get the most out of YouTube you'll need to know how to make videos. Read Chapter 13 to learn more about this.

12.3.1 How Many Social Media Platforms Do You Need to Use?

Roughly more than half of the public use more than one social media platform. That does not mean that you have to be on every platform because it is popular or new. Oftentimes business owners try to do too much at once and create social media accounts on every site at the same time. This is often too much work and will result in a decreased focus on a specific site, or the creation of lower-quality content.

To determine which social media platforms are best for you to reach and engage your audience, take some time to do some research about each one previously discussed.

Also, consider the following important factors:

- What type of product, service, or event are you promoting?

- How much time and money are you willing to invest on that platform after finishing doing your research on it?

- What type of content will you be posting? (i.e., text, video, etc.)

- What platforms are your target audience most active on?

- What are the channels your competitors use?

You should not use any platform you don't understand or can't explain how or why it can help you accomplish your online marketing goals. So, before you decide which platforms to use, create a clear plan to keep from losing your focus, which far too many business owners do. Remember it is better to be successful on one or two platforms than fail on five or six. If you believe in being on several social media sites, then you really need to consider hiring a social media manager to maintain all of your accounts.

12.4 How to Create a Realistic Plan to Achieve Your Social Media Goals

It is very easy to invest time on social media activities and accomplish very little. Spending your time on what you believe are necessary activities yet seeing little to no results can be discouraging. On the other hand, having a solid social media plan you can follow could be extremely effective in getting the exposure and sales you want for your business.

Your social media plan should consist of the following steps:

Step #1 Set Goals: The main thing to keep in mind is if you don't have a goal to aim for when using social media—or any strategy meant to promote your business—successful results will be impossible or very difficult to achieve. Think of your goal as a destination and the plan is your roadmap. Without a destination, you will just be going around aimlessly.

As discussed in Chapter 2.5, you should create goals that are SMART— specific, measurable, attainable, realistic, and timely. This will make creating your plan a lot easier. As you are thinking about which goals to set remember that social media is about building relationships, engaging, and solving problems. So, your goals should not always be focused on sales and making money. When you focus on helping people sales will come.

Here are some examples of SMART goals:

Acquire New Customers: Get people to discover your business as a result of your social media activity. This is the best measurement of how effective your efforts have been.

- **SMART Goal Example:** Generate 10 sales from Twitter per month by September 28th, 2022.

- **Metrics to Track:**
    - Number of sales made
    - Revenue generated
    - Source of web traffic (traffic sources)
    - Revenue by traffic source
    - Average order value (AOV) (Total revenue/total number of orders = AOV)
    - Amount of website visitors (visitors)
    - Amount of web pages they've seen (pageviews)
    - Amount of time spent on website (session duration)
    - Percentage of visitors that left after seeing only one of your web pages (bounce rate).

Increase Social Media Reach: Reach is a measurement of the potential size of your social media audience from all of the channels you participate on. From this number you want to know how many of your audience have taken some type of action to engage with you.

- **SMART Goal Example:** Increase followers on our Facebook Fan page to 300 by the end of the 2nd quarter of this year.

- **Metrics to Track:** New fans/followers/contacts, comments, likes.

Increase Unique Website Visitors: Driving people back to your website gives them the opportunity to make a purchase. If they are not ready, they can request additional information in exchange for their contact details. Over time through email marketing and continued social media engagement they can be converted from a visitor to a customer.

- **SMART Goal Example:** Increase website visitors to 10,000 per month by October 25th, 2022.

- **Metrics to Track:**
    - New visitors
    - Traffic sources
    - Pageviews
    - Your most popular viewed web pages (top pages)
    - Session duration

- Last page visitor sees before leaving your website (exit pages)
- Bounce rate.

Grow Email List from Social Media: Leads are visitors that come to your website and usually exchange their email address for an exclusive resource or content. Growing your list means you can take the time to nurture a relationship with prospects you can turn into customers later.

- **SMART Goal Example:** Increase the number of new email subscribers from social media traffic from 5,000 to 10,000 by the end of the 3rd quarter of this year.

- **Metrics to Track:**
    - Number of new email subscribers from social media
    - Opt-in conversion rate (new subscribers/visitors = opt-in conversion rate)
    - Lead traffic source
    - Which posts or ads are sending people to your landing page (click-throughs)
    - Amount of sales generated from social media leads.

Start Implementing Social Customer Service: Also called social customer care, is providing customers support on the various social media platforms. This method of resolving customer issues is increasing as the use of social media continues to grow. To be prepared you'll need to have a Listening Strategy.

- **SMART Goal Example:** Create a Listening Strategy by June 30th, 2021

- **Metrics to Track:**
    - Number of support questions, complaints, reviews
    - Your response time
    - Scoring from 3rd party entities tracking customer support effectiveness such as:
        - Customer Satisfaction Score (CSAT)
        - Net Promoter Score (NPS)
        - Customer Effort Score (CES)
        - Service Level Agreement (SLA) Compliance.

Step #2 Choose Tactics: Once you have identified a goal you want to pursue, the next step is determining what activities are required to accomplish your goal. Start by selecting which social media channels you plan to be on. Your decision will depend mostly on the audience you're trying to reach. Then break down how you're going to spend your time on the channel(s) you've selected. Your plan should have a detailed schedule of what tasks you are going to commit to on specific days and at specific times.

For example, you may create a simple social media activity schedule for Twitter that can look like this:

TIME	Mo	Tu	We	Th	Fr	Sa	Su	TASKS
9:00 am	x	x	x	x	x	x	x	Reply to direct messages, @mentions
9:10 am, 2:00 pm 7:00 pm	x	x	x	x	x			Tweet and retweet about industry news or link to newly created content.
9:30 am, 2:30 pm 7:30 pm	x		x		x			Identify influencers to follow and comment on their posts.
9:30 am		x		x				Post articles to your blog and tweet the links to them.

Step #3 Implement Tactics: Once you created your schedule of tasks, it's time to take action.

- Follow your timetable. It will serve as your to-do list.

- Don't procrastinate. Put your plan into action immediately, don't wait until 3 months from now. When you spend a lot of time planning it's just another form of procrastination.

- Prioritize important activities first. If you have an important task that you must do every day or each week, make sure that you include it in your schedule.

- You won't achieve your goal without a commitment to your plan. Make sure you don't create a timetable you can't keep or have to constantly change.

- Success with social media requires perseverance. Results may not come as quickly as you expect but you must trust the process and follow your plan.

If you already know you don't have the time or desire to implement some, or all of the aspects of your plan, then you'll need to delegate it or hire someone who can.

Step #4 Measure Your Metrics: Before you begin measuring your progress with any of these metrics, make a note of your starting point so you can accurately determine your growth from week one.

You can get started by checking these places:

• Website: Review metrics about your website traffic and visitor behavior. The easiest way to track and measure your metrics is to use Google Analytics.

• Email: Focus on metrics like the number of subscribers, open rate, click-through rate. Log into your email marketing service provider to see what metrics they track.

• Sales: For total revenue, average sales amount, and other sales-related data check your e-commerce software

• Social Media: Each platform has their own metrics they track that you can examine. There are also third-party, cloud-based apps like Dasheroo (https://www.dasheroo.com) that gather the insights from multiple platforms and consolidates them into one dashboard.

The social media landscape is constantly changing. What works this week, may not work the next week. So, testing what tactics are working must be a constant. Choose a particular time weekly or monthly to review your data periodically.

Step #5 Repeat Steps #1 through #4: If the tactics you used worked and you're happy with the results, then use them again. You can repeat the same goal but increase the desired outcome, or set a new goal. If you want to change a tactic, then only change one at a time so you can actually measure the impact that change has made on your future results.

12.5 12 Ways to Make Your Business Stand Out on Social Media

Whether you are just starting to use social media or have experienced a little success, you need to know that getting your business to stand out can be very challenging.

The following factors can affect how hard you have to work to get noticed even if you have clear goals as a solid plan.

- Location of your business (city, state, country)
- The industry you are in
- Your target audience
- What you are offering to sell
- Amount of competition you have
- How marketing savvy is your competition
- Your available time and financial resources
- Having a content strategy.

Here are some tips to keep in mind as you implement your social media strategy.

1. **Create Synergy:** Connect your social media accounts with each other for two reasons:

    • People can easily view your profile and content on other platforms and follow you on those places as well.

    • You can easily share what you post on one platform with your connected platforms.

2. **Username Consistency:** Try to get the same username for all of your profiles to develop a greater web presence as more people begin to search for you. There are resources available that will check a chosen username across all platforms and let you know whether or not it's available on all social media networks. Knowem.com and NameCheck.com are just two of these.

3. **Visual Consistency:** Use the same color scheme for all of the social media channels you have a presence on. Make the colors the same as your logo and website.

4. **Provide Better Content:** Learn to create content that is engaging and makes people want to share it. This is a really important aspect of social media. If you want to stand out and reach more people, the way to do it is through exceptional content. Especially if it is video.

5. **Create a Recurring Event:** Think of something you can deliver on a weekly basis and position as a can't miss event such as:

- A live Q & A via live stream or text post
- Industry news of the week video or slideshow
- Weekly customer case studies.

Develop something that will keep your followers coming back.

6. **Make Sharing Easy:** If you are using WordPress for your website, use a social share plugin that puts share buttons at the top and bottom of your blog post. This will allow readers to easily share your content with their followers.

7. **Voice Your Opinion:** Search the social media channel you are a part of to find thought leaders, influencers, and anyone talking about your industry. Read and watch their content regularly and comment on what they're talking about. As they become more familiar with you, they may view your content and leave a comment. Also, their followers may see your comment and visit your profile out of curiosity.

8. **Get Feedback:** Polls and questionnaires can be good discussion starters with your followers and subscribers. Ask interesting questions to stimulate interest and to get more responses. Use the feedback to learn how to better engage with your target audience.

9. **Respond Quickly:** Make sure you are monitoring what is being said about you and your business on the various social media channels. You want to respond to any positive or negative feedback fast. That will show potential customers how responsive you can be. Research has found being responsive prompts 48% of consumers to make a purchase.

10. **Outdo Your Competition:** Research how your competitors are using social media and develop a way to use it that is better and unique to you. If someone is using social media in a way that you like but they are in a different industry, borrow some of their ideas and incorporate them into your strategies.

11. **Share Your Passion:** If there is a cause or mission that you are extremely passionate about let people know about it. Is there some noble reason that you are in business or is there a problem that you are trying to solve? Talk about it but be authentic.

12. **Make More Videos:** Videos are the most engaging type of content and the sooner you become more confident creating them the better. This includes webinars, livestreams, etc. Experiment and find a style that allows you to be yourself while providing value to your viewers. Since there is only one of you, you'll certainly stand out.

12.6 Two Social Media Traps to Be Cautious of and the Common Mistakes That Set Them Off

There are two potential traps that are very easy to be caught in when using social media and they waste your time and money. Social media has the perception of being easy because so many people use it and you can usually get started without having to pay. But there is a big difference when using it for business compared to using it personally.

If you are not disciplined and committed, you will be caught in one or both of these traps:

1. **Time Trap:** By not following the steps for creating a realistic social media plan it will take you much longer to see any benefits, or you may see none at all.

2. **Money Trap:** If you are going to spend money, you'll need a plan to help calculate potential costs. Without one your social media marketing will turn into a money pit. On the other hand, if you try to hire someone to do this for you but insist on paying as little as possible it could wind up costing you much more later.

To get a better understanding of these traps that drain your resources let's examine some of the most common mistakes that get you caught in them.

Paying to Be Popular: Under no circumstance should you ever buy fake followers, fans, or subscribers for any of your social media accounts. There are 3rd party companies that offer services to increase your followers which they say will increase your exposure. This defeats the purpose of social media which is to attract real people who want to hear what you have to say, get to know you, buy your stuff, or partner with you. By having fake followers, you are likely to expose yourself and your true supporters to spam-filled comments, or you'll have a ton of followers with low engagement. In either case, you risk damaging your reputation and ultimately finding your account suspended, deleted, or banned.

Buying Cheap Social Media Management: If you have to choose between hiring someone to do your social media for cheap or not doing social media at all, then I say don't do it. You have too much to lose when it comes to the reputation of your business. The last thing you need is for a low-end company to buy fake followers which I just told you about. Just as bad is when they are unable to deliver on lofty promises. Successful social media marketing is an investment that takes time to develop, so if you are going to spend your money think in terms of smartphones. The better ones usually cost more. If you need help creating and executing your social media plan read Chapters 17 and 18 to learn more about hiring and working with experienced professionals.

Turning Over Social Media Marketing to Untrained Employees: In an effort to save money, many businesses won't hire someone with experience, but instead will assign the task to an inexperienced employee. Relying on them to create your social media plan, do research, implement tactics and manage their time on their own is not wise. Their lack of skill will cost you both money and time as you may not see any results at all or it may take a while to see any noticeable results. If you decide to outsource your social media marketing do yourself and your businesses a favor and work with a professional.

Spending Money without Having a Plan: In Chapter 12.4 I talked about the importance of having a realistic plan and how to create one. If you insist on spending money and you don't have a plan, you'll be wasting your money. Your social media activities must support your business goals. Otherwise, your actions will be random and so will your results.

Ignoring Your Metrics: There will be no way to knowing if your social media efforts are working if you don't track and measure them. Part of creating your social media plan is identifying which metrics you will track and how often you will check them.

Being on the Wrong Social Media Platforms: It may seem like a good idea to be on all of the social media sites, but many of them won't be useful to your business. By trying to be on every platform, you are using more resources than you need to, making your efforts less effective. This is one of the reasons most businesses come to the conclusion that social media does not work.

As mentioned before if you can't explain how a particular channel works you should not use it. Start with being on one or two relevant channels where your target audience exists, and you understand how it works. When you are ready to expand to another platform review the ones covered in Chapter 12.3, or do some research to see if there are new platforms or mobile apps that are better suited for your business. If you discover any, determine if the users match your target audience and the method used for engaging with them fits your communication preference (i.e., text, images, video).

Not Maximizing Social Media Opportunities: I see many people using social media, but their sales offers are poor, and their lead generation process is weak. If you are going to spend time using social media, make sure you are getting something out of it more than a bunch of followers. Have an idea of what actions you want them to take such as buying from you, joining your mailing list, watching a video, or visiting a web page. To get a boost in SEO put links in your social media profiles, content, and comments when appropriate.

Being Inconsistent: When someone visits your blog or one of your social media pages and they see the last entry was over a month ago they may get the impression that they don't have to come back to visit you for a while. Inconsistency with your posting means your content won't be as prominent as the content of other people your audience is following. In order to be top of mind of your fans, and to become an influencer, you need to be consistent with your postings. That's why creating an activity schedule that includes the days and time you will post is recommended. Ways to automate your posting will be covered in Chapter 12.7.

Trying to Sell All of the Time: Everyone understands that social media is used for selling but its primary purpose is to connect people who want to share passions and similar interests. . If the majority of your content is nothing more than sales pitches, then you will not get many followers. It's that simple Making too many promotional posts has caused 46% of people to unfollow a business. It's that simple. An easy guideline to remember is one or two out of every 10 posts can be promotional in nature. To further distinguish yourself from competitors is to make sure you post educating content that provides value to your audience. In time they will become more responsive to your call to actions.

Posting Click Bait and Irrelevant Content: One of the things I see a lot of SMB owners do when using social media is posting a lot of content that is meant to get a lot of attention but has no relevance to their business. They will use viral videos, provocative images or silly memes in order to get more likes and shares. Their rationale is that if someone takes the time to view that type of content, they are automatically a potential targeted follower.

Doing this once in a while may be harmless depending on the relationship they have with their audience. But using this as a legitimate strategy is going to build an audience that's only interested in this type of content. These types of posts do nothing to increase sales, generate leads or promote their business. These SMB owners don't realize they are conditioning people to treat their sales messages and offers as background noise. This audience they attracted will remain and continue to grow as long as they continue to post low-value content.

If people are not responding to content the answer is not to resort to clickbait. Matter of fact, one report discovered 41% of people will unfollow a business that doesn't share relevant information. Talk to your audience and ask them what they want. Conduct a poll. Do something that is going to show your true followers that you have something of value to offer and you're ready to share it. If you already did that and it did not work, then you need to honestly reevaluate your expertise, messages, business offers and how you present them. Consider getting help creating your content or having it done for you.

Targeting the Wrong Audience: The previous mistake shows what can happen when you do things that don't attract your target audience. Nothing wastes time more than talking to people who are never going to buy from you. There is no benefit to having 10,000 followers if none of them are going to take action. That's why buying followers is not effective. Don't follow just anyone. You want your feed to be relevant so that when you interact or share the content in your feed, you can be confident it's something your customers will be interested in as well. You are better off with a group of 500 to 1,000 targeted, engaged, and responsive followers than 5,000 people who are only half interested.

Your Niche Is Not Social: It's obvious that all industries, audiences and offers are not the same. So, to expect that the same amount of planning and execution in different niches will yield the same results is not realistic. Some niches benefit more from social media than others. Part of your research is to find out where your target audience is and then observe how they are responding on a particular platform. See how engaged they are? What content are they responding to? Find out how many of your competitors are using social media and what platforms they are using.

If you created a plan, followed all the steps in the process but still are not reaching your goals you can adjust your goals to meet your expectations or try another online marketing strategy. You certainly don't want to stick with a strategy that is not working for you.

You Don't Have a Social Media Policy: You should create a social media policy so that it is easy to understand what your goals are on social media, how you will address negative feedback, how you will interact with others, and how platform-specific actions like retweeting on Twitter will be handled. This policy will not only help you keep focused and on track but also help your employees who might help manage your accounts understand how to conduct themselves.

12.7 What Is Social Media Automation and How Is It Done?

Social media marketing can be very time-consuming especially when doing routine tasks such as:

- Managing multiple channels
- Engaging active users
- Responding to customers
- Posting new content
- Reaching out to influencers
- Monitoring for mentions.

Managing social media can quickly become a full-time job, especially if you're finding success at it. Luckily, there is a solution that can save you a lot of work and time making these processes a lot more manageable. Social media automation is the use of tools to automate or semi-automate some of the processes used in social media marketing.

Most of these tools are cloud-based (online), a few are software-based (on your computer). Many of them can be used for multiple platforms, and the others are created for only one platform. Depending on what your needs are there are tools that specialize in doing one or more of the following functions:

- Compiling analytics
- Posting content on a schedule
- Finding followers
- Finding mentions
- Identifying trends
- Measuring influence
- Finding influencers
- Discover relevant content

Some of these tools are free to use while others have a cost for using, but if you are going to be saving time it is definitely worth considering,

There are way too many automation choices to discuss here so I'm only going to list the ones that are highly recommended and used by social media experts into categories.

Social Media Management

- **AgoraPulse.com:** An easy-to-use social media management tool with unlimited reports to track your efforts.

- **Buffer.com:** Manage accounts and schedule posts to Twitter, Facebook, Instagram, Pinterest, and LinkedIn.

- **Hootsuite.com:** Keep your social presence active 24/7 by automatically scheduling hundreds of posts at once, across your social accounts.

- **PostPlanner.com:** Helps you find & schedule top-performing content to reach more followers.

- **SocialFlow.com:** Uses real-time data and business rules to determine what and when to publish to your social media properties for both owned & paid social posts.

- **SocialOomph.com:** A service that provides free and paid productivity enhancement services for social media users.

- **SproutSocial.com:** A collaborative social media management platform used by businesses to distribute their social communications.

Increase Followers

- **FollowerWonk.com:** Helps you explore and grow your Twitter followers.

- **Izea.com:** Monetize your content, creativity, and influence in the largest marketplace of its kind. Create a free profile and get the opportunity to partner with industry-leading food, fashion, beauty, and lifestyle brands.

- **SocialBakers.com:** Measure the performance of your business across social channels. Learn more from your customers, gain valuable insights into industry and competitor activities.

Social Listening

- **Agorapulse.com:** Discover trends and insights about your brand—and your competitors.

- **Brand24.com:** Discover what people are saying online about your business as it unfolds in real time. Get instant access to mentions about your business across the web.

- **Mention.com:** Get live updates about your business from the web and social media.

- **TagBoard.com:** Uses hashtags to search for and collect public social media within seconds of being posted to networks like Twitter, Instagram, and Facebook.

12.7.1 Should You Automate Your Social Media Marketing?

Automating your social media activities seems like is an easy decision, right? Who wouldn't want to streamline their workload if it were possible? Well, even with the obvious benefits automation offers, there are some drawbacks you should know about.

But, before revealing those drawbacks let me point out the pros of automation.

Advantages of Automating:

- **Convenience:** You can prepare content ahead of time that can be posted automatically at specific times on multiple channels without having to log into different accounts. Sending and responding to messages is a lot easier now and saves time.

- **Consistency:** The ability to schedule your posts means you can distribute your content on a more consistent basis. You can spend your time creating multiple pieces of content and release them on a more predictable schedule.

- **Grows Your Audience:** Scheduling your post gives you the flexibility to post at different times of the day. Instead of posting at the same time, you can post at various times when different users are most active and increasing the chance that your content will be seen.

• **Faster Engagement:** Since you'll be spending less time posting content, more time is available to engage with your audience. Also, if someone had some type of interaction with your content, you'll be able to see who it was, which platform they were using and then reply to them immediately.

• **Improves Readership:** As you get new followers, they may not be aware of your older content so you should recycle it. Some tools have the ability to do this or you can just schedule some of your older content to appear at a future time. This will introduce your content to people that have missed it and give it longevity.

• **Helps to Executes Your Strategy:** You can use automation to test and track various metrics such as new followers, most active engagement time, clicks on links in your posts, which content was most effective, etc. Review the metrics and change your strategy as needed.

Disadvantages of Automating:

• **Irrelevant Content:** Depending on your content source you may be automatically posting content that your audience is not interested in. If this happens too often you may lose some credibility. Monitor and review your automated post.

• **Not Authentic:** You are doing a disservice to your efforts when you automate personal messages, auto "like" irrelevant content, and auto-following people that don't fit your target audience. Customers and influencers are not going to be interested in connecting with you if you're responding like a robot.

• **Risk of Repetition:** Your true fans are going to follow you on all of the channels where you have a presence. When you post the same content on each of the platforms you risk being ignored because your post is redundant.

• **Disconnection from Your Audience:** Social media automation tools are meant to help you be more efficient, not replace you. Don't become complacent with convenience and stop engaging with your audience. Putting out a bunch of content means nothing if you are not responding to the comments people are making about it. Or even more problematic, not responding to customer questions. The extra time gained from using automation tools really should be spent on interacting with your followers.

• **Posting During Serious Events:** If your content is continuously being posted during an emergency or tragedy you may be viewed as being insensitive. People remember things like this and it may influence their decision to associate with you. This is not the type of attention you want.

So, What Should You Do?

Knowing the advantages and disadvantages of automating your social media marketing will prepare you for what to expect if you decide to do it.

Regardless of your decision here are some tips that you should always remember for increasing the effectiveness of your social media:

• **Stay engaged:** Social media gives you the opportunity to build a following and develop a relationship with your target audience. Automation is just a tool, it's not a strategy. The human element is what makes social media effective.

• **Consider your audience:** Be proactive and address your audience's needs and expectations by providing them with relevant content when they need it.

"Stop thinking of 'video marketing' as this separate entity that is optional for your business. Video is an effective form of communication that needs to be integrated into each and every aspect of your existing marketing efforts.

– James Wedmore, Author and Video Marketing Strategy Expert

13. Video Marketing Dos and Don'ts You Must Know

13.1 What Is Video Marketing?

More small business owners have started to realize the benefits of video marketing and how it can impact their sales. One of the reasons behind the rising use of video marketing is the way it differs from traditional TV commercials. These videos are delivered via the internet and watched on computers, mobile devices (phones and tablets) Smart TVs, and streaming media devices like the Amazon Fire TV Stick.

Video marketing gives more freedom to express ideas and concepts. It can be used to not only introduce you but also to explain your business, services, products and even show off your location. The idea is to let people know what you do and why they should do business with you.

13.2 Why Should You Use Video Marketing?

Video marketing is effective because of the way the human mind perceives and stores information. For some of your target audience, reading blocks of text can be boring and tiresome. Most readers tend to only skim through the first few paragraphs, and some won't even bother doing that.

Videos, on the other hand, are not just engaging but also very intriguing. They get more attention than other forms of online media. Viewers retain 95% of a message when they watch it in a video compared to 10% when reading it in text. Using video allows you to communicate the important points of your messages in a very short time. According to Forrester Research, one minute of video is equal to 1.8 million words to your audience. This may be the reason why 59% of executives say they would rather watch a video than reading text.

Not only that, video helps convey complex information more clearly. This makes it ideal content for sharing on social media. If enough people like and share your video it can create a viral effect and lead a lot of new people back to your website generating more leads and sales.

However, this is not the only benefit that makes video marketing effective. Additional reasons for using videos include:

- **Increases Conversion Rates:** Videos help customers make decisions. Including a video on your landing page can boost your conversion rate by up to 80%. If you want to increase the number of leads you get, create a video explaining what a prospect will get in exchange for their contact details. The same would be done for the products and services you offer.

- **Improves SEO:** As customers' demand for video increases Google, Yahoo, Bing, and other search engines are increasingly ranking websites that have videos on them over ones that don't. According to VideoExplainers.com, a business is 53x more likely to appear on the first page of Google results if it has a video on their webpage. Videos increase the amount of time visitors spend on your website and decrease the bounce rate.

- **Increases Online Visibility:** YouTube is the 2nd largest search engine to Google making it another resource for driving traffic to your website. You can also post your video on other sites like Vimeo, Facebook and anywhere you can submit videos for even more exposure. It's even possible for your videos to appear on the first page of traditional search engines when they are optimized properly.

- **Sets You Apart from Competitors:** Even though video marketing is more affordable and easier to do than ever, most small businesses still aren't taking advantage of it. By using videos in your marketing you're establishing yourself as a savvy businessperson that understands customers need to be communicated to in different ways—giving you an edge over your competitors that don't have videos.

- **It Builds Credibility and Trust:** Video helps you connect with your target audience. It provides a way for you to create a personality for your business and show who you really are. It's a good way to build long-term trust. The more videos you create to help educate and inform your audience, the more trust you will gain. And trust gives customers more confidence to spend money on your offers. Videos are so impactful 57% of consumers say that they gave them more confidence to purchase online.

13.3 What Type of Videos Can You Make to Promote Your Business?

Videos can be used for a wide range of purposes, including but not limited to selling, training and explaining content on your website. If your goal is to build and expand your web presence, then you can definitely take advantage of video marketing to increase traffic and sales.

So, how should you go about integrating video marketing into your overall online strategy? The first thing to start doing is every time you come up with a marketing campaign, start thinking of how to integrate video into it. Video created for online gives you more freedom to explore more unconventional ideas and concepts compared to ads made for television. This includes the video length, format, as well as the topic of the video.

There are many types of promotional videos you can use for your marketing campaign. Here are some examples of what you can do:

- **Live Action:** Recorded live action videos feature actors, but they don't have to be extravagant like the commercials you see on TV. It can be one person explaining something or a group of people acting out a script. Use this type of video to introduce yourself to your audience as it builds an emotional attachment with them and establishes your credibility. You can also create educational videos that not only promote your business but also offer value to the audience.

- **Live Streaming (livecasting):** It's the same as live action but the video is being broadcasted in real time. Live stream videos are becoming more popular as technology is making it easier and more affordable to capture live footage on mobile devices. Through platforms like Facebook Live, YouTube Live and apps like Instagram, businesses are able to broadcast live to their audience whenever they want. Another benefit of live streaming is you can interact with your viewer in real time which increases the level of engagement.

- **Talking Head:** Everyone is familiar with this type of video. It's the one where the person on the screen is speaking directly to the camera and is viewed in close-up. Usually from the shoulders up.

- **Screencasts:** A screencast is a recording of a computer screen using audio or text to explain what is being seen on the screen. Screencast are great for demonstrating how to use software, apps or navigate websites.

• **Animated Video:** Animated videos are often used because they're eye-catching. The most popular style of animated video is whiteboard animations. They explain complex products, services, ideas and information in a way that's easier to understand. Animated video turns serious topics into less intimidating and more interesting ones. This makes them better for showing how you would solve a problem rather than telling.

• **Photo/Video Montage:** This is one of the easiest types of video to create. Using websites like Animoto.com and Stupeflix.com you can create a video from photos, video clips, text, and music. The finished creation is a video slideshow that can get you started with video marketing.

• **Presentation:** Another type of video that's popular is the one that uses presentation slides to communicate a message. The video is created by the recording of slides created in presentation software like PowerPoint (PC) or Keynote (MAC) along with a narration describing what's on the slides. Presentation videos are primarily used when the objective is to educate and inform the viewer.

Being shy or uncomfortable in front of the camera are no longer reasons to keep you from getting the benefits of video marketing. If you know how to use presentation software these videos are easy to make.

13.4 27 Ways to Use Video to Grow Your Business

Most people are interested in knowing the 'best' content they should use to make their video marketing take off. It actually depends on various factors such as the purpose of the video, your target audience, and your budget.

A full-fledged video with a proper narrative and live actors may cost you just as much as a traditional commercial as far as the production is concerned. However, for smaller businesses and startups there are many other budget-friendly and equally promising options as well.

Here are the different ways to use videos in your business organized by category:

Product Information:

- **Video Sales Letters:** Video sales letters (aka VSL) are usually presentation videos on a website where the only content on the page is the video. Video sales letters should teach your viewer something that is important to them. Toward the end of the video, a buy button appears, and the video encourages the prospect to take action. They're an effective form of direct response marketing.

- **Tutorials:** Short "how-to" videos with instructions showing viewers how to do something. (Example: How to install software.)

- **Training Videos:** Training videos can be considered a series of related tutorials. You can create multiple videos that cover related topics or choose one topic and explore different aspects of it. (Example: Home exercise program.)

- **Demonstration (Demo) Video:** A demo video shows people how to use your products and services. Features are highlighted to show differences from competitors. Include an explanation of how the customer's problem will be solved, or their goal can be reached to persuade them to make a purchase.

- **Customer Support/F.A.Q. Videos:** Create short videos to answer issues your customers may experience. As new issues come up create videos that explain what to do.

- **Video Reviews:** Creating review videos can help your audience make decisions that save them time and money. Consider products and services that don't compete with your offers, but people would still find useful. Your review should be an informed and succinct analysis offering both pros and cons. When you consistently weed out the good products from the bad people will rely on your feedback rather than trying to figure things out on their own.

Promotional:

- **Promotional Video:** Promo videos are used to introduce or educate people about a particular product, service, cause, or business. The goal is to encourage the viewers to buy or know more about what's being promoted.

• **Explainer Videos:** An explainer video is a short, animated video that explains your business and what you offer in a simple, engaging and compelling way. They're ideal for your website's homepage.

• **Sizzle Reel:** A fast-paced video that's about 2 to 5 minutes long that uses audio, visuals, and messaging to promote a product, service, concept or person. They are used for sales and marketing presentations, pitches and website videos. Demo reels, showreels, media highlight reels, public relations videos, video pitches, electronic press kit videos and promo videos fall into the category of "sizzle" videos.

• **Video Tour:** Video tours allow viewers to see a place or locations without having to travel. They can be used to show offices, factories, retail space, or anywhere you conduct your business. Another way they're used is to promote places people want to visit or live in. Video tours are effective at selling hotel rooms, vacation packages, homes, events and more.

Authority:

• **Educational:** An educational video's primary purpose is to teach the viewer about something they want to learn.

• **Interviews:** Interview an expert in your market and get their perspective on a topic while building your own credibility.

• **Video Tips Series:** Video tips are like a combination of tutorials and educational videos. Tips you offer should be relevant, useful and best when they come from your own experience. They should be a mix of success and pitfalls.

• **Talk Show:** A talk show-style video has at least one show host that talks to one or more guests about various topics that are important to your audience. You can also do a round table type of talk show where four to six guests talk about industry trends, issues and outlook. An added element would be a call-in talk show that takes live phone calls from callers listening at home or on their mobile device.

• **News Video:** News videos inform your viewers about stories and trends that affect them. Share upcoming national and local dates and events in your industry. Ask your customers and social media followers to send in story ideas so you're always talking about what they're interested in.

• **Video Magazines:** A series of themed videos discussing information relevant to a particular topic or area of interest that are available online on a periodic basis. The video magazine can be created with curated content making the topic easy to research, organize, and present.

Entertainment:

• **Vlog:** A vlog is a video blog post. It also refers to a blog that only has video posted on it. People who create vlogs are known as "vloggers." Vlogs are created by getting in front of a webcam or using the camera on your mobile device to capture video. You can talk about things going on in your personal life, your business, or whatever topic that will interest your audience. Vlogs are low cost, easy to make and they help you connect with your audience.

• **Getting the word out:** If you have something important to say create a video and share it on social media. Ask your friends' associates to share it as well.

• **"Man On the Street" Interviews:** These interviews take place in public, or at a specific location, or event. The objective is to record the different opinions and spontaneous responses to questions on a topic or issue from the public. Sometimes these videos are serious, but usually, they're funny and offer a unique form of video content.

Testimonials:

• **Customer Testimonials:** Your best customers can share how using your products or services helped them solve a problem or achieve a goal. A video allows prospects to see themselves in the stories of other people.

• **Case Study:** Case studies are like testimonials, but you can give a more detailed explanation of how your business satisfied your customer's needs. You'll be able to highlight specific problems, solutions, and benefits so potential customers will know what results they can expect when working with you.

Event:

• **Event Video:** This is the recording of activities that happen at a live event. This includes but is not limited to conventions, conferences, seminars, and workshops. An event can be live streamed and recorded so it's available for viewing later. The videos bring the experience to viewers who couldn't make it and exponentially extends the reach of any single event.

- **Webinars:** They're video presentations that are live streamed. This allows your audience to get information in real time without having to travel. You can also record webinars so they can be replayed later. If you know how to use presentation software these videos are easy to make.

Public Relations:

- **Community Relations:** If your business is investing in the community, participating in local programs, contributing time and resources to valuable causes, then you should be capturing those efforts on video.

- **Public Service Announcement (PSA):** A message created with the objective of raising awareness, changing public attitudes and behavior towards a social or health issue.

Miscellaneous:

- **Repurposing Content:** Turn old blog posts, articles and special reports into videos and get more out of them.

- **Recruitment Videos:** Use this video to attract the best and brightest people to work for your company. Your video can contain what you have to offer, employee testimonials, insight into the work environment, and the direction the business is heading. Attracting top talent won't be hard when you not only tell but also show people what it's like to work for your business.

13.5 How to Create Videos for Your Business

There are many ways for you to get started with creating your videos. But first, you'll need to determine how involved you want to be in the creation process. The best way to ensure a successful video marketing campaign is to leave the technical work to the professionals. Many companies won't charge a fortune to make great videos for you leaving you with more time to work on your business. However, if you want to save money more than you want to save time, there are tools and technology available to help you create a great video.

Below is a list of action steps and tools you need to start getting your videos created.

Outsource Your Video Projects

Creating videos isn't for everyone. You and your staff may not have the necessary time, skill, or desire to continually make new marketing videos. So, here are two ways to get the job done for you.

- Hiring a video production company is an alternative to making your own live action videos. If you plan on doing a lot of on-location filming or you just want your videos to always look professional, then bringing in an expert is a smart move. You can do a search online for video professionals in your local area.

- Working with a video production company is not an all-or-nothing choice. You can have an effective video marketing plan by hiring freelancers to edit any footage you may have or create other types of videos for you like an explainer video. Learn how to find and hire freelancers in Chapter 18.

Hiring an expert means your projects will be high quality and done in less time. If either of these options appeals to you, then make sure you review the professional's portfolio and skill level before hiring them.

Creating Your Own Videos In-house

You may not have the budget to outsource your video marketing, but you still want to benefit from using the strategy in your business. The level of complexity for any DIY solution you chose will depend on:

- The amount of money you're willing to invest in the solution, and
- You or your team members' ability to learn what to do.

Hardware for Live Action Videos

If you plan on shooting live action videos, here's what you'll need to get started:

- **Video Camera:** Required for capturing live action video production. Camera choices are:

• Camcorders – Digital single-lens reflex cameras (also called a digital SLR or DSLR) shoot high-quality videos. They offer a lot of settings and options that are used mostly by professional video producers.

• Mobile Device Camera – Today the video recording quality on mobile devices is almost as good as on professional cameras. If you own the latest high-end priced smartphone or tablet, you'll be able to capture nice video footage.

• Webcam – These cameras are used with desktop and notebook computers. They're used primarily for capturing talking head style videos. The video quality is not as good as the ones on newer mobile devices but it's more than suitable for basic video projects.

• **Support Devices:** Using a tripod keeps your camera from moving while recording so your videos look very stable and level. Another option is a mount with a flexible gooseneck to take videos from different angles. Selfie sticks allow you to take videos of yourself from a greater distance rather that holding your camera in your hand.

• **Microphone:** Your videos need to have clear audio. Viewers will stop watching your video if the audio is bad. Video cameras, mobile devices, webcams and most laptops have built-in microphones with decent recording quality. Using an external microphone enhances the sound quality of recordings ensuring everything captured is clearly heard when the video is played back.

• **Lighting:** Like sound, lighting is very important so make sure the light in your shooting location matches your video's needs. When shooting indoors you'll need good lighting, so if your lighting is insufficient then you'll need to invest in additional lights or a "three-point lighting" kit.

• **Backdrop:** This is not a must-have but will certainly elevate the level of professionalism in your videos. Shooting video in front of a solid white background keeps the focus on the subject in the video and eliminates distractions. Using solid green screen backgrounds like they do in Hollywood allows you to digitally insert a virtual background adding some variation to your videos. The location where you are filming needs to be large enough to hold a backdrop and set up your equipment.

Video Editing Software and Apps

Depending on how you plan to use the recorded video, any mistakes and unnecessary parts may need to be edited out from the raw footage. By using video editing software, you can remove mistakes, copy, cut, and paste the footage in a way that completely rearranges the order the video was shot. While editing you're able to put some flair into your video by adding motion, transitions, music and sound effects to fine-tune it before you finish. It may take some effort to get things to look and sound the way you want, but the software makes it easy to produce professional-looking high-quality videos.

Here's a list of video editing software titles you can take a look at.

- Adobe Premiere (Windows, Mac)
- iMovie (Mac, iPhone)
- Lightworks (Windows, Mac, Linux)
- Vegas Pro (Windows)
- VSDC Free Video Editor (Windows)
- Windows Movie Maker (Windows)
- Wondershare Filmora (Windows, Mac)
- PowerDirector (Android)
- WeVideo (Cloud, iPhone, Android)
- VideoShop (iPhone, Android)

Video Creation Software

You probably already know that using footage captured from a camera is not the only way to make videos. Explainer videos, animations, whiteboards, and slideshows are created with computer software or cloud-based applications. Some of these programs will allow you to import your saved video files and add them to your project.

Most video creation software only produces a specific type of video, so you'll need to know what kind of videos you want to create before you make your investment.

- **Software for Computers:** Programs installed on your desktop or notebook computer. There are many to choose from, I suggest you take a look at these:

- Adobe After Effects (Windows, Mac) – A digital visual effects and motion graphics application used to create animation and other special effects for graphics-related projects. Adobe's After Effects program is versatile and creates different types of videos by using project templates that you can buy.

- Camtasia (Windows, Mac) – This software is used to record onscreen activity, webcam video, and audio for existing PowerPoint presentations. Through Camtasia, you can record, edit, produce and share content.

- Movavi Slideshow Maker (Windows, Mac) – A convenient tool that can help you turn your photos into memorable movies. Add video elements to make your slideshow more fun to watch.

- NCH PhotoStage (Windows) – Turns your photos, videos, music and text into stunning video slideshows.

- VideoMakerFX (Windows, Mac) – It is a professional software tool to create animated sales videos and sales letters. VideoMakerFX has integrated every customization option you will need in a professional video.

- **Web Applications:** Cloud-based programs that you can use on almost any computer that has access to the internet.

    - Animoto – Turns your photos and video clips into professional video slideshows in minutes.

    - Vyond – An animated video creation platform designed to allow businesspeople with no background in animation to quickly and easily create animated videos.

    - Jing – A screencasting program that takes a picture or video of the user's computer screen and uploads it to the web.

    - Magisto – Turns your digital videos and photos into movies that look and feel like living experiences.

    - PowToon – Make animated videos that look super professional in just a few minutes.

• Prezi – Presentation software that uses motion, zoom, and spatial relationships to bring your ideas to life and make you a great presenter.

Before you buy any software, experiment with free or trial versions first. You can find out if a particular program does all of the things you need for your project. Also, check the minimum system requirements needed for the computer the software will be installed on.

Buying Video Content

One of the resources you need to know about is the use of royalty-free content. Royalty-free refers to the right to use copyright material or intellectual property without the need to pay royalties or license fees for each use or per volume sold, or some time period of use or sales. If you're looking to save time and money on your video production, using elements such as stock footage, music, and images can be exactly what you need.

• **Royalty Free Media** – These are just a few of the many websites online that provide royalty free stock content for use in your videos.

• **Pond5:** An online marketplace for royalty free media. The company licenses stock footage, stock music, stock photography sound effects, after effects, images and 3-D models.

• **RocketStock:** Offers a curated collection of after effects templates for video editors and motion designers.

• **VideoBlocks:** A subscription-based service that provides members with unlimited downloads of stock footage, motion backgrounds, special effects, After effects templates and much more.

• **iStock Photo:** One of the world's leading stock content marketplaces, offering millions of hand-picked premium images.

• **Deposit Photos:** A stock agency with millions of premium high-quality stock photos, royalty free images, illustrations and vector art.

• **Fotolia:** Offers photos, illustrations, vectors and videos for use in creative projects

• **AudioBlocks:** A stock media website dedicated to everything audio.

• **Amazon:** Visit the popular online store, do a search for "royalty free music" and you'll see a large selection to choose from.

• **SoundStripe:** A service that allows you full access to their entire library of music.

13.6 How to Make Your Videos Effective So They Connect with Customers in Five Steps

Your marketing videos require more than just an idea and some moving images on a screen. Here are 5 steps that will make your videos more effective.

1. **Start with a Plan** – A successful video for your business starts with having a plan. Many people overlook this step, and you can tell by how unorganized and uninformative their videos are. No matter what type of video you create its purpose must always be clear to the viewer.

   Your plan should start with:

   • Identifying who is the video for. Is it for existing customers, prospects, or both? Knowing your target audience is a major factor in how effective your video will be.

   • Write down the exact goal you want your video to achieve. Is it to sell, inform, entertain, train, or something else?

   • Once you decide on the purpose of the video write down the topic for the video. The more you narrow down the topic, the easier and faster it will be to create your videos. A video about saving money for retirement is more specific than one that just talks about how to save money.

2. **Create an Outline** – Next create an outline for your topic. Don't just hop in front of the camera and start talking about whatever comes to your mind. Take time to think about the information you want to deliver and how you'll present it. Each of your videos should have a single message.

3. **Record Your Message** – It's time to use your camera or video creation software to capture and create.

• If you plan on being in the video be yourself and explain what makes you and your business different from your competition. When recording, shoot a lot of close-ups. On small screens like mobile phones, these close-up shots are more compelling than wide-angle shots.

• If you create a product or provide a service show people what you do. For example, if you were a dentist that specialized in restorative work, (i.e., dentures, crowns, bridges) you would show and explain to viewers the same thing you would to a person that came into your office.

• If you want to simplify a complex product, service, or idea then use an animated explainer video. The combination of visuals and complementing voice-overs will get the message across.

4. **Edit Your Footage** – Once you have the footage you need, it's time to edit what you've captured.

   • You want your video to move at a relatively quick pace to keep viewers from getting bored. This means cutting scenes out that you think are too slow. Adding transitions between the clips will make the video flow smoothly. If the video suddenly skips from one scene to another without some type of transition some people may become irritated.

   • Depending on the type of video you are creating, you may decide to use titles, captions, and text. If you do make sure they're easily visible especially on small screens. Also, keep the words on the screen long enough for people to read them.

   • During editing is when music can be added to your video. Music enhances your video even if you are doing a simple narration. Take movies for example. Think about how music makes them more interesting and entertaining.

   • Make sure the length of your video is ideal for its purpose so viewers won't lose interest. See Chapter 13.6.2 How Long Should Your Video Be?

5. **Use Video SEO** – SEO is necessary for any form of content you use for online marketing. This is the technical side that most business owners are not aware of when making their own marketing videos. Learning to research and use keywords for SEO is one of the most important things you can do to promote your video and business.

• When it's time to post your video online make sure you use the best keywords in the title, tags, and description to increase the chances of your video getting listed in search engines. Review Chapter 7.4.

13.6.1 Should You Use a Script or Not?

Should you use a script or not? It depends.

Some video marketing experts believe you should avoid using a script. They say it makes you sound stiff and formal when reading and the objective is to sound as natural as possible. The need for you to use a script is also lessened when you are very familiar with the topic you are discussing. One of the benefits of not using a script is that you come across as more authentic. This is especially true when appearing in front of the camera. A way to practice without using a script is to imagine that you're explaining your information to a close friend. This will give you a friendlier and more natural tone when you're recording.

Other experts including myself think using a script is especially beneficial when you are first starting to make videos. It helps you keep on message and ensures you cover all of the points you listed in your outline in a clear, concise, and compelling way. This is good if your videos are short so they get to the point as soon as possible. If your video is long like a video sales letter, a script keeps you from rambling, reduces the umms & uhhhs, awkward pauses, and brain freezes. You'll present yourself as being more prepared.

If you plan on using a script here are 4 tips to sound more natural when reading it:

1. Write short sentences – Long sentences don't sound so good when spoken. Break long ones down into shorter ones.

2. Alternate your delivery – Change your pace, add some pauses, speak quickly in certain moments to add some excitement and more slowly in others to allow time for contemplation.

3. Improvise a little – Leave spots in your script where you can adlib and insert a personal thought or experience from memory.

4. Practice – Read the script aloud a few times before you record, so you become comfortable with it. You want to sound conversational.

The purpose of your video will also determine if you use a script or not. If you're doing a vlog or interview, you wouldn't be using a script. So, start out by doing what you feel most comfortable with—script or no script—and then try a different format next time to see what works better.

13.6.2 How Long Should Your Video Be?

There isn't a right answer to this question. The length is subject to:

- **What is the topic of the video?** Your topic can answer one or all of the following questions: who, what, when where, why, and how.

- **Who is the target audience?** Customers, prospects, followers, subscribers, men, women, baby-boomers, Gen Xers, etc.

- **What is the purpose of the video?** To sell, review, inform, teach, promote, etc.

- **What type of video is being created?** Live action, live stream, screencast, animated, etc.

- **What do viewers expect to see?** Entertainment, commentary, demonstration, product information, you, or someone else.

- **Where is the video going to being used?** Your business website, social media websites, local business directories, mobile apps, video submission websites.

- **Where is the audience viewing the video?** Are they out of the house using a mobile device with a service that charges data fees? Or are they home on their computer?

- **What action do you want the viewer to take?** Do you want them to buy something, subscribe to your channel, like something, submit their email address?

According to an article written by Ezra Fishman posted on Wistia.com.

- "Videos up to 2 minutes long get a lot of engagement" (up to 70%).

- As the length of the video increases the amount of engagement decreases.

    • There is a significant drop-off between 2 and 3 minutes so you are better off editing your 3-minute video down to 2 minutes.

- Videos 6 to 12 minutes is the next best duration.

    • The loss of engagement levels off after 6 minutes and holds steady at 50% engagement up to 12 minutes.

- "Proceed with caution after 12 minutes."

    • There are times when a video needs to be as long as it needs to so don't cut a long video down to a short one if it's going to impact the value provided.

    • Videos longer than 12 minutes are usually tutorials, commentaries, or video sales letters and viewers expect them to be long.

    • If you develop a tendency to create long videos your audience will learn to expect it and their engagement will increase.

The length of your video will also be determined by the script that you've written. If you want a short video make sure your script is clear, concise, and compelling. Whatever you don't cover in the video can be put on your website or description section wherever the video is posted.

Start out making short videos, and get a feel for what your audience likes before venturing off into the realm of longer videos.

13.7 Where Should You Host Your Videos Online?

Once you're satisfied with your video it's time to show it to the world. Just like your website, your videos need to be stored (or hosted) somewhere online so people have access to them. There are two options for you to choose from, hosted and self-hosted.

Option #1 Hosted: A hosted video is one that is uploaded to a video sharing site like YouTube. This is a fast way to get your video online

Advantages of Using Hosted Video:

- **It's Affordable** – There is no cost to upload and share your video file.

- **Easy to Use** – Little technical skill is needed to upload a video and place it on a webpage or social media site.

- **Video Compression** – Your video file is reduced to the smallest size possible allowing it to load fast, stream smoothly, and retain a high quality in appearance

- **Unlimited Bandwidth** – Every time your video is watched you don't have to worry about bandwidth restrictions that can stop your video from being shown.

- **Device Compatibility** – Viewing your videos on different browsers and devices requires them to be available in different formats. Hosted videos are converted into multiple formats after they are uploaded and the correct version is shown depending on where it is being viewed.

- **Large Audience** – By uploading to a video sharing site your video can be seen by more people that never heard of you, your business, or your website. If they like what they see they will respond to your call to action or like and share your video.

- **SEO Benefits** – If your video title and description are optimized with a targeted keyword and the competition is not too strong, your video could appear in search engine results.

Disadvantages of Using Hosted Video:

- **Shared Ownership** – When you upload to video sharing sites almost all of them allow you to maintain the rights to your video. However, as part of the sites' terms & conditions, they have the right to use your video. They can determine how easy it is for other people to find it just like search engines. Your video can also be removed if someone complains about it because it violates the terms and conditions of the site where it is hosted.

- **Unwanted Feedback** – The idea behind video sharing websites is to share and discuss the content. While you may welcome positive comments, you may also get some undeserved negative comments you can't remove. You can disable the comment section on the page where your video is, but that may limit your ability to grow a following. They won't be able to engage with you.

- **Advertising** – Some free services will show unwanted ads before, during, and after your videos. Some of these ads can be from competitors.

- **Competition for Attention** – Your video is never the only one on the page. Viewers can get easily distracted by related videos. If people lose interest in your video, they will quickly move on to the next one. Make sure your video is at least interesting and informative so after it's watched people take the action that you want them to.

Here's is a list of common video sharing websites.

- **Dailymotion.com** is one of the biggest video platforms in the world, offering a mix of content from users, independent creators and premium partners. Business videos do have a higher risk of being deleted here than on YouTube.

- **Metacafe.com** is a video sharing website that specializes in short-form video entertainment in the categories of movies, video games, sports, music and TV.

- **Vimeo.com** is a video sharing website where you can upload, share and view videos. It was the first video sharing site to support high-definition video. If you're going to use video to promote your business, you'll need to use Vimeo Business otherwise, any personal account you use will be suspended.

- **YouTube.com** allows users to upload, view, rate, share, add to favorites, report, comment on videos and subscribe to other users.

Option #2 Self-Hosted: For a self-hosted video, you pay for a third-party hosting service to store your video. They'll provide you with a media player for you to embed your video on your website.This option is used when you want to put an exclusive video on your website. Especially if it has a call to action.

Advantages of Using Self-Hosted Video:

- **Complete Ownership** – Your video is hosted on a server you're paying for. You won't have to worry about your video being taken down from a complaint or getting negative comments you can't filter. The chances and ability for someone to use your video without your permission are significantly less.

- **Traffic Control** – If someone sees your video and wants to share it, they will need to provide a link to where the video is located on your website. This means you get all the traffic unlike using a video sharing site.

- **Increased Conversions** – Your video will not have other ones to compete against. There will be no distractions and no competitors. Now your call to action can be focused on and acted upon.

- **Zero Advertising** – Since you are paying for hosting you won't have to be bothered by ads appearing in your videos. Viewers will be able to get straight to the message.

- **Professional Appearance** – When your video is self-hosted you get to control how the video player looks on your web page. You also won't be required to have the watermark of the hosting company logo plastered on your video.

Disadvantages of Using Self-Hosted Video:

- **Cost** – Depending on the company you use the cost of self-hosting will depend on:

  - How many videos you plan to upload
  - The file size of your video
  - The type of tech support you'll need
  - Paying monthly or annually
  - Amount of cloud storage space you'll need
  - Bandwidth usage
  - The number of your team members that need access to your account
  - Access to statistics

• **Limited Exposure** – When you self-host your videos you'll need to apply web marketing strategies to attract your own audience. You won't have the easy access to viewers that comes with video sharing sites.

• **Free But Slow** – Another way you can self-host your video is to upload your video file to your web server where your website is stored. The challenge with using your web hosting for streaming your video is:

  • Based on your web hosting plan you probably won't have the resources (bandwidth, space, CPU speed) to store and stream videos.

  • You'll need to know how to set up and configure a video player to embed on your website that could show your video on different screen sizes.

  • If multiple people are watching your video simultaneously, playback and your website performance will slow down.

The following companies offer self-hosted plans for videos.

• **Wistia.com** is a video platform for businesses. It has free and premium video hosting solutions and supports video creation and editing tools like Soapbox.

• **Vimeo Business** is a valuable enterprise platform for businesses to share their high-quality, visual stories. Manage videos in one place. Upload all your videos with up to 5TB of storage, organize your library, and enjoy advanced privacy settings and player customization. (https://vimeo.com/business)

• **SproutVideo.com** is a video hosting platform for businesses that makes it easy to customize, publish, and track your videos online.

• **DaCast.com** is an online video hosting service that supports video streaming, embedding, sharing, and video storage. Its online video services are designed for business and other commercial operations.

Mix-up Your Video Hosting

Depending on your video marketing strategy, where you host your video can make a big difference. The best strategy is to do a little bit of both. Hosting most of your videos on sites like YouTube is not a bad move if you're trying to connect with its user base. Putting self-hosted videos on your website will give you more unique content and a reason for people to visit your website.

13.8 10 Ways to Make Sure Your Videos Are Seen by Your Target Audience

The demand for videos from consumers is constantly increasing along with the places you can share them. It doesn't do you any good to create a video that gets little to no views especially after you put so much effort into making it. You'll need to put just as much effort into getting your videos seen. When it comes to marketing and promoting your small-business videos, follow these 10 basic tactics:

1. Leverage the power of social media and post your videos on all of your accounts. Become active in groups and if your video is helpful then share it.

2. Put a call to action video on your home page.

3. Use video sharing sites like YouTube to give your videos more exposure.

4. When submitting videos to other websites and directories make sure they have:

    • A strong title that describes the benefit people will get from watching your video.
    • Keywords in the title, description, and tags that your target audience would be looking for. This will also increase the chance of your video appearing in search engine results.

5. Encourage people to like, comment, and share your videos so more people can find out about them. Start with family, friends, and customers.

6. Work on getting more fans, followers, and subscribers so they can be notified when you have a new video. Engage with them so they feel you're approachable and someone they can trust.

7. Include links to your video in any email marketing that you do. Adding video to your emails can increase click rates by 300%. Place a link to one in your signature file.

8. Put a link to a video on all of your printed marketing material. (business cards, brochures, etc.)

9. Include a link to a video in any online press releases you send.

10. Create videos regularly. If your audience knows you're consistently creating videos and they're good they'll come to view them.

13.9 What Video Statistics Matter the Most

Video marketing is one of the few types of marketing that you can easily track and know if it's effective or not. Depending on where your video is being hosted some of the things you can track include:

- How much traffic the video is getting
- How viewers discovered the video
- Gender of the viewer
- Age range of the viewer
- How many times the video was watched
- Average time spent watching the video
- How many people liked or shared it
- Viewership by County.

These are very useful indicators, but the one that matters the most is "did the video achieve its goal?" Did the video generate a sale or get a lead? Did you get a new follower on social media?

This is why you need to establish what does a "successful video" mean to you before you create any. If you don't you may be lulled into thinking a video with positive statics is doing well, but it's not delivering the results you created it for.

If a video has poor statistics and it's not producing results, then you know you need to go back to the drawing board and deliver better content. There are a few good tools to analyze how well your videos are performing. Wistia.com and YouTube Analytics are two of the best options. It's also a good idea to use a specific link from your videos to your website or landing page so you can track how many clicks and/or conversions the video is generating.

Putting a video on the web and hoping it does well is not going to work. Your video analytics can not only show you how your current videos are doing but also give insight on how to make future videos more effective.

"Doing business without advertising is like winking at a girl in the dark, you know what you are doing but nobody else does."

– Steuart Henderson Britt, author, professor of marketing and advertising

14. Understanding the Basics of Paid Online Advertising

14.1 How Effective Is Paid Online Advertising for Your Business?

Many digital marketers and business owners believe that digital marketing methods such as content marketing are stronger and have more impact than using paid online advertising. I believe that paying for online advertising is an investment that, when done the right way, can produce fruitful results.

Briefly put, online advertising is a marketing strategy where targeted promotional messages are used to attract consumers to get web traffic. A well-planned and executed paid ad campaign offers your business the following benefits:

- Immediately increases online visibility by having your ad appear where your target market is already spending a lot of their time. This is especially true with the tech savvy millennial generation.

- Provides a way to get more targeted traffic to your web pages quickly.

- Ability to create ads that focus on specific markets. Segment your offers by audience demographics, product and service variations, keyword, etc.

- Tests multiple ads (split test) to identify which ad or aspect of a specific ad (i.e., headline) is more effective.

- Offers methods for measuring and tracking results, unlike traditional offline advertising.

- Saves you money by using performance-based advertising where you only pay when a result can be measured from your ad.

- Continues to market to your prospects even after they already saw your ad or visited your website.

- Allows you to match the marketing efforts of competitors that were already using this strategy and get an advantage over the ones that haven't.

- Increases the credibility of your business. When your ad is seen consistently it reinforces that you are a legitimate business

But also know that while impactful, paid advertising can also be risky, as a poor campaign can end up costing you more than you intended, with little or nothing to show for it.

This chapter will help you understand paid online advertising and which method you should try first to get quality traffic for your web pages.

14.2 The Two Types of Online Advertising

Online advertising is not the strategy you jump into without having a basic understanding of which options are going to give you the most for your investment. Different types of ad styles can be used, and each has their own strengths and weaknesses.
First, let's talk about the two primary types of advertisements, search ads and display ads:

Location: The main difference between these two ad types is where they appear.

- **Search Ads:** You will only find these on search engine results pages. The ads may appear at the top and bottom of the screen for anyone that does a search using keywords with commercial intent (i.e., looking to buy something). Overall, ads that appear with these types of keywords account for 65% of clicks received on SERPS, compared to 35% for organic results. Businesses bid on keywords that will cause their ads to show and compete with each other for the best position on the page.

- **Display Ads:** These types of online ads are the ones that appear on websites with content or conversations related to the industry of the advertiser. They tend to promote things a visitor was not looking for, but the advertiser wanted to bring attention to. An example would be an auto parts ad on an automotive website. The ads can be seen in different areas of a web page (top, bottom, side or middle).

Appearance:

• Search ads are text-based ads that have these 3 features: a headline, brief description and a web address.

• Display ads are visual in nature but can also appear as text. Their layouts can be customized, and they use images, or interactive elements such as moving images, animation, audio, video, video games and more.

Pros & Cons:

Search Ads

Pros	Cons
Your ads only appear when someone uses a keyword that you have put a bid on. You won't waste money on untargeted advertising.	Ads are limited to a certain amount of characters.
They're faster to create and manage.	Some skill is required to write ad copy.
Able to test ads without making a large investment.	No way to make your ad visually stand out
Conversion rates are higher because the ad appears when someone is searching for a solution. They are more likely to click on it to see what you are offering.	Ad space is available through bidding and some industries are very competitive and expensive to get space for.

Display Ads

Pros	Cons
Effective at introducing or reminding people about you, your business and offers.	You can't target your audience using demographics. Not as effective as search ads.
They can reach a large audience within a target audience.	May not be viable for some businesses.
They're visual and can be interactive.	May require a larger investment to create effective ads.
Since they are not targeted, they may be cheaper to use.	Initial account set up may require more technical know-how than setting up for search ads

14.2.1 Understanding Clicks, Impressions and Conversions

When using online advertising there are some terms you need to be familiar with so you can decide which advertising method will work best for you.

- **Clicks:** A click is when someone uses a cursor on their computer screen or finger on their mobile device to click on your text or image ad. The term click-through (CT) is a measurement of how many times this has happened. Click-through rate is the percentage of people who click on your ad after they see it.

- **Impressions:** This is a measurement of the number of times your ad has been seen on a viewer's screen (either desktop or mobile) or displayed on a web page. Unique impressions measure how many times your ad was seen initially. So, if your ad is seen by one person using multiple devices, each impression will be considered unique.

- **Conversions:** This is the percentage of people who, after clicking your ad, go on to complete a desired action such as downloading an e-book or purchasing a product.

14.2.2 What Are the Different Ad Formats Used Online?

There are many best practices for paid online advertising that come from various channels and platforms. It is not realistic to cover them all here, but here is an overview of the paid advertising opportunities available to you.

E-Commerce Ads

If you have one or more consumer products you want to promote there are ad formats available specifically for that purpose. Search engines show shopping ads which are more than just a text ad. They show users a photo of your product plus a title, price, store name, and more. E-commerce websites such as Amazon and eBay offer promoted listings where you can get your merchandise noticed by their enormous audience. With e-commerce ads, your items are seen by customers at the time they are searching and browsing for what you are selling.

Email Ads

People who use free email services like Gmail or Yahoo mail will see ads incorporated into their inboxes. There will be image display ads on the side of the screen, but some ads will look like incoming emails at the very top of the screen. They are clearly identified as advertisements, but when you click on one of them, you'll be redirected to a promotional web page. There are different ways to target your audience like their age, gender, interest, domains of email senders, and specific keywords found used in their email.

Interstitial Ads

This type of ad takes up the entire screen of the device being viewed. On websites, they appear when browsing between pages, or while a webpage is loading. In mobile apps, they show up at different times that the developer chooses, such as during a loading screen.

Local Directory Ads

When people are looking for a local business the first place visit may not be a search engine. Some people have come to rely on local business directories so advertising on these websites is worth exploring. When you pay for an ad in a business directory like YellowPages.com or a review site like Yelp.com it's really to get prominent placement on that particular directory. Your business name along with a description and rating will appear near the top of the screen above other businesses in your niche. Along with favorable placement, you may also be able to get placement on your competitor's directory pages, and a top listing on the mobile version of the directory.

Local Search Ads

Search engines can feature a business location and lead users to call or visit it. When people search for nearby businesses on Google or Google Maps (for example, "coffee near me"), they will see ads that feature local businesses.

Mobile Ads

Millions of people rely on their mobile devices to search the web, check their social media accounts, and use mobile apps. It would be a missed opportunity not to advertise to them. Choose from text, graphic, video, or in-app ad formats for your campaigns.

Native Ads

These ads are designed to have the same appearance as the website they appear on. You may have noticed them at the bottom of posts of popular blogs, entertainment, and news websites. They may be under headings that say something like "Sponsored Topics" or "Around the Web." Some of those ads lead to other articles and some lead to advertorials which are ads presented in the style of an editorial. Other types of native ads are promoted tweets, sponsored posts and search ads that appear on SERPs.

Pay Per Click (PPC) Ads

PPC advertising has become a very popular way to promote online. As the name suggests, advertisers only pay when someone clicks on their ad regardless of how many times it's shown. Depending on where the ad is displayed it can be entirely text, a graphic, or a combination of both. Places you'll find PPC ads include high traffic content sites, search engines, and social media channels.

Podcast Ads

Podcast listenership is steadily increasing and is projected to continue for the foreseeable future. Podcast ads can be used to reach an audience that is passionate about a particular topic and will pay attention to their trusted host as they're promoting an ad. Promotions are done at the beginning, middle, and sometimes the end of a show. Shows with a lot of listeners will cost more but the rates are very reasonable.

Retargeting Ads

Have you ever seen an ad promoting something you recently viewed on a previous website? That was a retargeting (remarketing) ad. When a customer visits a website, it may leave a small piece of data (called a cookie) on the user's computer or mobile device. Cookies are created by the user's web browser and store information such as their preferences and browsing activities from that website. An advertiser can use the information from cookies to have their ads follow the user to other websites and continuously promote their offers.

Some may view this as an aggressive or invasive type of marketing, but it's a lot easier to market to people that already know about your product or service. In marketing, there is a principle called The Marketing Rule of 7 that states a potential buyer needs to hear or see a marketing message at least seven times before they'll consider taking action to buy from you. Using retargeting ads are a way to make that happen.

Social Media Ads

Ads appearing on social media make sense because that's where most people spend their time online. Different platforms have their own way of presenting ads, but they would typically function and be created like display ads. You'll be able to use data provided by users to target a particular audience with platform-specific ads such as promoted posts or sponsored stories. There are plenty of advertising options unique to social media that are very effective.

Video Ads

Video advertising can be described as the creation of a video for the purpose of promoting a product, service, event, message, etc. Another definition would be the appearance of display ads before, during, or after an online video. So even if you don't know how to make a video, you can still benefit from their growing popularity.

Unlike other types of paid ads, video ads are unique because you can inform, engage, and entertain your audience with them. They don't have to be fancy or long to watch, but you should try to make them memorable and always have a call to action. Forty-three percent of new customers buy something they saw in a YouTube ad.

14.3 What Are Online Advertising Networks and Which Ones Are Most Popular?

An online advertising network is a company that provides advertisers with places to put their ads on the web. Most networks offer various types of ad formats like the ones I just talked about along with diverse choices in ad placement on web pages across the internet. Unlike print and TV ad networks, they have a technological advantage that allows them to deliver targeted advertisements to consumers online. They also have the ability to track how many times an ad has been seen and clicked on. A report of that data can then be generated which is not possible with traditional advertising alternatives.

Ad networks provide advertisers with resources and tools to create ads and manage their campaigns in real time. Some ad networks also partner with content publishers who want to monetize their websites by promoting ads on them. This gives advertisers even more places for their ads to be seen in order to reach their audience.

There are a large and growing amount of advertising networks to choose from, but I will help you narrow down your choices by giving a breakdown of the 10 most popular ones used by advertisers.

1. **Amazon Marketing Services:** If you sell consumer products on Amazon, using Amazon's built-in advertising platform is a great way to promote your products throughout their site. Visit https://advertising.amazon.com.

2. **Bing Ads:** If you want to advertise on Microsoft's different properties, such as Bing, MSN, Yahoo, and AOL, you should use Bing. Visit https://www.bingads.microsoft.com.

3. **BuySellAds:** This company is small compared to some of the other ones, but it has an extensive publisher network that lets advertisers reach in-demand audiences at a pace that matches their growth. Some of the popular niches to advertise in include programming, design, business, and cryptocurrency. Available ad formats supported are native ads, sponsored content, display ads, and email advertising. Another ad format that's available is podcast ads where you can purchase a sponsorship where your promotion read during the broadcast. Visit https://www.buysellads.com.

4. **Epom Market:** Epom is an advertising platform that can place ads on a variety of reputable publisher's websites. They offer fantastic analytics and as much functionality as any of the other leading platforms. Their portfolio of publishers also includes some of the most popular mobile apps. Visit https://market.epom.com/advertisers.

5. **Facebook Ads:** When it comes to social advertising Facebook is the top ad channel for both B2C and B2B marketers. It offers an easy and affordable way to advertise online. Over 2.4 billion people use Facebook each month and 1 billion use Instagram. You can create and manage ads on

both platforms within Facebook. They offer different ad formats including their Facebook Audience Network used for promoting ads in mobile apps. Visit https://www.facebook.com/business.

6. **Google Ads:** An advertising service created by Google where you bid on keywords to determine the placement of your ad on the Google search engine and other integrated publishers. You only pay when someone clicks your ad. If you want to explore the various advertising options available on YouTube, you would also do it through Google Ads. Visit https://ads.google.com.

7. **InMobi:** A mobile ad network that reaches over 1.5 billion mobile users across 32,000 premium mobile properties. They gather and combine user behaviors from 1st, 2nd and 3rd party sources that enable them to provide more precise targeting and optimization for high lifetime value users. They offer advertisers unique ways to maximize their ad conversions. Visit https://www.inmobi.com.

8. **LinkedIn Advertising:** LinkedIn's self-service solutions lets you launch a targeted campaign in minutes. You can set your own budget, choose clicks or impressions, and stop your ads at any time. The platform is perfect for promoting to other businesses and professionals because when they are using it, they are in a business state of mind. B2B advertisers (58%) like the ROI on LinkedIn ads. Ad formats available are sponsored content, sponsored InMail, text ads, and dynamic ads. Visit https://www.business.linkedin.com.

9. **SharpSpring Ads:** A retargeting platform that lets marketers effortlessly bring back lost web visitors with Facebook ads on Facebook, banner ads across the web, and ads on Twitter. They help businesses get more sales and conversions by using their audience data to target ads with pinpoint precision. Visit https://sharpspring.com/ads.

10. **Taboola:** This content discovery platform offers native ad placement on many well-known high-traffic websites. The platform is good for reaching new audiences by sharing positive news about your business in order to bring awareness to it. Savvy advertisers create content that is useful or entertaining to drive traffic to their website to make sales or generate leads. Visit https://www.taboola.com.

On top of the different ad formats and ad networks to choose from, there are various ways to calculate the cost for promoting ads. Now it's time to explore different pricing models you must be aware of.

14.4 What Are the Three Most Common Pricing Models?

The cost of advertising online depends on a few things like the type of ad you want to create and where the ad is going to be seen. All online ad pricing is not the same so you will need to determine which pricing model is best for what you want to achieve, and your budget. Many pricing models are used, but three of them are more common than the rest. I'll explain the common ones first then briefly talk about the others.

1. **Cost per Click (CPC):** This pricing model is based on how much you pay each time someone clicks on your ad. Since you only pay when your ad is clicked it's considered a less risky way to advertise. Use this model when you want to drive traffic to your website.

2. **Cost per Mille (CPM):** Per mīlle is from Latin meaning "in each thousand." The "M" also represents the Roman numeral for 1,000. This pricing model is based on how much you pay to have your ad shown 1,000 times. The impressions can be on one website or across multiple websites depending on the advertising network. If bringing awareness to your business, an event, or cause is your goal then this will get your ad more exposure.

3. **Cost per Action (CPA):** Also called cost per acquisition. You pay when a specified action occurs such as: a sale, click, registration form completion, email subscriber, file download or some type of conversion determined before you start your campaign. This pricing model is usually more expensive, but if conversion is what you want then this is the one to use.

To get a better understanding of these pricing options, the table below shows how $500 of advertising dollars would be spent using basic metrics.

Pricing Model	Total Advertising Cost	Number of Impressions	Clicks on Ad	Click-through Rate (CTR)	Conversions	Conversion Rate	Ad Price
CPC	$500	25,000	250	1%	25	10%	$2.00
CPM	$500	50,000	250	0.5%	25	10%	$10.00
CPA	$500	25,000	250	1%	25	10%	$20.00

Here are the formulas used to calculate the advertising cost:

- CPC – Total Advertising Cost ($500) / Clicks on Ad (250) = Ad Price ($2)
- CPM – Total Advertising Cost ($500) / Impressions (50,000) x 1000 = Ad Price ($10)
- CPA – Total Advertising Cost ($500) / Conversions (25) = Ad Price ($20)

Other Pricing Models

- Cost per Lead (CPL) – Advertisers pay for a lead that comes from a consumer using a form to give their contact detail in exchange for the advertiser's offer.
- Cost per View (CPV) – You pay each time your video is viewed.
- Cost per Follower (CPF) – Used for building an audience on social media.
- Cost per Install (CPI) – Applies to the installation of mobile apps.
- Cost per Download (CPD) – Used when the advertiser wants to promote web-based apps or something that can be downloaded.

There are a lot of options available to you, however, I believe the CPC pricing model is the least risky to begin with if you are new to paid online advertising. Let's look at some of the benefits it offers.

14.5 What Is PPC Advertising and The Benefits of Using It?

Pay Per Click or PPC is the most popular type of paid advertising used by both large and small businesses for promoting products and services. The terms PPC and CPC are used interchangeably. CPC refers to the pricing model and metrics (the amount you pay). PPC is used simply to describe the advertising method.

With PPC advertising ads appears on SERPs, social media sites, and other publisher websites where advertisers only pay when their ad is clicked on. When someone searches for a specific product or service, ads are shown alongside search results or web content. Ads can also be set up to appear based on a person's interest introducing them to something they didn't know was available.

The way PPC advertising works is you bid against other advertisers for the top position where you want your ad to appear on search engine results pages or web pages. You do this by buying or bidding on keyword phrases that are relevant to your products or services. The higher the bid, the higher your ad will appear when it is shown exposing it to more people who will find the ad (and click on it) to go to your website. You would then pay your bid price every time a visitor clicks through your ad. The ad space on any screen is limited, so being among the top bidders is essential.

There are many benefits to PPC advertising, making it an effective way of promoting a business online. Here are 5 reasons why you should use PPC for your business:

1. **Speedy Results:** Unlike organic search and SEO results, PPC advertising can start giving you rapid results soon after the campaign launch, bringing in quality traffic and leads to your website.

2. **Expand Your Reach:** You reach a larger audience and increase your online visibility. As your business grows you can scale your advertising and expand to international markets if you are not already in them.

3. **Targeted Traffic:** PPC campaigns can be set up to run during a specific time period and in specific geographic regions, dramatically increasing the quality of targeted traffic to the website. Half of the people that visit a website as a result of clicking on a PPC ad are more likely to buy something than visitors that came from an organic link.

4. **Testing Capability:** PPC is a great way to test the market potential and traffic for a variety of keywords, landing pages and sales opportunities.

5. **Maximize Return:** The best part about a PPC campaign is that it can be tracked, making it easier to manage costs, measure conversions, determine your ROI and compare them against other marketing strategies.

PPC advertising is a fast and practical way to get visits to your website, fan page, or whatever offer you are trying to promote. Especially if you are just starting your business, you can't get traffic organically, or you want to reach more markets quickly.

14.5.1 What Types of Businesses Should Use Pay Per Click Advertising?

PPC advertising can work for almost any business, but there are some industries and situations where using this method of advertising has a greater advantage. Using PPC advertising is a good idea for your business when the following is true:

You Sell Products Online

- You sell rare and unusual versions of existing products that may be hard or impossible to find in local stores:
    - Custom fashion and jewelry accessories
    - Home decor products
    - Products for hair and beards.
- When you have a wide variety of products promote them with PPC by bidding on long-tail keywords to sell them and drive more traffic to your website. Long-tail keywords have less competition and a lower cost per click. Therefore, you can have a cost-effective ad campaign where you can make some money from your products with a lower profit margin. Review Chapter 7.4.1 which explains long-tail keywords.

You're Promoting an Event or Seasonal Occasion

- Events have a deadline which gives them a sense of urgency (concert, webinar, in-person workshop, etc.). If a person sees an ad for an event they're interested in, they're more likely to take action so they don't miss out.
- If you have a seasonal business (landscaping, weddings, pool maintenance, etc.) or you sell products people look for during holidays (flowers, costumes, fireworks, BBQ grills, etc.) PPC ads bring attention to your offers.

You're Selling in a Highly Competitive Market

- Being in a competitive market means you will need to use multiple web marketing strategies to reach your target audience. Adding PPC advertising to your marketing arsenal means you can take on your toughest competitors.

Putting your ad up means taking one of your competitors down. Some of the most competitive industries include:

- Cleanup Services
- Health
- Insurance
- Legal
- Loans

Your Business is Location-Specific

- Is your local business experiencing the following challenges?

    - It's not appearing in local listings of search engines, directories, or online maps.
    - Your business does appear, but it's ranked toward the bottom of the list under your competitors.

- If you're having either of these challenges, then using location-specific keywords in a PPC ad can have your business shown prominently on relevant websites. This is a viable option if you're waiting for improved results from any Local Search Marketing (Chapter 8) or Reputation Management strategies (Chapter 9) you may have in progress.

You Use Direct Response Marketing

- Direct response marketing is the use of compelling messaging that asks prospects to respond to a specific call to action immediately (i.e., complete a form, call a phone number, make a purchase).

- This type of marketing relies heavily on tracking and measuring results. PPC advertising matches perfectly with it because of the metrics tracked when ads are viewed and clicked.

You Rely on Repeat Business

- If you offer . . .
    - A service (i.e., dentist, landscaping, web-based service, any type of ongoing training), or

• A product (i.e., food, beauty supplies, supplements, any type of consumable item).

You're in an Industry with High Profit Margins

• Some businesses don't rely on recurring sales from a single customer to generate revenue. Instead, they focus on getting single sales that have high profit margins which sustain their business. For example, real estate agents, home remodelers, attorneys, etc. Using PPCs can bring in more customers in need of big-ticket services.

You Want Web Traffic Immediately

• Most online marketing strategies take time to set up and once done it may still take some time to see results. PPC campaigns can be set up relatively fast and customers can see your ads in a couple of hours. Whether your website is new, you're waiting for another web strategy to kick in, or you just want to boost your traffic because you are having a sale, PPC marketing will get your ads in front of the people you want to reach.

If any of the scenarios listed above apply to your business, then PPC advertising is a strategy worth looking into. It's worth trying a couple of different strategies to see which works best for your business.

14.6 What Are the 10 Steps to Setting Up a PPC Campaign?

Getting started with your first pay per click campaign is not difficult at all. With some research, practice and patience you'll be able to set up campaigns whenever you need to. If you can add a profitable PPC campaign to your marketing that increases your sales and grows your business you've found a winning solution.

To set up a successful PPC advertising campaign, it is essential that you know:

• The product and/or services that you're selling

• Your competitors in order to gain an understanding of what is trending in the market

• The needs of your target audience and what they are looking for, and

• Where is the traffic to your website coming from? What websites are sending traffic and what keywords are being used?

Once you know that information, use it when following these 10 steps to set up your PPC campaign:

1. **Determine Your Goals:** Before you begin your PPC campaign it is necessary to define goals so you can stay on course by knowing exactly what you are trying to achieve. Do you want to generate leads, increase sales, or get more subscribers? When defining goals make sure they are SMART (specific, measurable, attainable, relevant and timely). Review Chapter 2.5.

2. **Select an Online Advertising Network:** The next, most important step for a successful PPC campaign is to decide on the advertising network you want to use. Initially, you should explore the most popular ones offered by Google, Bing, Facebook, and LinkedIn.

   However, deciding on which ad network to use should not be based solely on its popularity. You want to advertise on the one that has the widest reach to your target audience.

   Read the free information available online for each of the ad networks. They have plenty of resources and tools to help you set up your first PPC campaign. It may take some time to review all of the information but it's definitely worth it, and I strongly recommend it.

3. **Do Your Keyword Research:** One of the most important aspects of PPC marketing is doing keyword research. Choosing the right keywords will impact the success of your campaign and how much you will be paying per click.

   Comprehensive keyword research will allow you to build a keyword list that will be relevant to your industry and audience. Choose long-tail keywords for your campaign as these will have a higher conversion rate and avoid using low-converting generic keywords. Some keywords you want to use may be very competitive and cost more to bid on.

   If you are using Google Analytics to track the traffic to your website, you may see some keywords people are using to find you—so make sure to use those as well.

   Keep your business and PPC goals in mind. By doing so you will be able to select the best keywords. Review Chapter 7.4.2 How to Choose Keywords for SEO as a reminder.

4. **Plan Your Budget:** Set your budget based on what you can afford, your PPC goals, and the keywords you want to bid on. The keyword research you did in the prior step will give you an idea of how much you can expect to spend on each one. Try not to overpay for clicks by overbidding on keywords.

   Keep in mind that cost per click varies depending on the bid amount of your key phrases and the number of clicks you are receiving. Always measure your ad spending and profit margin to know if you are spending more or less on your PPC campaigns.

5. **Set Up an Ad Network Account:** To set up an account on any of the PPC platforms you are required to complete a sign-up process where you'll provide your billing information and method of making payments.

6. **Start a New Campaign:** Each online advertising network is different but each one has the following steps or some variation of them:

   • Select Your Campaign Type – Choose what type of campaign you want to run:
   - Search
   - Display
   - Shopping
   - Video
   - App

   For right now start with a search campaign. It's easier to manage and not as technical as the other campaign types.

   • Choose a Campaign Goal – Next, select a goal for your campaign (sales, leads, web traffic).

   • Name Your Campaign – Give your campaign a name to make it easy to identify.

   • Select a Location to Target – Choose the region where you want your ads to be displayed (globally, nationally, locally).

   • Select Languages – If your target audience speaks a different language add it to the settings.

• Choose Your Bid Strategy – This is where you decide how much you want to spend on your ads. There are different options to choose from based on your experience as an advertiser. Review the description of each option found on the ad network you're using.

• Enter Your Budget – What is the average amount you want to spend each day? Take your monthly budget and divide it by 30.

• Campaign Schedule – You can select a start date and end date for your campaigns.

• Ad Rotation – If you have more than one ad per keyword you can rotate showing them, or set it up where the one that performs the best is shown the most.

• Set Ad Schedule – Choose the day you want your ads to show. If you are a local business and you are closed on the weekends and your store hours are 9 am to 5 pm, you can have your ads shown based on the schedule of your business.

• Location Option – If a person who lives outside of your targeted area shows interest in areas that you targeted in your ad set up, they will be able to see it. If you have a local business, you don't want to pay for a click for a person that is not in a position to buy. With this option, you can make your ads visible only to people who live in your targeted location and exclude people who don't.

7. **Set Up Ad Groups:** Ad groups are like folders for your ads. If you're promoting multiple products, you might divide up the ads for each product into ad groups. These groups will target specific keywords and have their own individual settings and budgets.

Here are the steps for setting up an ad group:

• Determine how many ad groups you want to use and give each one a name describing a product or service.

• Enter the keywords you want to use for each group. For example:

Ad group #1	Ad group #2
bluetooth speaker	bluetooth headphones
bluetooth speaker brands	bluetooth headphones android
bluetooth speaker car	bluetooth headphones for ps4
bluetooth speaker cheap	bluetooth headphones for swimming
bluetooth speaker clock	bluetooth headphones for tv
bluetooth speaker cooler	bluetooth headphones for working out

8. **Create Your Ads:** Now it's time to create the ads that will be triggered to display when someone does a search using one of the keywords you won a bid on. Your objective is to create persuasive ads with attention-grabbing headlines, compelling ad copy and a strong CTA (Call to Action). Even if your targeted keywords are great and generate a lot of traffic, very few people will click on your ad if the copy is poor.

   For a successful PPC campaign, the ad copy must encourage customers to take the action you're requesting of them. This is essential if you want to have good conversions and get a high ROI. There are a lot of components to the step. You'll find them in the following subchapter.

9. **Choose Your Landing Pages:** When setting up your ads you'll need the URL (web address) of the web pages you want people to visit after they click your ads. Some ad networks rank the quality of your landing page so make sure it is relevant to the ad, and delivers what the ad copy promised.

   Content on your landing pages should include the same keywords used in the ad and a clear call to action so visitors don't get distracted and click away from the page. Your copy must explain the benefits clearly to the visitor making it easy for them to do what you want them to do. This is where good copywriting skills come into play. If you're not proficient in writing copy or don't have the time to learn, consider outsourcing this part to a professional copywriter.

   Getting your landing page right and ready for your campaign, like everything else in online marketing, will take time and testing to find the winning combination. However, it is definitely worth it to your business in the long run.

10. **Follow the Rules:** Finally, it's important that you read all the rules and policies of the ad network before setting up your campaign. You don't want to do anything to get your account suspended or banned because a rule was broken, even if you didn't mean to do so. There are many regulations and important points on what you should do and shouldn't do with PPC advertising, so it's worth taking the time to read through the rules before starting.

    As I mentioned before each ad network has its own procedures for setting up campaigns. Some of the steps I listed may be done in a different order, executed differently or not at all. But now you have an idea of what to expect when working with PPC campaigns.

14.6.1 How to Write Effective PPC Ads That Get Clicked

When it comes to writing an effective ad for your PPC campaign, you need to ask yourself these three questions:

1. What's important for my target audience?
2. What do I offer that makes me stand out from my competitors? And,
3. What action do I want people to take after they read the ad?

Put yourself in your potential customer's shoes to get a better idea of what they want and why they would choose your product or services. Jot down the answers to the questions as you'll need them to create your ads.

Effective PPC Ad copy requires the following components:

An Attention-Grabbing Headline

Your headline is the most prominent part of your ad, so it is where most people are going to look at first. Here is where you focus on the benefits of your offer, not the features. Try using some of these tips when creating your headline:

- Ask a question
- Use trending topics
- Use emotional triggers to evoke anger, disgust, guilt, competition, affirmation, fear, etc.
- Add your location if your business is local

- Use quotes or testimonials about your product or service
- Avoid using jargon or slang people may not understand.

When possible use numbers such as prices, discount percentages, dates, or statistics to make your headline more specific which will catch a reader's attention.

Strong Body Copy

After your headline is the body copy. This is where you give a description of your offer. You'll be able to use more words here than you did in your headline, but you want to keep your copy clear and concise.

Your ad has to stand out if you expect people to click on it. That's why you need to have a strong copy and call to action to keep the reader interested after they see your headline. Mentioning promotional offers is another way to catch people's attention. They entice customers to try things out they may have otherwise passed over. So, if you offer free shipping or some type of discount mention it in your ad.

Your call to action must tell the person reading your ad what instructions you want them to follow or what they'll receive. Examples of phrases that get people to respond are:

- Buy Online Today
- Register Now
- Free 30-Day Trial
- Contact Us Today to Learn More
- Sign Up Today
- Compare Prices
- Browse Our Sections
- Join Free for a Month
- Get Started
- Find Out More

Display URL

The display URL is the web address that appears with your ad but is more simplified so as to be more attractive. For example, if your display URL is www.example.com, your actual URL might be http://www.example.com/bluetooth-speakers?ref=googlead2. The actually URL must be the web page visitors will go to after they click on your ad.

Keywords in the Ad Copy

The most effective PPC ad will contain actual keywords in the headline, body copy and display URL. Don't use too many keywords in your ad. That would be considered keyword stuffing by the ad networks and your ad will most likely not be displayed. Use a relevant keyword in the headline and another keyword in the ad description.

Some experts believe adding descriptive keywords to display URLs may reduce the number of clicks that your ad gets. The only way for you to know is to create multiple ads testing the addition of a keyword to the display URL. Your results may be different.

Careful Spell Checking

Even a minor typo or spelling error on your ad won't go unnoticed. Many advertisers have fallen victim to simple mistakes and grammatical errors on their ads or landing pages, which have led to them getting fewer clicks and lower conversions. Always double and triple-check your copy and content for errors.

Research Your Competition

Keeping an eye on the type of ads your competition is running will give you ideas for your ads and introduce you to new markets you may have overlooked. To see what ads your competitors are using, visit a search engine and type in one of the keywords you're using for your ads. As you are looking over the ads answer the following questions and take notes:

1. How many competitors are running ads?
2. Do their ads have keywords in them? How many?
3. Which ads stand out from the others?

To speed up this process and get some really detailed intelligence about your competition there are services you can use to analyze the ones you know about and reveal competitors you were not aware of.

- **Ispionage.com:** Uncovers your competitors' strategies, how much they spend on ads, and how you can address your blind spots.

- **SEMRush.com:** Helps you get insights into your competitors' strategies in display advertising, organic and paid search, and link building.

- **SpyFu.com:** Will show you every keyword your competitor has bought on Google Ads, show every ad variation in the last 14 years, and monitor your paid and SEO rankings on the major search engines.

- **Serpstat.com:** Benefit from your competitors' experience in attracting leads through organic and paid search, track your main competitors, and improve your content, as well as your SEO and PPC efforts.

- **Wordtracker.com:** A research tool that will tell you which keywords are most popular based on the keywords you have researched and it will show you differences in results depending on the search engine.

Remember you are not doing your research to copy the competition but to learn from them and incorporate successful techniques into your own PPC campaigns.

Simply choosing the most popular keywords won't translate into clicks and profits. You have to convince people that you can solve their problems and give them what they're looking for. Having an effective ad will do exactly that.

14.7 How to Keep the Cost of PPC from Skyrocketing

One of the things you should strive for when using PPC advertising is to lower the price of your CPC whenever possible. When you first get started with PPC advertising the bid price you pay for your keywords will be based on where you want your ad to appear. It can appear first, last, or somewhere in the middle. As you gain more experience working to optimize your ads and landing pages, you'll be able to see the effects that changes have on campaign cost.

Conversely, if you don't optimize your campaigns, and track and monitor what is going on you'll spend a lot of money, won't get results, and probably stop using PPC believing it's not effective. I don't want that to happen to you.

Here's how you can keep PPC ad cost under control and even lower them:

Understand the Ad Network

It's important to know the rules and best practices of any of the ad networks you want to advertise with. Before joining an ad network make it a point to find out these details:

- Which ad types do they offer, search or display?
- Where will ads be displayed? Search engines, websites, on social media?
- Which ad formats do they specialize in? E-commerce, mobile, text, video, etc.?
- How much does it cost to get started?
- What type of measurable results are available? Clicks, click-throughs, impressions, etc.?
- Can multiple campaigns be created and tested?

Don't Pursue the Wrong Goals

When initially setting up your campaigns you're asked, "What is your goal?" Match your goals with your PPC campaign in order to determine the budget you are willing to spend. The strategy for driving traffic to your website is different than one trying to get more people to opt into a mailing list.

Don't Target the Wrong Audience

All customers are not your customer just like all keywords are not relevant or useful to your campaign. Just because a keyword gets traffic does not mean it's targeted traffic. Don't get lulled into a situation where you're paying for ads that are getting clicks but they are not converting into sales. If this does occur, you can use Google Analytics and your campaign analytics to turn this challenge into an opportunity to determine what part of your campaign needs to be corrected.

Beware of Not Spending Enough

When first starting with PPC many business owners want to minimize their financial risk so they start by investing the minimum amount required by the ad network or just a little bit above that. The challenge with starting that way is they won't spend enough to gather sufficient data to evaluate the performance of their ad campaigns. Their daily budget will be too small and therefore their ad won't be shown enough times.

What happens is when a bid for a keyword is not high enough compared to other advertisers the ad will not be displayed. For example, if the daily budget for the campaign is set to $10, but all the keywords in that campaign have a CPC over $12, you would need a daily budget of $60 to afford to get 5 clicks per day.

The best way to approach using PPC is to manage your expectations when you start. Take time to learn how things work and suspend your need to make a profit immediately. Learn all the ins and outs and treat this time as your initial investment in your digital marketing education.

As you learn how to tweak campaigns you can start to create campaigns with the intention of making a profit. If you happen to make a profit while you are learning that would be a bonus.

Keep Ad Groups Relevant

When creating ads within a group make sure it's relevant to the keywords in that group. Try to have no more than 15 to 20 keywords per ad group to keep them focused. Select only a few long-tail keywords that best define your products or services for a particular demographic. Work on those for a higher chance of converting and stop using the ones that are performing poorly. Use keyword tools to help identify keywords that have a buyer intent (i.e., buy bluetooth headphones online).

Put Restrictions on Your Ads

After your ads have run for a while you will have enough data to make critical decisions to improve the performance of your campaigns. Over time you will be able to determine:

- Which days and times are your ads performing best?
- What devices are people viewing your ad with?
- Which targeted locations are sending traffic and which ones are not?

If there is any aspect of your campaign that is not working change it or stop it. Don't waste money on showing your ad when it's not converting.

Switch from Automatic Bidding to Manual Bidding

Most ad networks have different ways you can bid for your ads. The tactic you choose depends on what is most important to your business. Most businesses want the highest number of clicks, impressions, or views on a video. There are two types of bidding: manual and automatic.

- **Automatic Bidding:** This is the simplest way to bid because you just set your daily budget and the ad network automatically manages your bids to bring you as much engagement as possible. The challenge with automatic bidding is there's no incentive for ad networks to show your ads for the least expensive bid price. Also, if your market suddenly becomes increasingly competitive, you may see a sudden spike in your CPC that will increase the spend of your daily budget.

- **Manual Bidding:** If you know the keywords that you want to use and which are more profitable than others, you can set the maximum bid you would make per click and the ad network will not go above it. Manual bidding gives you control over your budget and you can make changes to your campaign that go into effect immediately. If you have an ad that is getting a lot of impressions but not converting, lower the bid price to save money while you see if you can optimize the ad. The disadvantage with using manual bidding is it takes more time to manage especially when you have a lot of ad groups and keywords to manage.

When starting with PPC using automatic bidding makes setting up a lot faster. But if you start with manual bidding once your campaigns have been optimized and your CPC is favorable, you can switch to automatic bidding so managing them is a lot easier. Whenever changing bidding strategies do it one campaign at a time so it's not overwhelming and you can carefully monitor any effects of the changes.

Improve Quality/Relevancy Score

Quality Score is an estimate used by ad networks to measure the quality of your ads, keywords, and landing pages. The more relevant your ads and landing pages are to the user, the more likely it is that you'll receive higher Quality Scores. Improving all aspects of your ad groups can lead to lower prices and better positioning for your ads.

Improve Landing Page Quality

The landing page you send traffic to for your PPC ad counts for part of the quality score used by ad networks to determine your CPC cost. Your landing page is an extension of your ad so making them similar is beneficial to your campaigns. The more relevant that particular page is to the ad, the lower your CPC.

Steps to making your landing pages relevant to your ad include:

- Having web page elements such as page titles, meta descriptions, headlines and body text that match the keywords used in the referring ad.

- Creating a different landing page for each of your products that have the characteristics just mentioned.

- Making sure they're optimized for viewing on mobile devices for traffic from mobile PPC ads.

- Getting the page ready for visitors by having a clear call to action on it.

- Having contact details about your business especially if you are advertising locally.

Every effort should be made to have a professional-looking landing page that has been checked thoroughly. The page design should be simple, easy to navigate, quick to load, with image links and hyperlinks that are not broken. Use Google Analytics to measure your results, test, and tweak your landing pages to improve their performance.

Many advertisers don't get this part of ad optimization right and end up wasting a lot of money with PPC. When landing pages are not relevant to your ad your bounce rate is likely to increase. So don't deceive prospects by making an offer in your ad like a free trial, and then don't deliver on your promise anywhere on your landing page. It will not only cost you a customer but also potential increases in your CPC rates.

Conduct Split Testing

You can learn about what your audience responds to and improve the performance of your ads by doing split testing. Regarding online marketing split testing (also referred to as A/B testing), it's the activity of driving random traffic to a campaign where two elements are tested to see which one gets better results.

With PPC, the elements that are tested the most are the headline, body text, and destination URL of the ads. Two or more versions of the ad are created where different elements are used in each ad.

For example: two ads are created in an ad group that are exactly the same except for the headlines. Both ads are triggered to show alternately for a particular keyword with each ad getting an equal amount of traffic. Over a predetermined amount of time or impressions, you will be able to determine which ads performed best. Then you can run another split test to check a different element. Even the elements used in landing pages can be tested.

Testing various aspects of your campaigns gives you more opportunities to succeed which in turn can lower your CPC. If you don't test ads, you won't know what's possible and will be stuck paying higher prices for clicks.

Track and Monitor Campaigns

You must pay attention to the performance of your PPC marketing campaigns especially when you are split testing. This will give you an opportunity to optimize them so they're more productive. At the same time, any campaign ad that has not proven effective can be immediately discontinued. You'll be able to put a value on your campaigns and know how much each one is costing you to get conversions.

14.8 What Are the Seven Biggest Challenges with Paid Online Advertising?

Even with all of the positives that paid online advertising has to offer your business there are some disadvantages to using this marketing strategy.

1. **Requires Skill:** While there are aspects to setting up an ad campaign that's easy, online advertising requires a calculated and systematic approach to setting up ads. Knowledge of keywords, bidding, target audience, and competition is required.

2. **Increasing Cost:** As more business owners find out about the benefits of paid online advertising the cost for placing ads is increasing. That's why knowing how to optimize campaigns is critical so you can maintain and possibly reduce the amount you pay.

3. **Larger Competitors:** Depending on the industry you're in and the size of your business you may be at a disadvantage trying to keep pace with bigger businesses that have larger advertising budgets and paid experts managing their campaigns. If the particular type of online advertising you want to do has too much competition or is too expensive, then explore the different kinds of ad formats available. There are enough choices for you to find one and make a profit using it.

4. **Ongoing Cost:** Since your ads only show when you pay for them, the moment you stop they will no longer be displayed. Unlike other marketing online channels, you are paying for immediate placement. That's why it's good to use more than one type of digital marketing strategy to complement this one.

5. **Too Many Choices:** Is it possible that there are too many options? With so many places to advertise and different ways to advertise doing the research is becoming more time-consuming. To keep from being overwhelmed seek the advice of a digital marketing consultant to go over your goals and online marketing needs.

6. **Ad Blockers:** This software is an extension that can be added to most web browsers and will prevent most ads from appearing on web pages. The number of people using them is increasing, not only on desktop computers but also on mobile devices. If a potential customer never sees your ad, then you can't expect to make a sale. To overcome the negative effects of ad blocking, then use native ads. These ads are designed to blend in with the surrounding content making a reader more likely to read and click on it.

7. **Needs Constant Monitoring:** More than other types of digital marketing consistent tracking, analyzing and optimization is necessary in order for a campaign to achieve maximum success. It's easy to overspend and get no results if you don't keep your eyes on what is going on. If you don't have experience, time, or the desire to do this yourself, but want to give the strategy a try then get help. Working with a digital marketing consultant that has experience with online paid advertising is advisable. They'll be

able to get things set up and maintain your account, or immediately point out problems with any existing campaigns you may have. To learn how to hire a web marketing consultant to work with read Chapter 18.

There is no doubt that paid online advertising works, but it requires a commitment to the entire process. Diversifying your web marketing with more long-lasting strategies ensures you are not caught by surprise by any changes in the paid online advertising industry.

Step 4: Implement

Carry Out Your Digital Marketing Strategy

In this section, you will learn what to do after you've reviewed the digital marketing strategies you have at your disposal. After reading Chapter 15 you'll understand the importance of doing market research and how to gather information about your target audience and competitors to use for your campaigns. You'll see why having a marketing budget is so important and how to set a budget. You'll also find out how to tell if your web marketing campaigns are effective or not. Then we will go over some tips for choosing which web strategies to get started with for your campaign(s).

While the focus on this book is on digital marketing it's important to know how to get even more from these high tech strategies you learned about by combining them with low tech strategies your competition often ignore. Chapter 16 reveals three game-changing ways that make your digital marketing even more impactful.

"Vision without action is a daydream.
Action without vision is a nightmare."

–Japanese proverb

15. Key Components and Tips to Start Implementing Your Digital Marketing Strategy

15.1 Why Market Research Matters and What Information Should You Gather?

We're going to shift gears and focus on your target audience. When you have a good understanding of your market, you'll feel a lot more confident in selecting which digital marketing strategy you want to use independently or combine as part of an overall online marketing campaign.

Before starting your marketing campaign, you must conduct some marketing research to gather information about your target market.

With market research you can:

- Identify potential customers
- Understand the needs of your current customers
- Identify problem areas in your business
- Set realistic goals for your business
- Make better decisions about your marketing strategies
- Learn about new market trends
- Discover economic shifts
- Examine the spending traits of your customers
- Use the information in your business plan and marketing plans.

Market research can also be used to find new business opportunities and create marketing campaigns that will focus on the interest of your potential consumers. You can use it to evaluate the progress of your business as well as the performance of your competitors when you monitor them.

Start your research by gathering the following information:

- **Your Ideal Customer:** Decide who you are marketing to based on their gender, geographical location, economics, age, or other demographic. Get even more specific by creating a customer avatar. This is a fictitious character that represents your ideal prospect. Having a customer avatar helps you target the right people.

- **What Are Their Pain Points:** Customer pain points is another way of referring to the problems or challenges that they have You can find out what is troubling your target audience by simply asking them. Contact them via social media or by email. If possible speak to them in person, maybe after they just made a purchase. You can also find this information by reading what they post online.

- **Where They Spend Their Time Online:** Part of building a customer avatar is knowing where they spend most of their time online. Do they spend most of their time on Facebook, YouTube, or a specific industry website? Another way to look at this is how do you expect customers to find your business? Do you expect customers to find you through social media shares, online ads, online directories, search engines, review websites, or some other method? Wherever they are that's where you need to be.

- **Keywords Used by Your Target Audience:** Marketing online is a lot harder and often unsuccessful when you are not aware of the keywords being used by your target audience. Many digital marketing channels rely on knowing what words people are using to search on various websites so campaigns can be targeted, increasing their chances of success. Review Chapter 7.4.2 (How to Choose Keywords for SEO) as a reminder.

- **Trends, News, or Hot Topics You Should Know About:** Keep your finger on the pulse of what's going on in your industry by following any trends or news that will assist you in connecting with your target audience. Social Media is a good way to find out what people are talking about. Use Google Trends to examine search trends dating as far back as 2004. Set up a Google Alert to notify you by email whenever the Google search engine finds new results—such as web pages, newspaper articles, blogs, or scientific research—that match your search term(s).

- **Your Competitors and What Are They Doing:** You need to do some type of competitive analysis on both your current and potential competitors.

> Knowing their strengths and weaknesses gives you an advantage you can use to protect your market share or take some of theirs. Observe which online strategies they're using or not using. How is their audience responding? Are they doing anything successful you can try to emulate?

Market research helps decrease the chances of wasting time and money to a large extent. Before introducing a new product or service, you can identify possible problems and have an opportunity to solve them.

15.2 Eight Business Building Questions You Must Answer That Can Make the Difference Between Your Digital Marketing Success or Failure

After you've done your market research, you'll have a better idea of the potential of your business and the types of goals you'll want to set. But before you begin to set your goals some questions can further narrow down your choice of digital marketing channels. You want to use the ones that are most likely to produce tangible results.

By answering these questions, you are already ahead of the internet marketing game. Instead of rushing into things, your ability to step back and think about how you should approach your goals is key.

Answer the eight questions below and use them to better understand your business and online marketing needs.

1. **Is your target audience aware that your product or service exists?** If you were offering things like "tee shirts" or "DUI lawyer" services, there is already a demand and awareness for these. People know what they're searching for. If your product or service is new and has never been available before or only available locally, you'll need to get the word out.

2. **What problem are you solving?** When you identify the customers that you want to target, determine what their pain points are. Customers want to know what you can do for them and sometimes they don't even know the problem you need them to solve. With this information, you can determine how to reach them and the message that will be most effective for that audience.

3. **How is your product or service unique?** Your customer wants to know the best features of your product and what makes your product stand out from the rest. When you identify this, you can construct the best marketing message.

4. **Is your sales cycle long or short?** A short sales cycle is if you have a product or service that people would purchase with very little research. The features and benefits are easily communicated. This usually consists of inexpensive offers like shampoo or haircuts.

   A long sales cycle is for a product or service that customers need to see repeatedly over a time before they decide to make a purchase. There is a lot of information available about the offer and customers may have a lot of technical questions. These are mostly going to be expensive offers like rental property or plastic surgery.

5. **Do you need to make repeat sales?** If your business relies on repeat business from existing customers, you need to stay in contact with them. You must remind them that they need your product or service again.

6. **Is your marketing budget large or small?** If you have a small marketing budget, the channels you can work with will be limited. So, choosing the right one is important since you really can't afford to experiment. With a larger marketing budget, you'll have more options but that doesn't mean you should frivolously advertise on multiple channels. You should still be diligent in selecting strategies that are not risky for your type of business.

7. **What is your Customer Acquisition Cost (CAC)?** This is a measurement of the cost for converting a potential lead into a customer. This metric is used to determine how profitable a business is by dividing all the costs spent on acquiring more customers (marketing expenses) by the number of new customers acquired in the period the money was spent.

   For example, let's say your company spent $3,000 on marketing in a quarter and acquired 100 customers within that same period of time, your CAC is $30 [$3000 / 100 = $30].

   This is a simplified version of the formula and there are different ones based on the type of business you have and the industry you are in. Use this metric to help to pick your marketing channels by measuring the CAC for each one you implement.

8. **What is the Lifetime Value (LTV) of your customer?** This metric represents the total gross profit that your business will take in over the course of your entire relationship with a customer. LTV gives you an idea of how much money you should be investing in customer acquisition by showing you how much value you can expect from a single customer over time.

   Before calculating LTV there are a few variables you need to know:

   - **Average Value of Sale:** This is the average value of a customer transaction.

   - **Number of Transactions:** The average number of transactions a customer makes during a particular time period (i.e., one year).

   - **Average Customer Lifespan:** This is the amount of time a business typically retains each customer.

   There are multiple ways to calculate LTV, here is one method:

   Let's say a software company charges $25 per month for customers to use its program, and the average length of the time a customer uses the software is two years. The lifetime value is calculated as LTV = $25 x 12 (months/transactions) x 2 (years) = $600. This number does not take into account the cost to acquire the customer which needs to be subtracted to get the final value.

   You can use the LTV figure to estimate your future cash flow and to find out how many customers you will need for your business to become profitable.

15.3 Set Marketing Goals to Help Decide Which Strategies to Use

You already know the importance of setting goals for your business. Having a clear set of goals, you want to achieve through the implementation of your marketing strategies will help in choosing the right channel for your business. After doing your market research and answering the 8 business-building questions some of the goals you can target are:

Increase Sales: Bringing in more money to your business is always a top priority. Especially if your business is new, where sales growth is especially important.

Determine where you want the increase to come from. (i.e., a specific product or service; online vs. offline.)

Improve Conversion Rate: Focus on getting more people to buy from you whenever they are exposed to your marketing and content. You don't want them to see just your offer, you want them to make a purchase.

Increase Targeted Traffic: You don't want to spend time or money on driving traffic to your website if it's not going to generate sales or leads. You want to focus on getting visitors to your site that are actually interested in what you offer. Get control over where they come from.

Retain Customers: If your business depends on repeat sales then you'll need a strategy that will convince existing customers to keep buying at a more predictable and quicker rate.

Increase Customer Interaction: Encourage and monitor conversations about your business. Ask for reviews, feedback, likes, shares, follows, subscribers, etc. Increasing engagement makes it easier to achieve other goals.

These are just examples of goals to set. Your goals should be based on the specific needs of your business.

After having defined your goal, you'll have better insight into which marketing channel(s) to use. You might have to use more than one channel to reach your objectives, so be prepared to prioritize. Make sure your goals are SMART (specific, measurable, achievable, relevant and time-bound).

15.4 Why You Must Have a Budget for Digital Marketing

Whether you run a small business or a big corporation, online marketing is essential to your profitability and growth. Yet many small businesses don't allocate enough money to marketing or, worse, spend it haphazardly. A marketing budget is a guide to ensure that you are staying on target with estimated costs vs. the actual costs. Not only does it help you manage your costs, but it also helps you determine whether your profit goals are within reach and keeps you on the right track from month to month.

When you have a budget and you're committed to it . . .

- You're forced to measure the progress of your business. You have a basis for assessing actual results.
- It gives you and your sales department measurable targets.
- It causes you to focus on specific marketing strategies based on objectives.
- It makes you look for additional sources of revenue (i.e., new product/service, market segment, or price point).
- You can allocate scarce financial resources more effectively.

15.4.1 Six Crucial Considerations for Setting Your Online Marketing Budget

Here are some factors to consider when determining your digital marketing budget for the coming year.

1. Do you currently have an online presence? If you currently don't have an online presence and need to complete the Acquire step of the BASIC process, you'll need to allocate more money to your budget than if you were partially or fully up and running online.

2. How long have you been in business? Your online marketing budget will be influenced by how long you've been in business. In your first year, you'll want to allocate your online budget differently than you will in later years. In year one, you may need to spend most of your online marketing budget on foundational things like your website. Within the first five years of your business, ramp up the marketing efforts in order to grow your business fast. Once your business becomes established you may be able to cut back on your marketing budget.

3. Who are your customers? If you are selling to consumers rather than businesses, you will likely spend more on your marketing efforts. When you are selling to consumers you have a wider audience to reach with your marketing operations to get to all your customers. When you're selling to a business, you can be more targeted. There will be more consumers that you need to reach versus the number of businesses you need to market to.

4. What can you afford? For a company that is bootstrapping, the type of business they're in will determine their budget differently from a company that is starting with a seemingly endless supply of cash. Companies that are bootstrapping look at it as what they can afford versus how much they

devote to online marketing. Luckily a lot of the online marketing efforts are free for people that do need to bootstrap.

5. How much of your budget is devoted to online marketing? A lot of medium and small-size companies are choosing to spend a significant amount of their marketing budget on web marketing because there is a greater return on investment. You can cast a wider net with online marketing efforts and have a larger impact on your audience. Large companies have the resources to spend on print and broadcast marketing, along with digital marketing. If you have the financial resources, then incorporate online marketing into your plans.

6. What were the results of past efforts? If you were in business last year what online marketing strategies did you invest your money in? Which were successful and which ones failed? Which one showed potential and you would try again? If a strategy was effective in the past, perhaps you should increase the efforts you put into that channel.

15.4.2 How Much Should You Budget for Your Marketing?

Based on the research and expert opinions, marketing budgets should be determined by how old the business is.

- For a business that has been operating for less than five years, it is suggested that 12 to 20 percent of gross revenue or estimated revenue is used on marketing. If your business is less than a year old, you'll need to invest more in order to get things started.

- For those businesses that have been operating for more than five years and are known by customers in their market, it is recommended that 6 to 12 percent of your gross revenue or estimated revenue is allocated to your budget.

Another budget recommendation comes from the US Small Business Administration (SBA.gov):

As a general rule, **small businesses with revenues less than $5 million should allocate 7–8 percent of their revenues to marketing. This percentage also assumes you have margins in the range of 10–12 percent** (after you've covered your other expenses, including marketing). If your margins are lower than this, then you might consider eating more of the costs of doing business by lowering your overall margins and allocating additional spending to marketing. It's a tough call, but your marketing budget should never be based on just what's left over once all your other business expenses are covered.

Typically, the smaller your business is the larger of a percentage you will need to invest above this range to make any type of meaningful impact in your market. Below is a chart of what a 7% to 10% annual marketing budget looks like for businesses of varying size:

Total Revenue	7%	8%	9%	10%
$25,000	$1,750	$2,000	$2,250	$2,500
$50,000	$3,500	$4,000	$4,500	$5,000
$100,000	$7,000	$8,000	$9,000	$10,000
$250,000	$17,500	$20,000	$22,500	$25,000
$500,000	$35,000	$40,000	$45,000	$50,000
$750,000	$52,500	$60,000	$67,500	$75,000
$1,000,000	$70,000	$80,000	$90,000	$100,000

Remember that your spending does not need to be fixed. You should be ready to change it at a moment's notice. Definitely give yourself time to see if your strategy is working. But if it's not, or if one strategy is working remarkably better, update your plan to focus on the tactics that work. It's good to review your budget and your results on a monthly basis. Make sure your spending and your tactics are actually achieving results.

Keep in mind that if your business is new and you are trying to gain a share of the market it is going to be more expensive. But once your business becomes established you can decrease the amount you spend on marketing.

You can visit the Small Business Administration (SBA.gov) for more guidelines and information.

15.5 What Are the Four Main Reasons Why You Need to Measure the Effectiveness of Your Web Marketing Campaigns?

Once you've started an online marketing campaign, you'll need to monitor its performance. You can't have a "set-it-and-forget-it" mentality. Instead, you need to remember these four crucial reasons why routinely performing campaign analysis is needed.

1. Online marketing can be a big expense for your business, so you want to make sure you get a return on your investment.

2. You need to confirm your campaign has hit its overall objectives.

3. You must gain insights into your consumers and their behaviors so you can use that information in future campaigns.

4. Knowing what's going on in your campaign gives you the ability to make informed decisions in the present and future.

15.5.1 Three Terms You Should Know before You Start Measuring Your Campaigns

In your web marketing campaign, a measurement you track can be the number of sales made or leads generated. But until you start analyzing your data and making comparisons, they're just numbers.

There are three terms you should be familiar with before we continue talking about measuring your campaigns.

1. **Benchmarking:** Is comparing your company's success against how it performed in previous campaigns, time periods, or competitors.

2. **Forecasting:** Is an estimate or prediction of future developments in business such as sales, expenditures, and profits.

3. **Key Performance Indicators (KPIs):** Are your company's measurable goals that are associated with your online marketing strategy.

Metrics are important because they give a numerical snapshot of the performance of your campaign and can help with benchmarking and forecasting. They are used to track and access the status of a business. While they may seem similar, there's a difference between business metrics and KPIs. Metrics offer a historical look at what took place, but they don't identify what future actions to take. KPIs on the other hand specifically target certain areas to measure, predict performance, and give insight on what to do next.

For example, a metric may monitor the number of leads acquired compared to a set goal, whereas a KPI would monitor how many leads contributed to increased sales. A metric becomes a KPI when it leads to a specific action.

KPIs are more than just statistical data, they add detail to your analysis, so using ratios and percentages often makes better KPIs than just raw numbers

15.5.2 How to Measure the Effectiveness of Your Web Marketing Campaigns in Seven Steps

Measuring the results of an online marketing campaign has several steps that are involved. Here's an easy way for you to do it.

Step #1: Start with a Well-Planned Campaign
Identify and set your business objectives

- Have the information from your market research available
- Use your answers from the Eight Business Building Questions in Chapter 15.3
- Refer to the keyword list you made for your business
- Gather details from past and present marketing campaigns.

Step #2: Set Targets for Each of Your Business Objectives
Once you've identified your business objectives set specific goals for each one. For further impact from your campaign choose a specific demographic to target.

Step #3: Select the Channels You Want to Use
Identify and pick the channels that can best achieve the results of your business objectives.

Step #4: Set Your Budget Accordingly
Calculate how much you are going to commit spending on digital marketing. Remember you may need to allocate more money than anticipated if your business has just started or is relatively new.

Step #5: Identify Your Key Performance Indicators

- By tracking the right KPIs for your business, you'll be able to make more educated marketing decisions. Each channel has their own metrics that can be converted to KPIs. Here are some standard KPIs you can establish for your campaign along with how they are calculated:

- Online Marketing Return on Investment—evaluates the performance of the campaign.

$$\text{ROI} = \frac{\text{revenue generated by the campaign} - \text{total cost of campaign}}{\text{total cost of campaign}} \text{ X } 100$$

- **Conversion Rate:** measure the percentage of visitors to your website that takes a desired action.

  - **Lead Generation:** (number of leads collected / unique website visitors) * 100 = Lead Generation Rate

  - **Lead Conversion:** (number of new customers / number of leads) * 100 = Lead Conversion Rate

  - **Sales Conversion:** (number of sales / number of visitors * 100 = Sales Conversion Rate

- **Click-Through Rate (CTR):** the ratio of users who click on a specific link to the number of total users who view a page, email, or advertisement. (number of click-throughs / number of impressions) * 100 = CTR

- **% of Sales from Digital Marketing:** calculate total amount of revenue generated by the campaign; (revenue generated by the campaign) / (total sales) = % of Sales

- Customer acquisition cost (CAC) and lifetime value (LTV) are also good KPIs to track.

- Set numerical targets and timeframes for your KPIs.

Step #6: Use Software Tools to Track and Report Campaign Data

- In order to track your metrics and KPIs efficiently, you'll need analytics software. Without it, the job would be too tedious (or almost impossible)

to do manually. You can only manage what you measure, so track all of your metrics for future analysis.

Understanding the data you collect is a lot easier when using an analytics dashboard. This is software that creates charts and graphs from the metrics that are most important to you. All of the details are available to view on the same screen making it much faster and easier to review.

• Here is a list tools used for tracking and reporting:

  • **Cyfe.com** is an all-in-one business dashboard app that helps you easily monitor all your business data from one place (e.g. social media, analytics, marketing, sales, support, etc.).

  • **GoogleAnalytics.com** is a free and enterprise analytics tool to measure website, app, digital and offline data to gain customer insights.

  • **GoSquared.com** is the fastest way to grab simple, easy-to-understand reports on your website traffic. From visitor numbers to traffic sources, to trending hot content, GoSquared makes it easy to report on the metrics you need.

  • **Hootsuite.com** tracks your social media engagement and performance through various analytics reports. Hootsuite analytic reports are flexible and customizable, giving you the ability to decide which metrics are most important for your business.

  • **HubSpot.com** measures both the quantity and quality of traffic you're getting to your website as a whole, or on a page-by-page basis. Analyze how each of your pages is performing in terms of views, keywords, and inbound links, and identify which traffic sources bring in the most visits, contacts, and customers over time.

  • **SocialBakers.com** has comprehensive social media analytics with accurate competitive and industry benchmarking, best-in-class reporting, customizable dashboards and easy multi-channel publishing.

• When choosing software track and measure your data follow these tips:

• Sign up for a free demo so you can try it out before you buy.

- Choose software that monitors more than one channel.

- The program must be able to analyze individual customer behavior, not just raw stats.

- Get the one that's easy for you to use and understand.

Step #7: Make Adjustments Based on the Results

As you analyze your KPIs frequently you'll begin to recognize adjustments that you can make to your online marketing campaign. Once you've gathered enough data, take immediate action and don't wait to make changes. If your campaign is not having success roll up your sleeves and figure out why. If things are going well identify the cause and attempt to duplicate it in future campaigns. Use the information to:

- Add or remove marketing channels
- Adjust your budget
- Make changes to your offers, etc.

15.6 Choosing The Right Digital Marketing Channel for Your Business

No matter what type of online marketing channel you use remember to think of digital marketing as a marathon, not a sprint. Don't skip any of the suggestions discussed in this chapter and use the details you learned about your target audience and your business to get crystal clear about what results you want to achieve.

Review the following tips and consider them when deciding which digital marketing strategy you want to use in your campaigns:

Start Slowly: When it is time for you to start your own campaign don't try to use too many online marketing channels at once. Being too aggressive can cause you to lose a lot of money very quickly. You'll learn from each campaign you build and increase your understanding of how things work.

Get Your Feet Wet: Succeeding with online marketing means you'll need to familiarize yourself with the processes. So, whenever you see any form of online advertising or marketing that resembles a strategy you want to try then test it out. Take time to learn the customer experience for PPC, mobile, and video ads by clicking on them. Investigate what happens when you submit your email on a lead generation web page. Study the communication that you get. Determine what you like or don't like about the experience. How persuasive are other businesses when it comes to getting prospects to convert into paying customers?

Be Flexible and Scalable: From the beginning, you should keep in mind that your goal eventually will be to grow your company. You want to consider where you will be able to outsource to allow for fast, yet controllable growth. What jobs can you hand off to other people to free up your time to focus on the important things that can only be done by you?

Follow Your Audience: Don't assume they will always follow you or know where to find you. You must continuously go where they are and keep track of the people that they follow and listen to.

Don't Just Copy: If you are going to be doing your own marketing don't choose a channel you won't enjoy doing. Just because a certain channel may seem like it's working for others doesn't mean you should do it too. If you like watching videos but hate making them because you're bad at it, then don't do video marketing. Pick channels that you are comfortable with and hire someone else to do the others.

The digital marketing channels you select will also help determine the budget that you will set aside for implementing campaigns. Both selecting a strategy and setting a budget depend on each other.

15.6.1 How Do Digital Marketing Channels Compare to One Another

Depending on the type of business you have, and the goal that was set, some strategies work better than others. Use this comparison chart as a guide in your channel selection.

CHANNEL	CHARACTERISTICS						
	Flexible Spending	Sales Cycle	Easy to Implement	Allows Engagement	Increase Awareness	Lead Gen	Speed of Results
Content Marketing	✓	Both	✓	✓	✓	✓	Depends
SEO		Short				✓	
Local Search Marketing	✓		✓	✓		✓	
Online Reputation Management				✓	✓		
Mobile Marketing		Short		✓	✓	✓	✓
Email Marketing	✓	Long	✓	✓			
Social Media Marketing	✓	Both	✓	✓	✓	✓	✓
Video Marketing		Both	Depends	✓	✓	✓	✓
Paid Online Advertising	✓	Both			Depends	✓	✓

Definition of Characteristics:

- Flexible Spending: Cost can be modified during the campaign.
- Sales Cycle: Select the channel that best fits with the sales cycle of your offer.
- Easy to Implement: Doesn't require a lot of technical skill.
- Allows Engagement: Audience is able to easily give feedback.
- Increase Awareness: Use when you want to get a message out quickly.
- Lead Gen: Use to generate leads.
- Speed of Results: Results from campaign can be noticed in a short period of time.

The reason some strategies have "depends" for their characteristics is that their effectiveness will be determined by how they are used.

Continue to become very familiar with these comparisons, so you can take action on your own or to easily communicate what you need to any digital marketing professional.

15.7 Should You Hire Someone to Run Your Online Marketing Campaigns?

This should be determined by your availability and commitment to perform the tasks needed to make your online marketing campaigns successful. Do you know how to perform the necessary tasks? Can you learn if you don't know how? Do you really want to do them? If you don't have the desire, time or technical resources to market your product or service you must hire someone to do all of the work for you.

This is a wise decision even if you are currently a highly respected thought leader in your industry. You'll never reach your full potential if you don't have time to create content, build a following online, or find more ways to speak in front of your target audience. Hiring a digital marketer to manage your campaigns positively positions your business and gives you the time to achieve maximum success.

Another reason to hire a professional is the fact that things change fast within digital marketing channels, consumer preferences evolve, and social media networks come and go. A digital marketing strategist stays up to date with such trends and will help you navigate them.

Hiring a consultant is a decision you must consider. Calculate the time and money it will take for you to do the work yourself and compare it to a digital marketing consultant's fee. Consultants are usually the more cost-effective choice.

"Successful people do what unsuccessful people are not willing to do. Don't wish it were easier; wish you were better."

– Jim Rohn, entrepreneur, author and motivational speaker

16. Ideas to Supercharge Your Digital Marketing

16.1 Three Ways to Significantly Increase Your Chances of Succeeding with Digital Marketing

Knowing what online marketing strategies to use is a tremendous advantage for your business. But what will really make them work is your ability to make your business unique and stand out from your competition. In this chapter, I'm going to discuss the 3 ways to make you and your business stand out so you can increase the success you have using online marketing.

The three ways are:

1. Branding
2. Becoming an authority, and
3. Being a Storyteller

16.2 What Is Branding?

Branding is what identifies your business and sets it apart from your competition. Consumers experience certain emotions or ideas associated with a company or a product whether good or bad; this opinion is fostered by the branding of the company.

Example of some successful brands are:

- Amazon
- Apple
- BMW
- Disney
- McDonald's

These companies are recognizable because they have strong branding.

Many different elements play a role in the branding of your business. Let's examine some of the prominent variables that impact branding.

Business Name: This name should be easy to pronounce and spell. You don't want people to have a hard time spelling the name every time they refer a friend to your business. A complicated name is not easy to remember. Especially if it's used as the domain name for your website.

Colors: The colors you use in your logo or on items that represent your company can play a significant role in your branding efforts. For example, the ketchup and mustard red and yellow of the McDonald's sign are known around the world. Brand colors improve recognition by over 80%.

Logo Font: The font that you use anytime your company name is seen in print can also impact how memorable your brand is for consumers. For example, Disney's font is very distinguishable. They use their font on everything they create.

Packaging: Companies use unique packaging as part of their branding. It helps customers to differentiate one brand from another when they see packaging that has the name, logo, and color scheme of the company.

Messaging: Brand messaging is the usage of verbal and written statements that quickly describe how you're different and what you do. Brand messaging can be used in elevator speeches, marketing material, press releases, taglines, slogans, and mission statements.

Examples of brand messaging in taglines:

- **Kay Jewelers:** "Every Kiss begins with Kay"
- **M&M:** "Melts in your mouth, not in your hands"
- **Subway:** "eat fresh."

16.2.1 Five Reasons Why Branding Is Important for Your Business

1. **It's Valuable**
   Effective branding can be a very valuable asset to a company. When someone wants to invest in an existing business, they have a far better chance of succeeding with that business if it already had exceptional branding before they made their investment. Consumers are already following and buying from well-branded companies, and that is why branding adds value to a

business. Eighty-two percent of investors want the companies they invest in to have a strong brand.

2. **Provides Recognition**
   Recognition is advantageous to a company because people gravitate to products or businesses that they are familiar with. Customers are more likely to use a company they trust when it is well branded and recognizable.

3. **Brings in New Customers**
   Great branding produces great referrals. When people are happy with a service, they tell their friends. For example, if someone recommends the services of a company like Amazon you instantly know what company they are talking about. This is because of their record of accomplishment and their branding practices.

4. **Generates Trust**
   Brand trust is a valuable intangible business asset. A company that establishes itself as professional, experienced, informative, and reliable gains trust within the marketplace.

5. **Employee Pride**
   When employees work for a company with strong branding, they develop pride in the company. That pride directly impacts their work ethic. In addition to wanting to work hard for the company, they will also spread the word about that company to their friends and family.

16.2.2 How to Build a Unique and Memorable Brand

When your branding is strong it will make it easier to promote your business. The trust gained from branding has such a strong impact that given the choice of two products, the consumer is willing to pay more for a product that has better branding. They are willing to go out of their way to get that brand. Great branding leads the consumer to believe they cannot live without that brand. It is easier for the company to sell their product when the product is backed by superior branding. Apple is a good example of this.

Ultimately people want to do business with companies they know, like, and trust. Strong brands are able to meet those requirements. There are several things you can do to build a strong brand online. I've broken them down into 3 phases so you can spend your time on the activities that complement and support each other.

Phase #1: How to Build Your Brand Awareness So Customers Know You

When people can identify your brand, this is a sign that you have been successful with building brand awareness. The more places your brand is seen, the more aware people are of your brand. Consistent branding across multiple platforms increases revenue by up to 23 percent. When they can find you on Facebook, Twitter, and YouTube the knowledge of your company is going to stick with them long term when it is seen repeatedly over a period of time.

- **Have a Unique Website Design:** When you make an excellent first impression on customers they feel a connection with you. You want people to see professionalism when they first see your website—while standing out from your competitors.

- **Optimize Your Website:** Ensure that your website is easy to find in the search engines for customers. A strong web presence is important in a day and time when there is an abundance of competition online. This is where SEO and the other digital marketing strategies come into play.

- **Get a Logo:** Your logo can be the first thing that people notice about your business. Therefore, it is important to have a well-designed logo that is memorable. Sometimes a simple logo is all you need. Often those are the cleanest and most unforgettable. It's important that you use the same logo throughout your online and offline marketing so that the image sticks with the customer and they don't get confused.

- **Create a Memorable Tagline:** A tagline is a repeated phrase, idiom, saying or expression that tells customers what your business is all about. As part of your brand messaging its purpose is to become synonymous with your company. The most effective taglines tell people the benefits of your services or products. I would recommend making this short to make it easy to remember. For example, when you say, "Just Do It," people know immediately that you are referring to Nike. You want people to be able to recall your company easily. A tagline helps accomplish this.

- **Write a Press Release:** This is an inexpensive method to get your company's name out there to make an impact on your branding. Not only will you be able to share newsworthy events and activities involving your business, but your press release may also get indexed in the search engines and bring additional exposure to your business.

Phase #2: Build Your Brand Appeal So Customers Like You

Once you've made people aware of your brand, you'll need to start working on getting them to like you. This is a lot easier to do today because of the ability to connect with people online. Customers want to feel like they can connect with you on a personal level. If they feel like they can do that, they'll feel more comfortable doing business with you. Customers who have an emotional connection with a brand have over a 300% higher lifetime value (LTV), stay with a brand for an average of 5.1 years vs. 3.4 years, and will recommend brands at a much higher rate (71% vs. 45%).

While continuing to build your brand, start working on making your business more likeable.

- **Create an "About" web page:** In Chapter 4.10 we learned the 12 Essential Features Your Website Needs. Another web page you can add to your website to build your brand is an "About Me/Us" page. You can use it to communicate who you are and the purpose of your business using text, photos, and videos. Focus on your brand and show visitors how they can benefit from what you offer and what you can do for them.

- **Use Social Media Connections:** Remember to add your social media accounts to your website so people have a chance to connect with you in this way as well. Thirty-seven percent of users will stick with a brand if they are part of a community. Try to determine which channels your target audience is most likely to be spending their time on. If you were talking to only business owners and certified professionals, you will certainly want to get on LinkedIn and Facebook at the very least.

- **Create Videos:** A business that is publishing videos is going to be more visible to customers and more memorable. When people can see your face or hear your voice while you show beneficial material on their screens, they'll begin to connect with you. When customers feel a connection with you, they are more likely to contact your company.

  Using videos, you can share your business values and create a likability for yourself and your business.

Phase #3: Build Your Brand Credibility So Customers Trust You

Based on the cost of a transaction a customer would prefer to interact with an individual rather than a faceless corporation or website. Branding can help you establish your online presence and give the consumer confidence in working with you. Finding ways to show you are reliable is another factor that plays into whether a client will work with you or not. If you have established trust in your brand people will be more likely to buy from you. As you're working on getting known and being liked, start doing things that will make you more trusted.

- **Create Compelling Content:** 46% of a brand's image comes from what they say, and how they say it. The best content is well written yet informative providing solutions to problems. Creating content should be a consistent staple of your online branding.

- **Offer Unique Freebies:** As your customers benefit from your compelling content adding free offers into the mix will increase that trust. Providing free offers like the ones mentioned in Chapter 11.6 creates an opportunity to obtain your customer's contact details such as their email address. You can begin communicating with your audience outside of your website or social media pages once you have their permission to use it.

- **Be Consistent:** Keep your brand messaging consistent. The messages that you use in any printed and digital marketing communication should be the same as what's used with an "in-person" experience you would have with customers.

- **Be Yourself:** Remember to be yourself when you're working on all phases of building your brand. You will not enjoy the process if you are pretending to be somebody you're not. When you're not enjoying what you do, it's difficult to remain consistent and perform necessary branding tactics long term or at a high level. When your audience knows that you are being yourself this becomes another factor in your audience's ability to trust. Remember no one can duplicate you.

Branding makes a huge impact on how people perceive your company. Successful branding makes it easier for customers to remember your business, products and services. If they have a good experience with you, they will be more likely to remember you, buy from your business and share their positive experience with others.

16.3 Why You Must Be an Authority in Your Industry

Becoming an authority in your industry is a great way to serve your customers and promote your business. As an authority and industry leader, potential clients will seek you out for your knowledge. When you demonstrate and share your expertise the path to profits becomes easier.

While there are advantages to being an authority it shouldn't be your sole objective. When you have a passion for developing your industry, there are things to gain from your contributions. If you are passionate about your business and your industry, then take the necessary time and effort to become an authority.

Before I discuss the ways you can become an expert, it is important to focus on why you should be aiming towards this goal.

You'll Become Highly Sought After: People want to meet experts. Peers in your industry will want to share ideas and explore ways you can work together in joint ventures. Talented and motivated individuals will want to work for you. You'll become a lot more attractive to traditional and new media outlets that constantly need experts to interview.

Your Opportunities Increase: When you are widely known new avenues begin to open for you. More people want to hire you. For example, if you currently speak in front of small groups your name will spread and if you market yourself correctly you could eventually speak at conferences and draw larger audiences.

Growing on Social Media Gets Easier: As you get more exposure people will follow the links that lead to your social media profiles. The desire to connect with you will bring more comments, likes and subscribers.

Search Engines Show You More Love: As more people search for you online and share your content, search engines will view you as a relevant resource and move your web pages and social media entries to the top of the results pages.

You'll Make More Money: The more name recognition, experience, and authority you have the more people will be willing to pay for your offers. You can command a higher price for your time. If you have multiple streams of income, more sales will be made.

The Sales Cycle Shortens: As an authority, you'll have the credibility that customers look for when they're deciding to work with you. This decision time is decreased as your credibility increases.

Now You Can Say "No": You won't have to settle for less when selling your products or services. Now you get to choose who you work with. Drop any services and products that you don't enjoy doing or aren't profitable. You get to be pickier about where, when, why, and for how much you will work.

You'll Have the Competitive Edge: Most of your competition are not authorities and have no aspiration to become an authority. Their laziness gives you an advantage. There is less of an urgency to compete with others in your field. You have the name recognition that others in your industry are struggling to acquire. You'll resonate with the customers you are targeting so there will be no feeling of desperation when it is time to search for new prospects.

Professional Accomplishment: Once you begin to hit the milestones you set for yourself as an authority, you'll start to feel a level of professional accomplishment. Becoming an authority takes a lot of work and some sacrifice. But once you start getting the recognition and rewards it will be well worth it.

16.3.1 How to Become an Authority Your Clients Know, Like and Trust

There's a mix of self-promotional strategies available for you to choose from when you decide to become an expert. Each strategy can be chosen based upon needs, available time and resources. I recommended incorporating more than one of the following methods in order to achieve a diversified promotional mix transforming almost anyone from a novice into an expert.

These methods of promotion are used by professionals and businesses to establish, grow, and maintain their status. A true expert can find value in all of the following strategies. Methods that can be new and exciting for you.

Create a "Signature Process"

A signature process is a specific set of instructions or steps created by you that will get your clients the results they're looking for easily and quickly. I created my BASIC signature process to take a complicated topic (Digital Marketing) and break it down into a series of steps. When followed, those steps will lead to a better understanding of what small business owners need to do when using the internet to market their business.

Creating your own signature process does the following:

- Demonstrates that you understand your area of expertise enough to simplify it and make it easier to understand.

- Quickens the implementation of other self-promotion strategies.
- You can incorporate your process into your branding.
- It creates another way to separate you from your competition.

While your competitors are trying to do the same thing everyone else is doing, you'll be promoting your own process. When a potential client asks you what makes you different or why should I hire you, you'll be able to quickly explain your method and how it will help them.

Here's a quick overview of how to name your signature process:

1. Identify the problem your target audience wants solved or the benefit they want to experience.

2. Think of a 4 or 5-letter word that best represents the solution or benefit. That will become an acronym for your signature process. The word should be powerful, meaningful, and memorable to your process.

3. Then think of a relevant word for each part of your process that corresponds with each letter of the acronym.

Another example is the process of making SMART goals. SMART goals are ones that are: Specific, Measurable, Attainable, Realistic, and Time-bound.

Your signature process helps your target audience understand all of the information about you, your products, and your services. It cuts through the noise and communicates who you are and what you do in a very memorable way.

Write a Book

Writing a book is a powerful way to establish yourself as an expert in your market and gain credibility. Just think about it, the ability to capture your accumulated knowledge and wisdom in an organized way for people to follow is very impressive. Most people assume authors who write books are experts so there is an instant status that comes with achieving this accomplishment. Your book should solve the biggest challenges your target audience has. It doesn't have to be a long book. Ten chapters with ten pages per chapter is a good start.

A published book is also one of the best marketing tools you could ever have. It will easily separate you from the competition and consistently show what you stand for, what you are good at, and why people should listen to you and purchase your products or services. Used as a lead generator a book will make you more money from the sale of the other products and services you offer.

Become a Professional Speaker

While it can be intimidating public speaking a good way to improve communication skills, confidence and further personal development. The ability to speak in front of a live audience and hold their attention is a very powerful and useful skill that positions you as an authority. Speakers are always in demand because companies and organizations constantly need new and fresh messages delivered to their live audiences.

If you're interested in getting started with this method of self-promotion start by writing an interesting description for one or more presentations in your field of expertise. Choose a subject then create a simple outline for it. You can start out by presenting on teleseminars and webinars. Then try out your presenting skills in live settings like adult education schools, networking groups and churches. As you gain more experience you can move up to bigger venues.

Get Media Interviews

Being viewed as an authority could not be more solidified than when being introduced as the expert on a radio or TV talk show. When a guest appears on a talk show they don't get on there by chance. Especially if they are a frequent guest. Similar to the need for public speakers, TV and radio show producers are constantly looking for guests for their programs. They want people that have something of value to add to the segment and will keep their audience interested.

Most producers of popular shows won't risk putting on an expert that has not done many podcast, radio, or TV talk show interviews. If you need to get experience, you can start by doing interviews on podcasts. To get on a radio or TV talk show, or podcast, contact the producer. You can usually find their contact information on the show's website. Here are a few internet radio show / podcast resources:

- BlogTalkRadio.com
- InterviewGuestsDirectory.com
- RadioGuestList.com
- WomensRadio.com

Find Joint Venture (JV) Partners

If you want to quickly boost your credibility and audience size connect with others who are already reaching your target market. Explore ways you can work together on short-term projects that can develop into long-term relationships.

One possible arrangement is the use of your JV partner's customer database to promote your products and services. In return, your partner may want a portion of the sales you make and the ability to make offers to your current and future customers. JV partners also benefit from being able to join forces in making purchases, exchanging resources, and sharing in research and development.

Potential JV partners include corporations, associations, organizations, small businesses, and current industry experts.

Implement the Web Marketing Strategies You Learned

Make sure you implement the strategies you learned about from previous chapters. Video marketing, email marketing, social media, and the various forms of content marketing can be used to further establish your authority.

Becoming an authority by using the methods just discussed, will differentiate you in a crowded market. That differentiation combined with your valuable knowledge will create a successful brand for you. As a bonus, all of these methods can be fun and build confidence.

16.4 Why Should You Use Storytelling in Your Marketing?

Humans are emotional creatures. They are drawn into stories as a form of communication because they can emotionally connect the characters and situations within a story.

Your personal and company story answers who, what, when, where, why, and how.

As a marketing strategy, storytelling allows you to sell without selling. It captivates listeners and it's a great way to hold their attention. Instead of trying to process statistics, data, and information stories helps your audience to grasp your points quickly.

16.4.1 How Do Stories Help Your Business Grow?

By telling the story about you and your business, you explain to customers how you're going to help them solve a problem. When you show them how you can help them achieve their goals the way that you achieved yours, they will join your journey and rally behind your cause.

Here are some additional reasons for telling your story:

- **Stories Are a Non-Threatening Method of Persuading Your Audience**
  A story is a gentler way to get your message across without the reader feeling pressured by the message. They can visualize the scenario. With an honest story, your reader is encouraged to trust you. When people can trust you, they are more likely to become a customer.

- **Consumers Can Experience Your Product or Service before Trying It**
  With a story, people begin to picture themselves using your product or service being described. The visualization allows them to connect with your offer.

- **You Can Gain Social Media Shares**
  The more your story resonates with the reader, the more likely they are to want to share the story with family and friends on social media.

- **Stories Are Memorable**
  When people emotionally connect with your stories, they are more likely to remember your story and therefore your message. It's easy to forget a name, but a good story is unforgettable.

- **Storytelling Can Work for Everyone**
  The great thing about storytelling is that you can use this strategy in any niche. You simply need imagination and creativity. If you don't have those two things, you can easily outsource the task.

When your stories take center stage, they're another tool for setting your business apart from the other businesses.

16.4.2 Effective Storytelling Tips

In order for your target audience to form a personal connection with you and your business, your stories must be authentic, creative and inspirational. So, before you develop your story, figure out how your products and services help your customers.

- What problems do they solve?
- What features do your offers have that are not available or offered by other products?
- What sets your company apart from your competition?

When you answer these questions, you can easily go through the process of creating your story.

Structure your story as you would a paper in school or a piece of fiction writing. Have a clear beginning, middle, and end. In the beginning, you want to establish the characters and introduce your story to the reader. In the middle of the story, you should go into the character's dilemma.
The end, of course, resolves the dilemma and ties up any loose ends. Stories are structured this way so that people can easily follow the story without getting confused.

Cater to your audience by considering:

- Who is your audience? If they are single moms, build your story around that. Include anecdotes that single moms can identify with.

- What problem can you solve for your audience? This question is most easily answered after you have a clear understanding of your audience.

- How are you going to solve the problem? Once you have identified the problem your audience is experiencing, the audience wants to know that you can help.

Create likable characters because people want someone to root for. This is the same reason there is always a likable character in a good movie. One good sign of a bad movie is that nobody is likable in the film.

Speak the language that your customer speaks. If your customers have a doctorate, you want to use vocabulary that is much higher than a high school level. Use the terminology that people in the market use that you are focusing on.

Don't always be selling. If you start to sound like you are trying to sell something to the customer throughout the story, the customer is going to lose interest and stop paying attention. Through your story, your audience will grow to trust you; if you are preoccupied with trying to sell to them, the quality of your story will suffer, and they will see through your ulterior motive.

Bring the characters to life with detailed descriptions. The best storytellers paint a picture of the characters and scenery for their audience. They can imagine the people and places that are depicted in the story. A thesaurus is a fantastic resource for expressive storytelling.

Tease your audience with anticipation. Try breaking stories up and making them available over time. You could also lead people to finish the end of the story on your Facebook page. Another option would be to have people subscribe to text alerts or your email list to get the remainder of the story.

Share your customer's stories. If you have customers that have experienced great results from using a product or service share their story. These case studies are extremely effective because they provide social proof of real-life results.

Add emotion to the mix. Humor, fear, sadness, and more can be captured by a great storyteller. Emotion adds an element that has the audience emotionally invested in the story.

Include photos with your story when possible so that the audience can visualize what is happening. It becomes a more entertaining story which encourages them to follow the story through to the conclusion.

Use videos to tell your story. If writing isn't one of your strengths, consider using video to tell your story. Video allows viewers to see what's happening instead of being told. What also makes it powerful is it's engaging, easy to consume, and sharable using social media. It's an ideal way to meet the growing demand for stories.

Backup your facts. If you are repeating something from a study, site the study. If research is necessary to find facts for your story, confirm the information from a couple of different sources so you can be sure you are reporting the information factually. Link to the web page where you got your information from.

A good story can boost your conversion rates and credibility when you genuinely connect with your customers. By painting a picture for them and creating personal relationships you will be on your way to establishing long-term loyalty.

Step 5: Consultant

Get Help with Your Digital Marketing

Even with the understanding of what digital marketing is, there is going to be a lot of work that needs to be done. In this section, you will learn about the importance of getting help with your digital marketing. You will find out why it may not be a good idea to have your employees do your web marketing and why working with a digital marketing consultant is a better option.

You will know where to go when you are ready to contact a digital marketing consultant and the questions you should ask before hiring one.

"Talent wins games, but teamwork and intelligence win championships."

– Michael Jordan, Six-time NBA Champion and Hall of Famer

17. Benefits of Working with a Digital Marketing Consultant

17.1 Why Getting Help with Your Digital Marketing Is Necessary

Now that you have an online marketing plan or strategy in mind, you need to find the right person to help you implement it. As a business owner, you can't be expected to be an expert in every aspect of your business, but you are still responsible for the marketing of your products. Without significant education and experience, it is difficult to develop a marketing agenda and execute it while simultaneously running a business.

If you plan on having a successful business, you will likely be too busy to market it yourself. You're probably juggling several balls in the air already. Digital marketing is an enormous undertaking and if you try to do it all yourself, you're bound to drop one of those balls, either in your online marketing or in some other area of your business. Also, if something gets overlooked, it's going to cost your business money in one way or another. On top of this all, the growth you want your business to experience may require multiple marketing strategies involving complex tasks, and multiple campaigns.

These are all great reasons to hire a digital marketing consultant (DMC) for your business. But there are also other benefits of bringing in someone new. Every time you ask your digital marketing consultant about their opinion, you're going to get a new perspective on your business and will have a new opportunity to see things from a consumer's point of view.

17.2 What Is the Role of a Digital Marketing Consultant?

A digital marketing consultant is a highly skilled professional that helps businesses develop and execute strategies to market or sell their products or services via the internet. Do not confuse a digital marketing consultant with an advertising firm. While a DMC may create ads as part of their duties, it is far from their only responsibility.

Digital marketing consultants will make suggestions regarding prices, packaging, product distribution, and how to sell products or services. These components are called the "marketing mix" and they take into account all of the aspects of a business when determining which strategies will resonate best with customers.

DMCs use their critical thinking skills to analyze the demographics of a business's customers. Being able to understand the thoughts and behavior of consumers is vital because the world of online marketing constantly changes, and what people do online today may change tomorrow.

Digital marketing campaigns need to be tailored to the individual business, product or service. Using the same offline marketing strategies that have been used before just isn't going to work, because a significant number of consumers are not responding to them. So, a marketing consultant that can think outside the box is going to be more valuable to a company than one that does everything by the book or uses a formula to come up with each marketing campaign. With consumers being constantly bombarded with advertising, uniqueness matters.

Web marketing consultants can either be proficient and knowledgeable in all areas of digital marketing, or they may specialize in one certain area of it such as social media, PPC, SEO, reputation management, etc. Large DMC agencies will most likely include services such as web design, e-commerce development, and they may also have separate departments for client services.

Other marketing consultants operate on a smaller scale where they take care of everything themselves, or with a small team. Either way, you shouldn't choose your marketing consultant based on the size of the company they own or work for. You'll need to do your own research to decide which marketing consultant is truly best for you and your business.

17.3 Why You Shouldn't Do Online Marketing Alone

Even after learning the impact a marketing consultant can have on your business, you may still decide to tackle the job of marketing online on your own. If you take on the huge task of doing your own online marketing and fail, not only will you lose the time it took to do the work, but possibly hundreds if not thousands of dollars. On top of that, your marketing budget may already be tapped, and you won't have the ability to correct any mistakes or try a different strategy.

Which campaign do you think will do better? A campaign completed with 50% effort or 100% effort? 100% of course. When you put the role of marketing solely on your own shoulders, you're forced to give this task a lower priority than someone whose only job is to provide marketing services. You're dividing your time and talents among the many roles that come with being a business owner. The more tasks you take on by yourself, the more your business suffers.

Do you really have the time to learn, invest in and try each of the different online marketing channels while you are trying to run your business? Probably not. Besides education, a marketing consultant comes with knowledge and experience working with other businesses. They know what works and what doesn't.

17.4 What Are the Challenges of Having Employees Doing Your Digital Marketing?

Another consideration is whether you should assign your online marketing to an employee. This may initially seem like a good idea, but you will find yourself facing the following challenges:

Never Enough Time or Focus

If your employee is working on managing your online marketing, they won't be working on what you initially hired them for. A lack of time, dedicated budget for training, and getting them reputable training can keep your in-house team member from getting the skills they need to achieve any online marketing goals.

A lack of time also means that most of the skills required will need to be learned on the job. This creates more problems because the combination of a maxed-out workload and a reduced skill set means there won't be time to keep up with changing needs in your online marketing campaigns.

No Direction

Who's going to create your online marketing campaigns, you or your in-house team member? You'll need to take the time to create the online marketing campaigns for your business and provide guidance on how to execute the strategies. Turning over your marketing to someone that doesn't have the right experience can be very costly.

Higher Cost

Speaking about increased cost there will be other necessities that need to be paid for in addition to the salary of your team member.

You'll need to consider:

- Training cost associated with learning what needs to be done. Even if you don't pay for formal training, if they have to learn on their own, they'll still be doing it at work while you're paying them.

- Software for creating content, automating processes, measuring results, etc. (and possibly computer hardware).

- Ramp up cost. This is for time spent at less than full efficiency while they learn your systems.

Plus, any cost that you can't predict.

As you add more duties to a current team member over time, they will expect an increase in pay as they take on more responsibilities and do more. If they decide to leave, you'll need to start this process all over again.

Scalability Problems

If you have a team member working on your online marketing and you want it to be scalable, the only way to do that is to enlist another employee for the task or hire more talent. With budgets already being limited for online marketing, it will be a challenge to find money for that additional investment—especially if your ROI is not above your goal.

Any in-house person you assign this responsibility will lack the necessary skills to do the job effectively. Digital marketing requires multiple talents. Having someone on your staff who is great at social media is different from the person who is a genius at website design, SEO, paid advertising, or creating campaigns. Someone who has an understanding and capacity to perform the broad range of the skills required will be hard to find, hard to keep, or very expensive.

17.5 How Hiring a Web Marketing Consultant is Good for Your Business

Digital marketing can be overwhelming, but when it comes to your online strategy working with a DMC can be extremely beneficial. Wherever your business ranks on the chart of online marketing readiness, you should consider speaking with a digital marketing consultant if you . . .

- Want to build your business
- Need to set well-defined short- and long-term goals
- Need help tracking key performance indicators to measure success
- Want to find new ways to improve relations with existing customers
- Want to attract new clients and enter into new markets
- Need an evaluation of your online presence and to get feedback on your web marketing efforts
- Need assistance with developing your brand and making your target demographic aware of it.
- Require damage control if something threatens to taint your company's reputation
- Want coordinated content created for multiple marketing channels that use targeted SEO keywords.

These are just a few of the ways that a digital marketing consultant can help your business. But there is so much more they offer in the way they support business owners. When working with a DMC you can expect the following:

Save Yourself Time: You're just too busy to do the work that's required by yourself. As the owner of a small or medium-sized business, you're already managing multiple tasks. Online marketing is a tremendous arena and if you try to tackle it by yourself, you're going to ignore or forget to do one of those tasks in either your online marketing efforts or somewhere else within your business. And wherever a task gets abandoned, it's going to impact your business in some way.

Save Your Business Money: On the surface, hiring a marketing consultant may seem like an unnecessary expense, but the more success you have in your marketing campaign, the more revenue you're likely to make. Yes, just like everything else in your business, marketing comes down to money. You may believe that investing in a digital marketing expert will cut into that extra profit, because you'll be spending it on your consultant. This is not the case at all. A weak campaign or no campaign at all is what's really costing you money. So, the money you lose by not hiring a web marketing consultant far outweighs the money you would spend on one.

Work with a Pro: Hiring a DMC means you get access to a professional that can create your campaigns and implement all of the web strategies you may need. They're responsible for keeping up with the latest trends, strategies and technologies for getting more sales, leads and engaging customers. Trying to keep up with the constant changes is like a full-time job on its own.

Help Keeping Your Business Focused: A digital marketing expert will set the ground rules, assign accountability, and bring productive order to your business. Through meetings, established goals, and a clear online marketing action plan, they bring much-needed clarity to confusing or stressful work environments. This can help you get employees to buy into the changes and to remain focused on the areas that they excel in.

Get Access to Specialists: A DMC will have access to a team of specialists that know what to do and when to do it so you can get the services that you need and don't over-pay for ones you don't need. This gives you more flexibility where your campaigns can ramp up and down quickly, change, or stop with very little notice.

Keep an Eye on Competitors: A savvy web marketing consultant will follow your top competitors and do competitive research to see where they invest their time and money, so you can keep pace.

Test, Measure, Optimize & Report: A web marketing consultant will conduct different tests on your marketing campaigns to see which strategies are doing well with your target audience. Using KPIs, they can make adjustments to the strategies to optimize the campaign to get the best outcome. Thanks in part to their experience and expertise, they can give you measurable results based on your return on investment (ROI).

Get a Valued Partner: Bringing in a web marketing consultant brings a fresh eye to your business. They will think of strategies that you may not have thought of because you have been so close to your business for so long. Sometimes you get so used to doing what you've always done, that you no longer think of new and creative ideas.

You can take their opinions with a little more weight than your employees and business partners because they truly understand what drives customers and why they buy products. The assessments they provide are very professional, insightful, and can make your business money.

Far too many SMB owners feel alone on their entrepreneurial journey when they don't have to. Hiring a web marketing consultant brings another person along for the trip. It's satisfying on so many levels to have someone else to discuss your plans, hopes, and dreams with. But don't hire just any DMC. Making sure they are the right fit for your business is equally as important as the results they produce. There will be many web marketing consultants to choose from, but if the chemistry between you is off, your expectations or desired results may not be met.

The logical conclusion is that it makes sense to hire an experienced digital marketing consultant. Their commitment to assessing and improving your business will be well worth the investment.

17.6 Seven Things You Should Know about Your Business before Contacting Any Web Marketing Consultants

Digital marketing consultants need a bit of direction. Before you interview and hire someone, you have to have a fairly good idea of what type of results you're looking to achieve. Here are seven questions you should know the answers to and keep in mind when looking for a DMC to work with.

1. **What Type of Online Marketing Do You Want to Focus On?**

   Are you looking to get 10,000 Facebook fans? Are you looking to increase your email list by 5,000 people? Maybe you just made a video and now you need help getting 100,000 views on YouTube. Whatever your goals are, have a couple in mind when looking for a DMC. This will help you not only communicate your goals to them, but you will also be able to pick consultants who have expertise in the type of marketing you would prefer.

2. **Do You Have an Established Brand?**

Your brand consists of anything that makes your business memorable and stand out from your competition as explained in Chapter 16.2. Branding includes your logo, packaging, tag line, jingle, or anything else that makes someone think about "your business" every time they hear it. If you don't think your business has a brand, a DMC can help you create one.

3. **Do You Know Who Is Your Ideal Customer?**

You should know who your ideal customer is by now. If you have identified your ideal customer prior to hiring a consultant, you can then concentrate on hiring one that specializes in that demographic. A good DMC will ask you who is your target audience in in order to make the best suggestions and recommendations for your business.
Work with your DMC to verify the demographics of your own customer base. They can help you focus on that demographic and narrow it down even further. They'll be able to create a targeted campaign that will truly speak to that audience.

4. **What Are the Four Budgeting Factors That Influence Your Investment in a Digital Marketing Consultant?**

A budget will provide you with a guideline of a price not to exceed. Having in mind the amount you will pay before you have any conversations makes it easier to pass on a potential consultant or negotiate for a better price.

These are four budgeting factors to be mindful of when deciding on your consultant:

• **Cost:** Some consultants can be quite costly, but you also don't want to scrape the bottom of the barrel by hiring a consultant that won't work hard for you or has no knowledge or experience. A consultant should be able to demonstrate their skills with examples of their work.

• **Experience:** If your consultant has many years of experience and/or schooling, that will add to their cost. But do keep in mind that if they provide strong examples of their work, you may find them to be worth the investment.

• **Task:** You must take into consideration the task you are asking the DMC to take on. Different tasks are going to require more of an investment because they will require more of the consultant. The task may take more time, resources, knowledge, etc.

• **Time:** If you need a website built in a week, a DMC is going to have to hustle to get it up and running. That will cost extra money. If you can wait 6 weeks, your price will probably reflect the forgiving timeline.

Get prices from a few different consultants so you can compare the budgeting factors above. Thinking about these four things ahead of time allows you to identify which ones are most important to you, and the success of your business before any negotiations.

You may realize experience isn't that important to you because you can help with some of the work. Thinking about the task before you go in will help you decide quickly in your meeting if that task can be modified to bring the price of the consulting services down.

5. **What Is the Timeline for Your Campaign?**

You'll need to put some thought into the timeline that will work for you. Do you want your campaign up and running in four months? Two months? Three weeks? This is another important detail that you'll need to discuss with any web marketing consultants that you talk to.

They'll tell you when they can start on your project and when you can expect it to be completed. They may also let you know if your timetable is realistic as some strategies like SEO and local search marketing take longer to get started and more time to see results.

6. **Will Anyone on Your Staff Be Available If Needed?**

When you decide to hire a DMC to work with changes will take place in your business that will affect your staff as well as yourself. If a potential DMC asks if your staff can help implement any marketing campaigns, you will need to evaluate your staff's capabilities to see if they're equipped to.

In most cases, your staff is busy doing the jobs they were hired for, so make sure you discuss the manpower and man-hours that might be needed from your in-house team. You should also know in advance which employees you think would be helpful, and how much time of theirs you're willing to commit. While there is no right or wrong answer in terms of whether your staff will be needed, going into the meeting with the knowledge of whether you can afford these man-hours is important.

7. **How Fast Should Your Business Grow?**

One of the main principles for entrepreneurship is to grow your business. This is probably why you are taking all the right steps to build yours and find the right professional to work with. While most business owners want to see rapid growth in their company, you need to consider just how much growth is too much and what's a healthy amount for your business. For most small companies—regardless of whether they sell products or services—they couldn't actually handle a massive influx of orders and requests. Make sure your marketing goals are in line with what you can actually handle at any given stage in your business.

If not, you'll be in a situation where the demand for your offer is more than you can supply. This will lead to disappointed customers because you can't follow through on what you promised in your marketing. One negative review from a customer can be extremely damaging to your business.

When customers have a bad experience, they are going to tell their friends. Without the proper preparation, your business can quickly go from many word-of-mouth recommendations to irate customers warning others about your ill-prepared company on social media.

Growth is definitely a good thing, but not being able to keep up with it is not. You need to know before you meet with your DMC just how much growth you're looking for. Make sure that with increased sales or service demands your company can continue to meet and exceed the expectations of your customers. An ideal scenario would be to steadily increase expansion so that you can gradually hire employees or increase your inventory to fulfill the extra business that is coming in from your new marketing efforts.

"Be strong enough to stand alone, smart enough to know when you need help, and brave enough to ask for it."

– Mark Amend, Author

18. Things to Consider When Hiring a Digital Marketing Consultant

18.1 What Information Do You Need to Have before Interviewing a Digital Marketing Consultant?

A DMC will want to know about your business and the goals that you have for it. Here's a quick reminder of what you should have ready:

- Market Research (Chapter 15.2)
- Answers to the Eight Business Building Questions (Chapter 15.3)
- Marketing Goals (Chapter 15.4)
- Budget Details (Chapter 15.5)
- Seven Things to Know about Your Business (Chapter 17.6)
- Keyword List (Chapter 7.4)

You'll need to have this available in a document for your prospective DMCs to review. If you only have some of these details or none at all, a DMC can assist in pulling together the necessary information. But this will put you at a disadvantage and you will almost be obligated to hire the one that does this for you, in addition to paying whatever they may charge for doing it.

18.2 What Characteristics to Look for in Web Marketing Consultants

Each potential DMC you consider will have their own set of intangibles they bring to the table. But there are some characteristics like the ones listed below you want to check for to ensure you hire a DMC that is most compatible with you and your business.

Experience and Specialization

It's a good idea to work with a DMC that has a lot of experience. Experienced DMCs have expertise in diverse areas of marketing. They've worked with businesses of various sizes and campaigns of various lengths. If your online marketing project is complex, you'll need someone that will be able to understand your needs and explain what steps they'll take to help you get your desired results.

Some DMCs have decided to become extremely proficient in only one or two online marketing channels. That means they may be great in social media and paid online advertising but may not be able to help you if you needed a video created. But, if there is a particular online marketing channel you want to succeed with then consider working with a DMC that specializes in that channel.

What Story Does Their Website Tell?

When choosing a DMC to work with, visit their website before you speak with them. They will usually list the areas of online marketing they are strong in and omit any they are not proficient with. If you are looking for a DMC that offers expertise in a particular web marketing strategy (ex: social media) that should be prominently located on their website.

Do They Have an Industry Focus?

Some DMCs are generalists meaning they work with all types of businesses. Others focus on working with business owners in a specific niche like lawyers or financial planners. Or businesses that are of a specific size. If your industry is very competitive or has regulations that need to be understood, then choosing a DMC that is familiar with your industry is the way to go.
Also, find out if the DMC does better at growing B2B (business to business) companies or B2C (business to consumer) businesses. You will want to talk with a DMC that works with businesses like yours.

Do They Prefer Full Control or Collaboration?

Some DMCs perform better when they have the authority to take full control of campaigns and do what is needed to get results. Others prefer to get input from the business owners during each step of the campaign from planning to execution. You should know ahead of time how involved you want to be in the process. Do you have the time and resources to give input on each campaign?

Or will you put your trust into the DMC you select to represent your business?

Are They Transparent with Their Reporting?

It is very easy to get bogged down with reports that show progress and wins, but they mean very little if there is no increase in your sales or leads. A reputable DMC will provide you with weekly or monthly reports highlighting key performance indicators. They will show you the good and the bad because they are committed to doing their best to increase the growth of your business.

Are They Passionate and Enthusiastic?

Your DMC should be passionate about online marketing and be enthusiastic when talking about ways to grow your business. They're not afraid to take risks and will be the driving force behind all of your campaigns and the implementation of your strategies. They keep up with the latest digital marketing trends and summarizes the details for you so your marketing knowledge can increase as well. They will do their best to make sure you understand what is going on.

18.3 Where to Look for Web Marketing Consultants

Like hiring for any position that is vital for your business, it begins with gathering a pool of qualified candidates. Where do you find these candidates? Here are a few options to help find qualified web marketing consultants:

• **Other Business Websites:** Look for small businesses that have online marketing ideas that you like. If you look at the bottom of their webpage, there should be a link to the company that developed the website and possibly all of the web marketing. If a link to the DMC is not available on the site (which would be unusual for a well-developed site), you could try to email the owner of the site and ask. If you don't hear back from the website owner skip that site as a resource and find another one that you like. It should not be very difficult to find a website with a link to the DMC at the bottom of the web page.

• **Social Media:** LinkedIn is a good place if you are connected to quite a few business owners. Ask your connections who did their web marketing and if they were pleased with the level of service. Your friends on Facebook that have businesses can be a wealth of knowledge when it comes to recommending resources. Ask them if they have any recommendations for digital marketing consultants.

• **Search Engines:** You can also use the internet as a resource. Use the search terms:

- digital marketing agency
- online marketing expert
- internet marketing consultant or
- web marketing professional

Interchange the words "digital" with "internet," "online," or "web" to expand your searches. If you want to use marketing that focuses on a specific strategy then type the name of the strategy along with the words "agency," "consultant," "expert," and "professional." (i.e., mobile marketing expert.)

You should find a nice size list that you can go through where you can look at their websites to see what they offer.

If you want to hire a consultant that has expertise in your specific industry add that industry in your search query. (example: digital marketing for law firms, email marketing for restaurants)

If you want to work with a consultant that's in your city or town, add your location to your search query to find local DMCs and narrow down your search. (example: Miami digital marketing consultant.) But unless you will need a lot of in-person meetings don't limit your search by location. Almost everything that needs to be discussed can be done by phone, email, or online using web conferencing software. If necessary, you, the consultant, or representatives from their business can have meetings at an agreed-upon time online.

A situation where a local DMC may be more beneficial is if you need to rank locally, in your own city, or in neighboring ones. They would have a thorough understanding of that region and already have strategies to help you get better rankings quicker. They would have an advantage in raising brand awareness for you locally.

Spend some additional time to find out if they have any poor reviews. Other business owners will share their opinions online, especially if they had a bad experience with a consultant. This will be easier to find if you are hiring a consultant that has a long track record.

• **Freelance Websites:** There are websites where business owners can contact a network of consultants and freelancers. Business owners can post short-term and long-term jobs and choose from skilled professionals who submit proposals on the jobs along with rate quotes. This is good for you because you have many candidates to choose from and you don't have to commit to hiring someone full time to work on your projects.

Here are a few freelance websites for you to look at:

- Crowdsource.com
- Freelancer.com
- Guru.com
- PeoplePerHour.com
- Trulancer.com
- Upwork.com
- WritersAccess.com

• **Ask Around:** Get referrals from related businesses that are similar in size. Ask people you meet at networking events. If there are any business owners in your area you feel comfortable approaching, you can simply ask them who does their online marketing, or if they hired a DMC.

Once you have narrowed down your list of DMCs contact at least 3 to 4 of them you got from your own research and/or referrals and start calling to set up face-to-face meetings, or phone interviews. If they have time you may be able to conduct your interview during the initial call. Have interview questions ready before calling to set up any appointments in case that happens. After you have communicated with the potential DMC, you will have a better idea of whether they may be the right fit for your business and worth the investment.

18.4 20 Questions to Ask a Web Marketing Consultant before Hiring Them

After doing all of your research and having some initial conversations with potential DMCs it's time for a phone call, face-to-face meeting or video chat with your top selections. After you you've contacted them and introduced yourselves you can begin the interview.

You want to be able to offer more to the conversation than just "make me more money."

Go into the conversation prepared by asking questions. By asking the right questions, it immediately sets the tone for what you expect, and the consultant will know what you are thinking.

Here are some questions that you should ask:

1. **Why should I hire you as my digital marketing consultant?**
   You want this answer to come across as confident. They should be able to tell you what sets them apart and makes them unique. If they cannot show themselves as unique, will they be able to position your company as unique?

2. **How long have you been a digital marketing consultant?**
   Almost anyone with a computer and the ability to build a website can claim to be a DMC. You want to make sure that you're working with a legitimate business that can do what they claim and can prove it. DMCs with less experience are more likely to make mistakes and not be able to fully think out strategies in their entirety. Just be aware that hiring an inexperienced DMC can have consequences you may regret in the future. Remember that your hiring decision is an investment in your business.

   The other risk you run when you don't work with a certified or experienced DMC is that you could be working with someone who is just in between jobs, or who is just looking for something to do to make some "side hustle" money. Should a better opportunity come along they could just pick up and leave, leaving you stranded.

3. **What online marketing courses have you taken?**
   You do not have to have a degree to become a web marketing consultant. It is recommended that your candidates have at least taken some courses to educate them on online marketing. If they have taken courses, you can feel confident that they understand the more complex digital marketing strategies and are able to map out a plan of action for your online marketing campaigns.

   Strategies and implementation are an integral part of a DMC's work. If they have not received training in these areas, it is difficult to rely on their knowledge alone.

4. **Do you just lay out the plan, or do you execute it too?**
   Some DMCs just give you a great plan but it's up to you and your team to execute, others handle the whole process. Most firms and DMCs can handle one or both aspects of online marketing: strategy and execution. If you hire a DMC that is strategy-focused this means he creates, develops and lays out a marketing plan for your business that you can execute without him/her. With the strategy-focused method, the marketing consultant's relationship with you ends at the point where the plan has been created. You would use your employees to do the work that the consultant has planned out.

   Other marketing professionals can be execution-focused where they take over most of the grunt work for you such as creating your website to your specifications

   Many DMCs will offer both options to be provided by themselves or the company they represent. With the competition among DMCs being as fierce as it is, it becomes more and more important that a consultant offer as many conveniences for their clients as possible.

5. **Do you prefer a selling- or education-based method of marketing?**
   If you sell gardening tools you may offer planting tips to your customers. Those tips should come free with their purchase. The idea is that the customer will enjoy the bonus information that comes with the gardening tools and choose your tools over your competition.

   This tactic is different from selling-based methods which simply ask, in different ways, people to purchase your products, without really offering information to assert your authority. Both tactics have their advantages, but obviously, a hybrid of the two is preferable.

6. **How will you reach the right audience instead of spending my advertising dollars on uninterested consumers?**
   You want the DMC candidate to be able to lay out a plan of how they are going to reach your audience. Tell them the demographics you are trying to reach and the experienced marketing consultant will know where and how those consumers can be reached. If they are familiar with demographics and how to target those demographics, that should ease your mind a bit that they will be able to reach your target audience.

7. **How will your marketing campaign help me stand out from the competition?**
   This question will give you an idea of the creativity the marketer has. Do not let them just answer with I am a creative person. You want them to describe what they would do to set you apart. Perhaps a new tool that they can add to your website that competing companies do not use. Maybe a new company slogan or logo to freshen up your website and printed marketing materials.

   For example, your marketing consultant will need to analyze your competition to see what is working for them. They can use that knowledge to plan out the best course of action for your marketing goals. Observing your competition provides the DMC with strategies they can borrow and reveals opportunities you can take advantage of.

8. **How will you measure the success of a marketing campaign?**
   With your assistance, the DMC will be able to come up with goals to work towards while they are implementing a marketing campaign. You want to make sure that they show their progress using reports and summaries of the changes to the KPIs they have been tracking. If you want them to increase website visitors by 10% in the next six months, ask what strategies they will use to accomplish this for you. Milestones and measurable goals should be included in the strategy.

9. **What is the longest period of time you have worked with a client?**
   This question provides further insight into the experience the marketing consultant has. While the answer should not dissuade you from hiring the consultant, it is a factor to consider. The standard marketing contract is one year for ongoing work with a business. If the longest time period is two years that is a good sign. It shows their longevity in the business in addition to the confidence other companies have in them and their talents. If past clients have stayed for less than a year, you can probably bet on the fact that many more have stayed for less time. Are you willing to work with a less experienced marketer that might be just doing this as a hobby? You will have to decide that after you have evaluated their answers to the other questions.

10. **What has been the biggest marketing mistake you have made?**
    No marketing consultant is going to be perfect just like no person is perfect. Finding out mistakes they have made assures you that they are human

and they can learn from their mistakes. How did they react or resolve the mistake? How did they perform that task differently the next time around? It may be difficult for the applicant to answer this question, but it is an important question that says a lot about the marketing consultant. Do not be afraid to use a consultant that has experienced the good and the bad. I would even consider it questionable if they cannot come up with any past mistakes. How likely is it that your applicant is flawless? Unlikely.

11. **Do you have any prior experience marketing your own business?**
It is easy to spend another company's money on a marketing plan but if the marketing consultant has never done marketing for themselves it can be difficult to pinpoint the level of talent you are working with. If the consultant has experience trying to market their own business, they'll understand how important it is not to waste your money. They'll also have experience with executing marketing plans that did not work. Some lessons can only be learned when they're happening to you, such as a poorly executed campaign, a complete lack of market research, or not having a marketing plan. When a DMC has walked in your shoes, they will know the importance of performing at a higher level and delivering the desired results.

12. **Do you have experience hiring a marketing consultant for yourself?**
They don't have to say yes to this, but it provides good insight into the DMC that you are interviewing. If they've put their company's reputation on the line with a marketing consultant in the past you know they can relate to your need for help and trust. They'll understand how imperative it is that they get the desired results.

13. **Do you work alone as a marketing consultant or are you part of a team?**
You want to know if you'll be relying on just one person to implement the marketing tasks that the DMC proposes. If they have a more involved marketing plan, it might make you feel better to use a consultant that has a team working behind them. However, if they are confident they can get the job done on their own or are willing to hire assistance that can help them get the job done without an increased cost this could still be a consultant to consider.

14. **On average, how many clients do you take on at one time?**
You will want to know how much time the consultant will be able to devote to your project. It will still be difficult to judge from your point

of view whether the consultant is overloaded. For example, if they have 25 clients that may not be a problem because perhaps they are only doing five minutes of social media for 10 of the clients every day and maybe very little maintenance on websites for many of the clients. So, unless this number sounds ridiculous, I would not be too concerned if they can convey their confidence that your work will be done.

15. **Will you sign a confidentiality agreement and abstain from working with my competition while I work with you?**
You do not really want your marketing consultant working with the competitors at the same time they are working on your campaigns. It would be a conflict of interest that would hinder your marketing campaign as well as the competition's marketing campaign. If they're working with your competition, they may share marketing ideas both of you discussed whether intentional or inadvertent. You want to know that your marketing consultant is giving 100% to your marketing campaign and not 50% to you and 50% to your competition.

16. **How do you charge for your services?**
DMCs may use one or more ways to charge for their services. See Chapter 18.6.1 (What are the Different Pricing Options Used by Web Marketing Consultants?) to understand what they are.

17. **Do you provide a reasonable rate for your services?**
You do not want to go with the marketer that is charging the cheapest rate because that speaks to their talents and experience. The cheapest marketing consultant is most likely the most inexperienced and most likely the least talented. On the other end of the spectrum, you will find consultants that charge an extremely high rate. Among all the bids for your business, you should be able to find a consultant that is willing to work somewhere in the middle.

18. **Will you provide milestones and payment terms within the final contract?**
Make sure your marketing consultant provides you with the schedule detailing when certain milestones will be met. If they cannot give you a timeframe for milestones, at least get a completed goal date. You may also be able to get an idea of when they are starting on the project and how long different steps within the project will take.

19. **May I see samples of your previous work?**
DMCs can say that they worked on thousands of other marketing campaigns, but can they show you the evidence to prove it. Do they at least have some fantastic examples? If they've implemented a lot of web marketing campaigns, they should have plenty of examples to choose from if you request them. Make sure that they can show you samples of marketing plans, websites, and marketing campaigns that they have done in the past. Also, make sure that they've worked on projects that are similar to what you're looking for and what your business needs. Then focus on whether or not you like the samples they provide you with.

20. **Do you have letters of reference for past work you have done?**
Letters of reference can have a major impact on a DMC's business. For this reason, it is important that a marketing consultant have a letter of reference on them whenever they go into interviews. You could look at testimonials on websites but those can sound a little fabricated.

You'll be collaborating with your DMC a lot, and you'll also be putting your business a bit in their hands. Because of this, it's important you really click with your consultant. Beyond whether they are nice and professional and highly recommended, do you understand them, and do you get the feeling they understand you? Do you like their personality and feel like they respect you? Having a good relationship with your consultant will go a long way towards helping you understand and appreciate their ideas, and it will go a long way towards helping them achieve your marketing goals.

It's important to get to know your DMC before you commit to working with them, so make sure your questions have been answered to your satisfaction and that you are clear about what was discussed.

18.5 53 Questions a Web Marketing Consultant Is Likely to Ask You to Help Get Better Results

At some point during the interview process, there are some details about you and your business that the DMC will want to know. They will use the information you give them to assess:

- What you are looking for? What do you expect?
- Can they help you? Are they the right solution for you?

- What they think you need?
- How long will it take to complete or get results for what is needed?
- What is your level of commitment?
- How much would they charge?

In order for them to make their assessment and provide better results for you they may ask the following questions initially or over a period of time if you decide to work with them:

Questions about Your Goals

1. Do you know what marketing goals you want to achieve each month?
2. What are your monthly sales goals?
3. What is the biggest challenge in your businesses?
4. What is the biggest challenge in marketing your businesses?
5. What is your biggest challenge in making sales?

Questions about Your Business

6. What problems do your product or service solve?
7. How competitive is your niche?
8. Who are your top three competitors?
9. What makes your business different from your competitors?
10. How do you want to beat them? (i.e., search engine ranking, social media engagement, reputation, etc.)
11. What do you want your business to be known for?
12. Is your business seasonal? Is there a time during the year that you sell more?
13. Does your industry have any restrictions or regulations on how you can market your business online?

Questions about Your Customers

14. Who is your target audience?
15. Do you have a customer avatar?
16. Where do they spend most of their time online?

17. How does your target audience find what you are offering?
18. What do you currently do to get new customers?
19. Do you have a strategy to upsell customers?
20. What strategies are you using to retain customers?

Questions about Metrics, Measuring, and Tracking

21. Do you know the lifetime value (LTV) of your customer?
22. What is your customer acquisition cost (CAC)?
23. Are you currently measuring the ROI for your current online marketing?
    24. If yes, what strategy was the most successful?
    25. Which strategy was the least successful?
26. If you sell online, how do you track new sales or leads back to their original source?
27. What systems are you using to track and measure your online activities and performance?
28. Are you currently tracking offline sales that originated online? (i.e., phone calls, coupons.)
    29. If yes, how?

Questions about Your Online Marketing

30. Do you have a website?
    31. When was it built?
    32. Is it updated regularly?
    33. Who updates it?
    34. Is it mobile-enabled?
    35. What do you want visitors to do after they visit your website? (i.e., Buy something? Give you contact details? Call you?)

35. Are the pages of your website indexed in the 3 major search engines? (Google, Yahoo, Bing.)
    36. If yes, what keywords are they ranked for?
37. What online marketing strategies are you currently using?
    38. Were there any you tried in the past and stopped doing?

39. Are you currently capturing leads online to follow up with in the future?
40. Is your business dependent on local customers?
41. If yes, is your business listed in local directories?
42. Are you currently using social media?
43. Who manages it?
44. Are you creating original content?
45. How often?
46. Do you know what type of content generates an increased amount of engagement from your target audience?
47. Are you doing any marketing for your business offline?
48. What methods are you using?

Questions about Working with a DMC

49. Why are you considering working with my company?
50. If you worked with another web marketing consultant or agency what worked in that partnership?
51. What didn't work?
52. Which type of communication do you like best? Phone, email, video, or text?
53. What is your response time for returning messages?

These are not all of the questions a DMC may ask. Some could ask more questions, some less. Most of them have already been asked and answered in this book. In any case, you want to be prepared so both of you can determine if you're the right fit for each other.

True understanding comes from asking good questions One of their questions may cause you to view a problem through a different perspective, or even spark a completely new way you want to approach a problem. That's why you need to be honest and realistic with your business goals in this partnership.

Their questions and your answers not only help them provide better results for you, but the act of asking questions creates productive conversations that build your relationship.

18.6 What Determines the Cost of Digital Marketing Services?

Once you've narrowed down your list of candidates. you'll want to consider the cost to hire them. If there a couple of DMCs that you feel really good about and they have the personality, experience, and education you need, then price may be the deciding factor.

DMCs will provide you with details about what they can offer your company, but they usually don't list the cost of their services because each client and project has different requirements. This is why you need to have a detailed conversation with them before you can find out what they charge.

There are several factors that influence the cost DMCs charge such as:

- The product or service are you offering.
- The competitiveness of your market.
- The current web presence of your business.
- The goals you are trying to achieve using digital marketing.
- Which online strategies will be used to reach your goal.
- How much research will they need to do for you?
- The experience of the DMC.

DMCs need to make sure they charge fees that will enable them to stay in business and at the same time make sure they are priced reasonably for their clients. They have to be compensated for their time and business overheads, such as office expenses, training, travel, software and more. It is easier for them to determine their fees once they have spoken with you and know what you need and expect.

18.6.1 What Are the Different Pricing Options Used by Web Marketing Consultants?

When setting their fees, DMCs have different options they may use, including hourly rates, working on a retainer, and project-based pricing. Let's review each one.

Hourly Rates: A DMC will estimate the number of hours it takes to perform tasks and then calculates an hourly rate based on that. The rate charged takes into consideration the experience of the DMC, overheads, and other expenses. When charged by the hour it's a little easier to understand what you are paying for. With the other pricing options, you may need more detailed explanations.

Hourly fees should be considered for small and short-term projects.

Working on Retainer: A common pricing option offered is a monthly retainer. Clients pay the DMC a set price each month in return for having a certain amount of work done for ongoing services such as the oversight and maintenance of their web presence. Retainer agreements can be month to month or for a set period of time. (3 months, 6 months, 1 year, etc.) Some DMCs may offer you a discount since you will be pre-paying for the work. This payment option should be considered for ongoing projects.

Project-Based Pricing: Project-based pricing is often used as an introduction to the services from the DMC and can serve as a bridge between hourly pricing and monthly retainer pricing options. With project-based pricing, a DMC will generally outline in detail what they will do for you, and what it will cost them to do it. What the fee ends up being will be completely dependent on how large the project is, and how detailed the plan is. It's favorable as it gives more time to accomplish tasks while still having a set date or goal for the conclusion. Since the cost is fixed you won't pay extra if the project takes a little bit longer to complete. However, there may be instances where last-minute changes or additions can incur an additional fee. Project-based pricing should be considered for building new websites, creating videos, and mobile optimization.

Performance-Based Pricing: With this option, the fees of the DMC are based primarily, but not exclusively, on the value they believe they offer their clients, instead of the hours or resources put into completing tasks. Rather than ask for a set price, a DMC may instead seek a percentage of the sales that come as a result of their involvement and contributions. The terms are discussed before the contract is finalized. Another variation of this pricing model is fees are set and you pay as results are achieved. If a DMC specializes in SEO, he may only bill you as your search engine rankings and web traffic increase. From a cost perspective, this is a good option but most of the DMCS that offer this are specialists and may not be able to support you in other areas of online marketing.

Package-Based Pricing: Some DMCS will offer web packages that include different services provided for different set prices. For example, a web design package may include setting up your website. Another package may include web design plus submission to local directories. These packages are not a one size fit all solution, but if one has something that you need it can be a good way to get it at an affordable price. Just be prepared to pay extra for customizations and any request for additional services.

18.6.2 Why You Must Negotiate, Even If You Hate Doing It

One of the most common questions business owners ask DMCs about their services is "How much do you charge?" While getting the best deal is important you don't want to sacrifice getting good services. Even if you're on a tight budget don't be cheap when it comes to choosing a DMC to work with. Online marketing takes a lot of training, skill, creativity, experience and hard work to become proficient in that field. So, if you are expecting a DMC or agency to do all of your online marketing for a couple of hundred dollars per month then prepare to be disappointed.

There may be a couple of DMCs you can choose from, but their fees may be too high for you. Don't be afraid to try and negotiate for a better offer. Negotiations are a part of doing business and honestly, they expect it. A lot of times they will come up with different price points depending on the services that they provide. But, in order to work with clients that have different budget requirements or limitations, DMCs know they need to be flexible with their fees. Part of your negotiation may be refusing a service that you know you don't need, how much transparency they need to have, or how often you are contacted. This is why you are asking each candidate for quotes and doing interviews before deciding. You're getting an idea of how much the services you want cost, their value, and the experience of the DMC. Use this information to your advantage and be prepared to negotiate.

18.7 Five Simple Things to Look For before You Sign a Web Marketing Contract

After you have done your due diligence and determined which digital marketing consultant is the right fit for your business and yourself, it is time to get a contract for the work that will be done. Be sure to read the contract and look it over before you sign it.

Here are a few things you want to look for when the time comes to sign that contract:

1. The contract should include the basics like what work will be done, and what will be provided by the DMC.

2. The contract should include different milestones so you can measure the progress made from the beginning of the contract to determine if the DMC is delivering what they promised on time.

3. All fees should be itemized and described so you won't be surprised by additional fees when the project or campaign is completed.

4. Include any payment dates in the contract. You do not want work on your projects to be held up for nonpayment especially if a payment is not due for another 30 days.

5. It should clearly state that you are the sole owner of everything created for you and your business and anything created on your behalf can only be used with your permission.

Conclusion

Congratulations!
You made it to the conclusion of this book, and you are now ready to begin a very exciting journey; a journey where your ideas and plans become tangible and they impact the lives of many people. This is also a journey where you can experience financial success at a very high level.

With the BASIC process, you now have a clear picture of how to accomplish all of your digital marketing objectives. You now know:

Step 1: Begin – Understand Why You Need to Have the Right Mindset Before You Use Digital Marketing

- 25 reasons why most small business owners fail at marketing online and how you can avoid the same fate
- the BASIC process and how it solves digital marketing challenges
- the SMARTER process for setting and achieving goals

Step 2: Acquire – Get The Tools You Need to Succeed Online

- the importance of having a good domain name, reliable web hosting, and a Google account
- you must have a mobile-friendly website that is created to make sales and capture leads
- how to get started with e-commerce and grow your online sales using affiliate marketing

Step 3: Strategies – Use The Most Effective Digital Marketing Channels

The different types of digital marketing channels available for you to use independently or as part of an overall web marketing campaign:

• Content Marketing involves the creation and sharing of online material (such as videos, blogs, and social media posts) that is intended to stimulate interest in a company's products or services.

• Search Engine Optimization (SEO) is the process of affecting the visibility of a website or a web page in a web search engine's organic, unpaid results.

• Local Search Marketing is the use of specialized internet search engines that allow users to submit geographically constrained searches against a structured database of local business listings.

• Online Reputation Management (ORM) is the act of monitoring, addressing or mitigating SERPs (search engine result pages) or mentions in online media and web content.

• Mobile Marketing is promotional activity designed for delivery to cell phones, smartphones, and other handheld devices, usually as a component of a multi-channel campaign.

• Email Marketing is the act of sending email messages with the purpose of:
  • Enhancing your relationship with current or previous customers
  • Encouraging customer loyalty and repeat business
  • Acquiring new customers or
  • Convincing current customers to purchase something immediately.

• Social Media Marketing is the use of social media platforms and websites to promote a product or service.

• Video Marketing is incorporating videos into your marketing campaigns to promote your company, product or service.

• Paid Online Advertising is a strategy used to direct traffic to websites, in which you would pay to have your ad shown on other websites or only when it is clicked on.

Step 4: Implement – Carry Out Your Digital Marketing Strategy

- how to conduct market research on your target audience
- the importance of having a marketing budget and how to set one
- how to measure your digital marketing campaigns for effectiveness
- how to choose the best digital marketing strategy for your business
- how to enhance your digital marketing efforts by branding, becoming an authority, and by storytelling.

Step 5: Consultant – Get Help with Your Digital Marketing

- why it's important to get help with your digital marketing
- the benefits of hiring a digital marketing expert and what you should know before contacting one
- where to find digital marketing experts and what questions to ask them
- how much does digital marketing cost and what to look for before you sign a contract for services?

There is a lot that I covered in this book and I hope it puts you in the mindset to do the work required. My advice is to start working on what you learned immediately. As you are working on it, refer back to the book throughout the process and you will learn something new every time. Don't get overwhelmed, just focus on the information you need every step of the way.
Don't be like the person that says they are going to start doing things next month. Start today!

Finally, as far as our journey together goes it does not have to end here. I have been with you up to this point and would like to be with you when you start working on your digital marketing campaign. If you are already on one of my email lists, you'll be hearing from me regularly with additional ways that I can support you and your business. If you are not on one of my email lists and got this book online, from a bookstore, library, or as a gift, please do get in touch! You can visit www.YourWebSolutions.com to find out the many ways I can help you. Whether you just want a complimentary strategy session with me, or you want me to manage all of your digital marketing, I'd love to connect.

I look forward to hearing from you soon, and hope you enjoyed reading this book as much as I enjoyed writing it.

References

Chapter 1.1 – 25 Reasons Why Most Small Business Owners Fail at Digital Marketing, and Why You'll Fail Too If You Don't Use This Book – Lack of Knowledge
Anon. "Mobile Share of Search Traffic by Platform 2019 | Statistic." Statista, 2019, https://geni.us/4UnDc7

Chapter 4.1 – Why Having a Website Matters to Your Business
Rosenbaum, Eric. "You'll Be Shocked to Learn How Many Small Businesses Still Don't Have a Website." CNBC, CNBC, 6 May 2019, https://geni.us/cdDi

Anon. "Small Business Marketing Trends for 2018 - 10 Stats and Insights." Ironpaper, 31 Dec. 2017, https://geni.us/AfGrh

Anon. "GoDaddy-Global-Small-Business-Report-2015.Pdf." GoDaddy, 2015. https://geni.us/9QwhTT

Chapter 4.5.1 – How to Know If You Should Redesign Your Website
Kocurek, Kat. "The Truth About B2B Web Design and Why You Should Invest in It." Kinesis The Truth About B2B Web Design and Why You Should Invest in It Comments, 3 July 2013, https://geni.us/b204LB

Chapter 4.10 – 12 Essential Features Your Website Needs
Agius, Aaron. "3 Critical Principles of Effective Calls to Action." Entrepreneur, 28 Jan. 2015, https://geni.us/8fxKp25

Chapter 5.2 – 10 Reasons Why You Should Consider E-Commerce for Your Business
Smith, Aaron, and Monica Anderson. "Online Shopping and E-Commerce." Pew Research Center: Internet, Science & Tech, 27 Dec. 2017, https://geni.us/H45dkb

Anon. "NRF Launches New Quarterly Report on Consumer Behavior." NRF, 27 Sept. 2017, https://geni.us/8jRW

Chapter 6.3 – Five Reasons Why People Ignore Content
Economist Group's Marketing Unbound. "Missing the Mark: Global Content Survey of Brand Marketers and Their ..." LinkedIn SlideShare, The Economist Group, 7 Oct. 2014, https://geni.us/cUkhoF

Chapter 6.4.3 – What Is the C.U.R.V.E. Method and How to Use It for Your Content Creation
Williams, Alex. "The C.U.R.V.E Method For Engaging Email Subject Lines." Oracle Marketing Cloud, 7 Feb. 2014, https://geni.us/8Cp1Cj9

Chapter 6.5.1 – Why Your Business Website Needs a Blog
Hood, Eddy. "The #1 Small Business Marketing Idea [Infographic]." The #1 Small Business Marketing Idea [Infographic], IgniteSpot, 7 Aug. 2013, https://geni.us/LzIyA

Chapter 6.7 – What Content Curation Is and How to Get Started Doing It
Anon. "Content Curation Can Inform, Engage Customers." EMarketer, 4 June 2012, https://geni.us/Ca88W9

Chapter 7.1 – What Is Search Engine Optimization?
Gesenhues, Amy. "Search Outpaced Social for Referral Traffic Last Year, Driving 35% of Site Visits vs Social's 26% Share of Visits." Search Engine Land, 23 Feb. 2018, https://geni.us/2SA7H

Chapter 7.3.1 – What Are the On-Page Elements That Affect SEO?
Prudhomme, Andre. "Non-Mobile-Friendly Share of SERPs Decreases 21% with April 21 Mobile Algorithm Change." BrightEdge SEO Blog, 28 Apr. 2015, https://geni.us/7onOzRz

Dean, Brian. "We Analyzed 1 Million Google Search Results. Here's What We Learned About SEO." Backlinko, 2 Sept. 2016, https://geni.us/jaoz

Childs, Matt. "Create Compelling Video Experiences." Brightcove, 10 Aug. 2015, https://geni.us/CBH9bJ2

Chapter 7.3.2 – What Are the Off-Page Elements That Affect SEO?
Anon. "Improve Your Local Ranking on Google." Google My Business Help, Google, https://geni.us/UFh3t

Chapter 7.6.1 – What Does Bounce Rate Mean and Does It Impact Where You Rank?
Lahey, Connor. "What Is Bounce Rate and What Is a Good Rate?" Semrush Blog, SEMrush, 14 Dec. 2020, https://geni.us/ptZsYTA

OMalley, Deborah. "Bounce Rate Basics: Everything You Need To Know." GuessTheTest, 2019, https://geni.us/K5yBoa

Hunter, Gillon. "Understanding Bounce Rate & How to Audit It." Search Engine Journal, Search Engine Journal, 15 Mar. 2018, https://geni.us/h5mybjt

Anon. "Usage Statistics and Market Share of Google Analytics for Websites." W3Techs, "2013 Email Marketing Benchmark Report." MarketingSherpa, 2013. https://geni.us/TACWM3

Chapter 8.2 – Eight Reasons Why Local Search Marketing is so Important
Schwartz, Barry. "Did Google Say 46% of Searches Have Local Intent?" seroundtable.com. Search Engine Roundtable, October 17, 2018. https://geni.us/KXeZ

Anon. "Understanding Consumers' Local Search Behavior." Google, May 2014. https://geni.us/nIsAUmz

Anon. "Mobile Path to Purchase - Five Key Findings." Google, November 2013. https://geni.us/i1Yn9A2

Chapter 9.2 – How Influential Are Customer Reviews?
Collinger, Tom, et al. "How Online Reviews Influence Sales - The Medill IMC Spiegel Research Center." 2017. https://geni.us/dGjNITI

Charlton, Graham. "Ecommerce Consumer Reviews: Why You Need Them and How to Use Them." Econsultancy, 20 Mar. 2012, https://geni.us/gNmQSt

Hinckley, Dan. "New Study: Data Reveals 67% of Consumers Are Influenced by Online Reviews." Moz, Moz, 2 Sept. 2015, https://geni.us/9hnj

Chapter 9.4.2 – How to Deal with Questions, Problems, Unhappy Customers, and Fake Reviews
Cox, Toby. "How Social Media Is Transforming PR and the Consumer-Business Relationship." How Social Media Is Transforming PR and the Consumer-Business Relationship | Clutch.co, 1 Nov. 2018, https://geni.us/Lrz2p

Anon. "Local Consumer Review Survey | Online Reviews Statistics & Trends." BrightLocal, 2017, https://geni.us/kiLBA8

Streitfeld, David. "Why Web Reviewers Make Up Bad Things." The New York Times, The New York Times, 15 July 2013, https://geni.us/GAnZ9xA

Chapter 9.4.3 – How to Build a Rock-Solid Reputation and Gain Customer Trust
Anon. "EventTrack 2018 Annual Report." Event Marketing Institute, June 2018. https://geni.us/huY33

Kolsky, Esteban. "CX for Executives." LinkedIn SlideShare, 3 Sept. 2015, https://geni.us/A2dlaI

Anon. "Local Consumer Review Survey | Online Reviews Statistics & Trends." BrightLocal, 2017

Chapter 9.6 – How to Protect Your Online Reputation against Hackers and Cyber Attacks
Anon. "Infographic: Top Online Threats to Small Businesses." SCORE, October 3, 2018. https://geni.us/yeYBBgu

Anon. 2021 Ransomware Statistics, Data, & Trends. PurpleSec. (2021, May 11). https://geni.us/MIC20FJ

Anon. "Berkeley Lab Commons." SSL Certificates - IT Frequently Asked Questions (FAQ) - Berkeley Lab Commons, n.d. https://geni.us/k4mJ2

Chapter 10.2 – Why You Should Not Underestimate the Importance of Mobile Marketing
Enge, Eric. "See Our 2018 Study of Mobile VS Desktop Usage." Perficient Blogs. Perficient Blogs, October 7, 2018. https://geni.us/mg5Ju

Rainie, Lee, and Andrew Perrin. "10 Facts about Smartphones as the IPhone Turns 10." Pew Research Center, Pew Research Center, 28 June 2017, https://geni.us/68h6

Flurrymobile. "U.S. Consumers Time-Spent on Mobile Crosses 5 Hours a Day." Flurry Blog, 3 Mar. 2017, https://geni.us/3uzq6sY

Anon. "Offer Holiday Shoppers the Assistance They Crave." Google, Google, https://geni.us/ofs6D2

van Rijn, Jordie. "The Ultimate Mobile Email Statistics Overview." Email Marketing Consultant Emailmonday, https://geni.us/okuNR4k

Anon. "The Inbox Report: Consumer Perceptions of Email." Fluent, 12 Sept. 2018. https://geni.us/zpBo4Ar

Kemp , Simon. "Digital in 2017: Global Overview - We Are Social." We Are Social USA, 24 Jan. 2017, https://geni.us/gRZU

Sridhar, Sridhar. "How Micro-Moments Are Changing the Rules." Google, Google, Apr. 2015, https://geni.us/SLicm

Chapter 10.3 – Why Your Small Business Needs a Mobile Friendly Website
Anon."What Users Want Most from Mobile Sites Today." Google, Google, Sept. 2012, https://geni.us/jlquZA

Chapter 11.2 – Why Should You Use Email Marketing?
Anon. "Email marketing is a double win for customer acquisition, Retention." eMarketer. 21 July 2016, https://geni.us/cqwGB

Anon. "2013 Email Marketing Benchmark Report." MarketingSherpa, 2013. https://geni.us/KVFBA

Riggs, Larry. "DIRECT MAIL GETS MOST RESPONSE, BUT EMAIL HAS HIGHEST ROI: DMA, But Email Has Highest ROI: DMA." Chief Marketer, Chief Marketer, 22 June 2012, https://geni.us/gEQV6

Anon. "24 Email Marketing Stats You Need to Know." Benefits of Email Marketing | Campaign Monitor, Campaign Monitor, https://geni.us/TFaAk

Chapter 11.3 – Why Is It Important to Generate Leads?
Kim, Larry. "7 Conversion Rate Truths That Will Change Your Landing Page Strategy." Search Engine Land, Search Engine Land, 15 May 2014, https://geni.us/8R8MSs

Chapter 11.5 – What Are the Tools Needed to Capture Leads and Build Your Email List?
Burstein, Danie. "Web Usability: Long Landing Page Nets 220% More Leads than above the Fold Call-to-Action." MarketingExperiments, 17 Apr. 2013, https://geni.us/AuZO

Chapter 11.9 – Five Ways to Tell If Your Email Marketing Is Working and What to Do If It's Not
Anon. "What Are the Average Click and Read Rates For Email Campaigns?" Campaign Monitor, https://geni.us/9SA86Fg

Anon. "Why You Want High Email Unsubscribe Rates." Norbert, 2 Sept. 2020, https://geni.us/zDoJQ

Smart, James. "Making Sense of Email Bounce Rates (2019 Update)." Campaign Monitor, 9 May 2019, https://geni.us/My9PHd

Chapter 12.3 – Which Social Media Channels Should You Use for Your Business?
Anon. "For Social Media Marketers, Facebook Produces the Best ROI." EMarketer, 5 May 2016, https://geni.us/oiG1ZoL

Anon. "Why Brands Should Embrace Instagram Instead of Facebook ." Ecommerce CEO, 1 Aug. 2018, https://geni.us/JtXcBIn

DeVries, Henry. "The Best Social Media For Lead Generation." Forbes, Forbes Magazine, 16 Nov. 2018, https://geni.us/9A9u

Anon. "Here's How People Shop on Pinterest." Pinterest Business, https://geni.us/8GkE.

Midha, Anjali. "Study: Exposure to Brand Tweets Drives Consumers to Take Action – Both on and off Twitter." Twitter, Twitter, 14 May 2014, https://geni.us/6Wpdxu

Anon. "More Spending on Social Video Ads Is Planned." EMarketer, 23 June 2017, https://geni.us/2BEZlA

Chapter 12.5 – 12 Ways to Make Your Business Stand Out on Social Media
Sprout Social. "The Sprout Social Index: Edition XI: Social Personality." Sprout Social, 30 May 2017, https://geni.us/8nVBKC

Chapter 12.6 – Two Social Media Traps to Be Cautious of and the Common Mistakes That Set Them Off
"The Sprout Social Index, Edition VIII: Turned Off." Sprout Social, Sprout Social, 14 June 2016, https://geni.us/KjBTT91

Chapter 13.2 – Why Should You Use Video Marketing?
Anon "50 Must Know Stats About Video & Animation Marketing." Insivia, Insivia, 2013, https://geni.us/YCXN71O

Anon "A Minute of Video Is Worth 1.8 Million Words, According to Forrester Research." Yahoo! Finance, Yahoo!, 17 Apr. 2014, https://geni.us/ue1bcO

Lister, Mary. "37 Staggering Video Marketing Statistics for 2018." WordStream, 9 June 2019, https://geni.us/7uFno

Anon. "The Benefits of Using Video on Landing Pages." Unbounce, https://geni.us/h6nlkiA

Anon. "Impact of Video on Internet Buyer (Infographics)." Video Explainers, https://geni.us/sIVsU

Loechner, Jack. "Product Videos Online Boost Purchase Confidence." 03/27/2013, 3 Mar. 2013, https://geni.us/r21BYoo

Chapter 13.6.2 – How Long Should Your Video Be?
Fishman, Ezra. "Proof That Humans Have a Two-Minute Attention Span." Wistia, 5 July 2016, https://geni.us/904zf

Chapter 13.8 – 10 Ways to Make Sure Your Videos Are Seen by Your Target Audience
Hussain, Anum. "22 Eye-Opening Statistics About Sales Email Subject Lines That Affect Open Rates [Updated for 2019]." HubSpot Blog, 2019, https://geni.us/OFRLK

Chapter 14.2 – The Two Types of Online Advertising
Gabbert, Elisa. "5 Reasons to Diversify Your Search Strategy with PPC Advertising." WordStream, 3 Apr. 2015, https://geni.us/RACB

Chapter 14.2.2 – What Are the Different Ad Formats Used Online?
Walgrove, Amanda. "Infographic: The Beginner's Guide to YouTube Advertising." Contently, 10 Feb. 2015, https://geni.us/ZQ30aA

Chapter 14.3 – What Are Online Advertising Networks and Which Ones Are Most Popular?
Stelzner, Michael. "2019 Social Media Marketing Industry Report." Social Media Marketing | Social Media Examiner, 31 May 2019, https://geni.us/PZBI

Anon. "Facebook, LinkedIn Ads Deliver Best Value to B2B Social Marketers." EMarketer, 8 Nov. 2016, https://geni.us/TK3Y1

Chapter 14.5 – What Is PPC Advertising and The Benefits of Using It?
Gardner, Oli. "SEO vs PPC - Time for a Fight! [Infographic]." Unbounce, 20 June 2012, https://geni.us/bwddMyN

Chapter 15.4.2 – How Much Should You Budget for Your Marketing?
Beesley, Caron. "How to Set a Marketing Budget That Fits Your Business Goals and Provides a High Return on Investment." | The U.S. Small Business Administration | SBA.gov, 4 June 2012, https://geni.us/EH2UYUC

Chapter 16.2 – What Is Branding?
Moir, Diane E. "Trademark Protection of Color Alone: How and When Does a Color Develop Secondary Meaning and Why Color Marks Can Never Be Inherently Distinctive." Digital Commons @ Touro Law Center, 19 Oct. 2011, https://geni.us/jNE05SA

Chapter 16.2.1 – Five Reasons Why Branding Is Important for Your Business
Drengberg, Charles. "The 4 Most Likely Ways Your Business Is Failing." Big Presence, 22 Aug. 2016, https://geni.us/c4Hj

Chapter 16.2.2 – How to Build a Unique and Memorable Brand
Shaoolian, Gabriel. "10 Marketing, Web Design & Branding Statistics To Help You Prioritize Business Growth Initiatives." Forbes, Forbes Magazine, 10 Aug. 2018, https://geni.us/3VrcB

Anon. "New Retail Study Shows Marketers Under-Leverage Emotional Connection." PR Newswire: Press Release Distribution, Targeting, Monitoring and Marketing, 27 Sept. 2018, https://geni.us/83Rf

Anon. "Millennials 'Would Spend More' If Part of a Brand's Community, According to Dialogue." Marketing. Communication. News., November 28, 2017. https://geni.us/3AMw01

Raghavan, Lulu. "Does Your Brand Sound as Good as It Looks?: Thinking." Landor, 10 July 2010, https://geni.us/hLcA

Index

About the Author:

Darrell C. Boyce knows that delivering the right information to the right person at the right time can change lives. He strives to light a fire under individuals ready to take that first step to enhancing their businesses and their lives. With years of research, hands-on learning, and a natural talent, Darrell brings critical information to readers in a succinct manner that's easy to understand—even for beginners.

Darrell lives in New Jersey and in his down time devours books and audiobooks on various topics. He's committed to helping SMBs and entrepreneurs reach their business goals through on and -offline marketing. While online marketing can be confusing, intimidating, overwhelming and time-consuming, his passion and enthusiasm—as well as knowledge in the field—make him a great fit for anyone needing help in these vital areas. Without marketing, businesses simply can't succeed. With Darrell's BASIC signature process, he'll break everything down and turn even a novice marketer into a pro that takes their business to the next level.

Made in United States
North Haven, CT
05 November 2026

21766802R00215